HOUDINI:
A MIND IN CHAINS

Also by Bernard C. Meyer

Joseph Conrad: A Psychoanalytic Biography (1967)

HOUDINI:
A MIND IN CHAINS

A Psychoanalytic Portrait

BERNARD C. MEYER, M.D.

E. P. Dutton & Co., Inc. | New York

Acknowledgment for permission to excerpt passages is made to the following: Milbourne Christopher. From *Houdini, The Untold Story,* by Milbourne Christopher. Copyright © 1969. Reprinted by permission of Thomas Y. Crowell. | Sir Arthur Conan Doyle. From *The Edge of the Unknown,* by Sir Arthur Conan Doyle. Reprinted by permission of Baskervilles Investments Ltd. | Robert Graves. From *The Greek Myths,* by Robert Graves. Reprinted by permission of Robert Graves. | William L. Gresham. From *Houdini: The Man Who Walked Through Walls,* by William L. Gresham. Copyright © 1959 by William L. Gresham. Reprinted by permission of Holt, Rinehart and Winston, Publishers, and by Brandt & Brandt. | Harry Houdini. From *A Magician Among the Spirits,* by Harry Houdini. Copyright 1924 by Harry Houdini. Reprinted by permission of Harper & Row. Also from *The Unmasking of Robert-Houdin,* by Harry Houdini. Copyright 1909 by Harry Houdini. Reprinted by permission of Routledge & Kegan Paul Ltd. | Harold Kellock. From *Houdini: His Life Story,* by Harold Kellock. Copyright 1928 by Harold Kellock and Melville H. Cane as Executor of the Will of Beatrice Houdini; renewed, © 1956, by Katherine Kellock and Melville H. Cane. Reprinted by permission of Harcourt Brace Jovanovich, Inc. | Theodore Reik. From *The Temptation,* by Theodore Reik. Copyright © 1961 by Theodore Reik. Reprinted by permission of George Braziller, Inc. | Robert-Houdin. From *The Memoirs of Robert-Houdin, King of Conjurers,* by Robert-Houdin. Reprinted by permission of Dover Publications, Inc. | Thomas R. Tietze. From *Margery,* by Thomas R. Tietze. Reprinted by permission of the author.

Copyright © 1976 by Bernard C. Meyer, M.D.
All rights reserved. Printed in the U.S.A.

First Edition

10 9 8 7 6 5 4 3 2 1

Library of Congress Cataloging in Publication Data

Meyer, Bernard C
  Houdini: a mind in chains.

  Bibliography: p.
  Includes index.
  1. Houdini, Harry, 1874–1926. 2. Conjuring.
GV1545.H8M48 1976   793.8'092'4 [B]   76-12631
                         M
                      Cop 1
            ISBN: 0-8415-0448-2

Published simultaneously in Canada by
Clarke, Irwin & Company Limited, Toronto and Vancouver

To Leonore

Contents

(ILLUSTRATIONS FOLLOW PAGE 102)

Acknowledgments

In citing my extensive indebtedness to the many individuals who have assisted me in this work, it is fitting that at the outset I should mention Doctor Olga Knopf, a colleague now in the ninth decade of an unceasingly vibrant life, who suggested that I might find Houdini an interesting subject for a psychoanalytic study. When she subsequently presented me with Harold Kellock's biography, like Houdini upon discovering the wonders of the *Memoirs of Robert-Houdin,* I became promptly fascinated and hopelessly ensnared.

My research has brought me the good fortune of an acquaintanceship with Mr. Milbourne Christopher, the celebrated magician and historian of magic, who has been exceedingly generous in sharing with me his vast library and materials.

I owe much to the generosity of Mr. Walter B. Gibson, whose prolific writings in the field of magic are matched by an encyclopedic familiarity with the world of Houdini. I also offer thanks to his occasional collaborator, Dr. Morris N. Young, as well as Mr. Sidney Radner and to Mr. Henry Muller, and his associate Mr. David Hagarty, of the Houdini Museum in Niagara Falls, Ontario.

Thanks are offered to Mr. Leonard Beck, Curator of Special Collections at the Library of Congress in Washington, Mr. Louis Rackow of The Players, and Mr. Richard Ernst, who gave me access to many volumes of Houdini's diaries and scrapbooks. I also wish to thank Mr. Melville Cane, Bess Houdini's sister, Mrs. Marie Hinson, and her daughter Ruth Kavanaugh, and Mrs. Marguerite Elliott, who served as technician and secretary of Houdini's brother, Dr. Leopold Weiss.

Thanks are also extended to Mrs. Elsie Rosner of *MD* magazine, to Judge George Starke, Rose Bonanno, Crystal Dunninger, Harry Houdini Hardeen, and the writer Maurice Zolotow.

Many colleagues have rendered me invaluable assistance. I wish to thank Dr. Jacob Arlow, Dr. Phyllis Greenacre, Dr. Charles Fisher, and Dr. Louis Linn for reading and criticizing the manuscript. My work has been enriched by the stimulating suggestions of Dr. Paul Pressman and Dr. Marcel Heiman. Dr. Emanuel Rice, Rabbi Gerson Cohen, Chancellor of the Jewish Theological Seminary, and Mr. Harold Manson have offered especially important ideas concerning the religious and Jewish aspects of this study.

I am also grateful to Dr. Dale Boesky, Ira Belfer, Pepa Bak, Lillian Mackesy, my sister, Marcelle Bier, Professor Harold Cherniss, Stanley Palm and Charles Reynolds.

For their excellent photographic work I wish to thank Deena Rubinstein, Richard Beller, Thomas Merrill, and Robert Campanile.

I extend thanks to Mr. Gordon Stone, Librarian of the Costume Institute of the Metropolitan Museum of Art in New York, and to Mrs. D. Langley Moore, Founder of the Museum of Costume in Bath, England.

Affectionate thanks are offered to Susan Rubenstein for her encouragement and valuable criticisms.

I write a special note of appreciation to Nancy Crawford for her invaluable editing of the manuscript.

Finally, I wish to express my gratitude to all the members of my family, who have endured my disappearance into the world of Houdini with patience and good humor. My son, Nicholas, has been generous with support and suggestions. For her discerning criticisms, I offer special thanks to my wife. Lastly I thank my daughter, Deborah, for her help in suggesting the title of this book.

Introduction

I've read that things inanimate have moved,
And, as with living souls, have been informed
By magic numbers and persuasive sound.

— Congreve

"A magician is not a juggler," wrote the celebrated French conjurer, Robert-Houdin. "He is an actor, playing a role—the role of a sorcerer." Had Robert-Houdin been as richly favored with the gift of prophecy as he was in the art of conjuring, it might be supposed that this Father of Modern Magic was foretelling the advent of his namesake Houdini, for in the annals of the art of necromancy, no actor has been more acclaimed. Nor was Houdini a brief meteor that streaked across the sky only to turn to dust when new magicians caught the public eye. He belongs in the select company of those personages whose names are legendary throughout the world of entertainment: Paganini, who was said to be in league with the Devil; the Divine Sarah Bernhardt; Charlie Chaplin; and Babe Ruth, the Sultan of Swat. Others have equaled, and perhaps surpassed, the radiance of these stars, but few have eclipsed their fame or burned so bright an image on the public memory.

So it was with Houdini, the universal emblem of wizardry and illusion, whose immortality rests not on feats of sleight-of-hand, but on the magic of his presence and the spell of his charisma. As a conjurer, Houdini was undoubtedly outclassed by such virtuosi as Thurston, Blackstone, Dunninger, and other magicians. Indeed, he looked with evident disdain upon that designation, for he once told some newsmen, "Don't insult me by calling me a magician. I am an escape artist."

This was no idle boast, for it was his incredible ability to effect seemingly impossible escapes from crates and boxes encircled by steel bands, from safes and bank vaults secured by combination locks, from restraints employed by the police, and from strait-jackets used to subdue the insane that earned him his dazzling reputation. Not without reason was he billed in the theaters of several continents as The Monarch of Leg Shackles and The Undisputed King of Handcuffs. In recognition of the aura that embraced his name, a dictionary coined the verb "Houdinize," which was defined: "To release or extricate oneself (from confinement, bonds and the like) as by wriggling out." In the language of the street, to "do a Houdini" became a common expression for vanishing or breaking away.

How did it come about, one may wonder, that in the enactment of the drama of necromancy, the role elected by this extraordinary performer was that of "escape artist?" At first blush one might argue that it was determined largely by the practical demands of successful entertainment and the capricious vicissitudes of show business. From the moment he discovered that the public thrilled to the spectacle of a hair-raising escape, it might be supposed that Houdini realized he had hold of a good thing, and as his career unfolded and his fame grew, his resourceful and imaginative gift spurred him on to create ever more ingenious variations on that arresting theme.

However tempting it may be to accept this eminently reasonable hypothesis, to the psychoanalytically informed observer, aware of the multiple determinants of human behavior, it inevitably proves to be too simplistic. Any explanation of a desire to hoodwink the public, of an urge to risk one's life, or of a wish to become a creative or performing artist, demands a search for unconscious motivations as well as an inquiry into deliberate intent and the play of chance. When, in his teens, Houdini gave up his job as a cutter in a necktie factory to become a magician, he revealed an irresistible attraction to the world of mystery and illusion. Yet there were avenues in the world of magic other than the performance of daring escapes that he might have traveled had they exerted sufficient appeal. Nor can his persistence in pursuing that road be ascribed to the prompt attainment of material rewards, for many years would elapse before he achieved success and fame.

Hence it may be suspected that, in choosing to become an "escapologist," Houdini was obeying the dictates of his own heart—intuitively he understood the strong emotional component in the public's response to the spectacle of confinement and release. He was surely aware of the widespread human tendency to respond sympathetically to the plight of a man trapped in the accidental cave-in of a mine, or of a child stuck in an underground pipe. He knew that during such crises reports of the fate of the victims dominate the headlines, and that the barely audible voice of a child trapped at the bottom of a well can drown out the combined cries of millions of children dying for want of food. No doubt he could also sense the cruel suffering of those who look on helplessly, and the unspeakable relief and boundless joy that burst forth when rescue is finally at hand. Once when a colleague asked him why it took him so long to execute his escapes, he replied, "If I get out too quickly the audience would reason that it was easy. Every second that ticks by during my struggle builds up the climax. When they are sure that I am licked, that the box will have to be smashed to give me air, then—and only then—do I appear."

In the performance of his escapes Houdini undoubtedly exploited that general susceptibility to such ordeals, but it seems that he did so armed with the sensitivity of one who shared in it himself. For reasons that will presently appear, it may be suspected that the emotional response of the audience evoked by him—the unbearable tension giving way to heaven-sent reassurance—was an echo of kindred feelings contained within himself. If this impression is valid, it follows that the choice of his calling as an escape artist arose not by chance or expediency, but as an inevitable expression of psychological forces that dwelled within the secret confines of his mind, and which originated within the experiences and memories of a distant past.

It is in order to explore the hidden sources of these mental currents, and to trace their sinuous course throughout the broad expanse of Houdini's complex history, that this book will employ the instrument of psychoanalytic psychology, that indispensable key to the locked secrets of the human mind, which, aside from its usefulness as a therapeutic tool, has often proved to be an invaluable aid in deepening our understanding and enlarging our vision of the subjects of biography. For self-evident reasons, moreover, this book will offer neither a detailed and sequential account of Houdini's career nor an exposé of his tricks. Concerning the former there are several biographies, of which the most complete and authoritative is Milbourne Christopher's *Houdini, The Untold Story,* which was published in 1969. In view of Christopher's extensive familiarity with his subject, and of his encyclopedic knowledge of the history and literature of magic, it would be folly to pretend that an amateur in the field, lacking these endowments, could hope to increase the scope of Christopher's scholarship or greatly widen the range of his research. By the same token, there are a number of books that offer authentic and detailed explanations of Houdini's methods.

Although both these sources provide rich and valuable material on *what* Houdini did and *how* he did it, neither pretends to deal with the question, *Why?* It is this aspect of the Houdini story that this book will seek to explore, pursuing the same aims alluded to by the scholar Herbert Muller, who, when speaking of the writing of history, declared, "The main problem is not to fill in the many gaps of our factual knowledge, as to make sense of the vast deal that we do know." [1]

Unfortunately, in seeking to apply this sound precept to the life of Houdini, there are vexing difficulties, for the "vast deal" is not so vast, and the raw data concerning especially the crucial early years of his life are singularly untrustworthy. Until comparatively recently even the country and date of his birth were a matter of uncertainty, and in some quarters still remain a matter of controversy. It is a curious commentary on this dilemma to realize that although he is dead but half a century, far greater reliance may be placed upon the presumed facts of the life of Charles Dickens, who died twice as many years before, and even of Samuel Johnson, who died a hundred years before that, in 1772. It is this very quality of unreliability that is the hallmark of the Houdini story, which from its very beginning is a medley of fact and fancy—a not surprising state of affairs, come to think of it, in the life story of an illusionist who died on Halloween.

Even when the "vast deal that we do know" possesses a fair degree of probability, it is still no easy matter to compose with confidence what is now fashionable to designate as the "definitive" biography, that bold effort to discard the rumor and the rubbish of romance and replace them with a meticulously researched study, set down and annotated by a precise and conscientious reporter. For a number of reasons this goal is not easy to attain.

First, the stated facts of any subject's life are not always reliable or free from the *Rashomon*-like bias of different observers, even when they are based upon autobiographic material or upon the testimony of a Boswell or other intimates. It is questionable, too, whether even the most secret diary is ever written without one eye on the hoped-for curiosity and titillation of the potential reader. Houdini's extensive diaries were far from secret, and occasionally contain marginal notes added by his wife.

Aside from the elusive nature of the truth, the emotional needs of the biographer (including the psychoanalytic biographer) may in-

fluence the image of the created portrait, which, like the idealized
paintings of some royal personages, may prove to be unrecognizable
save to the prejudiced eye of the idolater. Freud was aware of such
temptations and warned the biographer against idealizing his subject
in order to gratify his own infantile fantasies—most notably the re-
vival of the childhood image of his father. The urge to engage in
such idealization has led not infrequently to what has been aptly
called the "cherry-tree" style of biography, characterized by touched-up
chronicles in which the contradictions and the unpalatable realities
of the subject's life are sifted and censored in order to unveil a hero
who is revealed not only *sans peur et sans reproche* but also *sans* human impulses, and especially *sans* unconscious thoughts and feelings.
Such a disregard for complexity of character has occurred in some accounts of the life of Houdini, in which he has been presented with an
unwarranted two-dimensional simplicity. There was nothing simple,
for instance, about his much-publicized attachment to his mother,
which has often been depicted as a supreme example of filial devotion.
By the same token, the true cause of his bitter feud with his brother
Leopold was, in all likelihood, far more complicated than what has
generally been accepted. It has also been customary to view him as an
uncompromising foe of Spiritualism, but a closer view of the matter
reveals that on this subject he was caught in a severe inner conflict.

At times such distortions in character depiction arise from an unconscious desire by the author of a biography to use it as a luxurious
vehicle for self-portraiture. "A biography can never be objectively
true," wrote Julian Symons in the introduction to his brother's life of
Frederick Rolfe, *The Quest for Corvo*. "That is what distinguishes it
from a record of social or historical fact. The features of a biography
are all distinct enough, and they are recognizably the features of the
subject, but the hunted eyes and the hunting nose, the wafer-thin
mouth and the rocky chin are the biographer's own."

The impulse to engage in mythmaking is not uncommonly abetted
by the unseen complicity of the subject himself. This was surely true
of Houdini, who allowed dramatic falsehoods concerning his history
to flourish with the same flamboyance with which in later years he
designed and decorated his prospective tomb. A striking example concerns the variations he composed on the story of his bold leap from
the Belle Isle Bridge into the Detroit River, toward the close of the
year 1906. As far as can be determined, this event took place on November 27, a cold day but well above freezing. Locked in a pair of
handcuffs, Houdini jumped from the bridge into the river 25 feet

below, soon rose to the surface and, triumphantly waving the unlocked handcuffs to the cheering crowd, swam safely to a waiting boat.

Never one to overlook the possibilities for sensational elaborations and embroideries on his exploits, Houdini eventually subjected this experience to some interesting and imaginative revisions. To begin with, he shifted the date of his leap to December 2 and lowered the thermometer to zero degrees. Then he claimed that the river was frozen solid, despite which he dismissed any suggestion of canceling the performance, calmly insisting that a hole be cut in the ice so that he might plunge through it into the frigid waters below. This he supposedly did, but now he was beset by new troubles: after freeing himself from the handcuffs and rising to the surface, he was unable to locate the precious hole in the ice. Soon, after swimming about vainly in search of it, he began to need air. Although this "bothered" him, he later declared, he luckily did not panic. He let himself come up gently, and between the surface of the water and the undersurface of the ice he found a small space of trapped air, "about half an inch wide. Now by lying on my back," he continued, "and poking my nose into this gently I could fill my lungs." [2] Finally, after what seemed like an hour of swimming about in circles, he found the opening and escaped from his icy prison. (In a motion picture on the life of Houdini, the scenario indicated that he located the elusive hole by following the guiding voice of his mother, a latter-day Ariadne. According to this same source his mother died at the very moment of his escape—six and a half years before her actual death!) Like an inspired troubadour, Houdini related this experience with considerable flexibility: sometimes he shifted the locale of the event to Pittsburgh. All history, said Doctor Johnson, "so long as it is not supported by contemporary evidence, is romance."

In spite of the comparatively few details in Houdini's life story that can be accepted as unvarnished truth, and although a conscientious biographer is obliged to dampen his text with a shower of qualifiers like "alleged," "supposed," and "presumed," these limitations do not impose an insurmountable barrier to the creation of a valid and vivid portrait. Although, like a hazily recollected dream, such portraiture may be wanting in photographic exactness, the half-remembered, half-invented vignettes, such as his jump into the Detroit River, lend themselves to a psychoanalytic exploration of their potential hidden meanings.

Seen through the eyes of the psychoanalyst, the spurious version of Houdini's leap is not to be dismissed as an entertaining but useless piece of braggadocio, but should be viewed rather as a fantasy or daydream that is rich in hidden meaning. In the course of this book it will become clear that such distortions of truth lie in the cradle of a complex of fantasies; if properly understood, they can furnish the biographer with insights into the character of Houdini far more revealing than what may be discerned by attending strictly to the presumed historical facts. In the fashioning of such reveries Houdini may be linked with creatively gifted individuals whose poems and paintings reveal their personalities in a manner that is often wanting in those men of action who hide their visions and never tell their dreams.

It was not only as a highly imaginative and versatile performer but also as a storyteller and maker of motion pictures that Houdini left a legacy rich in clues concerning the secrets of his mind and heart. These stories and films of which he was the author, or at least the co-author, are for the most part obvious self-portraits which, while not qualifying as great art, often provide a revealing and often surprising glimpse into the darker corners of his character, apparently unsuspected and unexplored by some of his biographers.

As a magician, and especially as an escapologist, his art invites an interpretation of its meaning, demanding the same attention to gesture and symbol that is accorded the dancer or the mime, for his performances, despite the patter that accompanied them, consisted essentially of the mute enactment of a few simple themes. This was no less true of those daring stunts executed away from the stage and in the open air. Whether he was hanging by his feet from the cornice of a tall building, risking his flesh while tied to the stake within a ring of burning faggots, buried six feet below the ground, or plunging from a bridge into the chill waters below, he was not merely playing for publicity, as many people believed; he was living out a dream, an imagined horror that guided the sudden and unforeseen twists and turns of his strange existence, a nightmare as old as human history that linked his tragic fate with legendary figures of antiquity and myth. "He was not an ordinary magician, like Thurston, Kellar, Blackstone or Cardini," wrote Zolotow. "He was not an entertainer. He was playing Prometheus. He was playing Christ. He was playing allegorical charades in which he died and was resurrected." [3]

Take for example his extraordinary adventure within the belly of a "sea monster." A huge marine creature, described as "a cross between a whale and an octopus" (!) was washed ashore on a Cape Cod beach in the fall of 1911 and brought in a truck to the theatre in Boston where Houdini was playing. Responding to a challenge, Houdini allowed himself to be handcuffed and shut up inside the strange beast, and then sewn into this grotesque prison with chains secured by padlocks. Because the carcass had been treated with preservatives, its cavernous interior presumably reeked of fumes that were said to have made him "sick and dizzy," and at one point, choking and in a near panic, he supposedly tried to kick his way out. But then he composed himself, and a quarter of an hour after he had entered the monster's belly, the incredible Houdini was once again free.

To be sure, there are some who might ridicule the idea that this exciting exploit contained either symbolic or mythological significance. No need to seek deep meanings here, it might be argued, for all that drove Houdini's inventive genius was a passion for fame and a hunger for money—goals that this master of entertainment knew quite well how to attain. Yet for those who would dismiss this strange adventure as mere show business, it should be pointed out that in his encounter with the sea monster Houdini had, inadvertently or not, re-enacted a drama that is as old as recorded time.

It was told of the Greek hero Heracles, who rescued the king's daughter, the beautiful Hesione, from a sea monster sent by Poseidon. When the monster opened its vast jaws, Heracles leapt fully armed down its throat, and after spending three days in its belly, cut his way out and left the monster dead. It is the theme of the tale of Jonah, who remained in the belly of the whale for three days and three nights before he was regurgitated,* and of "The Story of Little Red Riding Hood." Symbolically it may be discerned in the destiny of Jules Verne's Captain Nemo. Joseph Campbell mentions other versions of it among the Eskimos and the Zulus, and in the legend of the Irish hero Finn MacCool. In poetry, Longfellow sang of it in *Hiawatha:*

> Mishe-Nahma, King of Fishes,
> In his wrath he darted upward,
> Flashing leaped into the sunshine,
> Opened his great jaws and swallowed
> Both canoe and Hiawatha.

It is doubtful whether Houdini himself understood the ancient origin of his adventure within the belly of the sea monster, or recognized that in this reiterated drama of incarceration and escape he was

---

* To the early Christians, Jonah's deliverance "out of the belly of hell" after that interval served as a foretaste of the later story of Christ's resurrection after three days in His tomb. On Holy Saturday, the day between His Death and Resurrection, Jesus is also described as residing in the "Belly of Hell."

enacting his own version of death and resurrection, but there were chroniclers of his life who understood it well. Responding to these allegorical charades, Zolotow, the author of a fictional re-creation of the Houdini story called *The Great Balsamo,* contrived to have his hero drown, entrapped by his own carelessness in a packing case submerged in the sea; in a movie depicting the life of Houdini, the scenarist subjected him to a similar fate, but ordered him to murmur in a dying voice, "I shall come back."

In both of these artistic re-creations of the Houdini story, his biographers signaled their awareness that, ulterior to the insistent proof that no walls could contain the bold hero of this awesome drama, they heard the muffled echo of grim claustrophobia. It is not strange, in view of the seeming prominence of this somber theme, that, like Daedalus, who escaped from the claustral labyrinth of King Minos on the wings of his own invention, Houdini embarked upon a passionate—albeit brief—career in aviation, and became the first person ever to fly a plane in Australia.

"The latest incarnation of Oedipus, the continued romance of Beauty and the Beast," wrote Campbell, "stands this afternoon on the corner of Forty-second Street and Fifth Avenue, waiting for the traffic light to change." [4] Not far from that corner, at the crossroads of the world of entertainment known as Broadway, Houdini, one of the great showmen of all times, electrified the spirits of thousands of spectators with the feverish excitement that sprang from his own invented re-creation of legends of antiquity. It is to trace the origins of those re-born myths within the tangled skeins of his own psyche, and to unravel the multicolored strands that were woven into the complex and fascinating tapestry that told the story of this man who danced with death, who played with punishment, and toyed with madness, that this book is written.

HOUDINI:
A MIND IN CHAINS

The Family Romance

Pretending is a virtue. If you can't pretend, you can't be a king.
—Luigi Pirandello: LIOLA

One day, toward the end of January 1901, in the course of his triumphant English debut, Harry Houdini, rising star in the firmament of magic and entertainment, happened to notice an elegant gown displayed in the window of a London shop. When he stepped inside he learned it had been designed for Queen Victoria, but she had died a few weeks before it was finished and hence had never worn it. Seized by a sudden inspiration, Houdini persuaded the shopkeeper to sell it to him, after agreeing to the condition that it was never to be worn in Great Britain. He promptly wrote to his mother in New York, inviting her to join him in Europe, where she might bear proud witness to his growing fame, and in addition participate in a private little drama of his own invention. She accepted his proposal, and a few weeks later was in Hamburg, where she watched her magician son perform to a sold-out house.

At the conclusion of that engagement they traveled to her native Budapest, where in the Palm Gardens of the Royal Hotel, which Houdini had booked for the occasion, his mother held court wearing the gown designed for the Queen of England, while her son stood proudly at her side. "How my heart warmed," he wrote, "to see various friends and relatives kneel and pay homage to my mother, every inch a queen, as she sat enthroned in her heavily carved and gilded chair." [1] (Figure 1) Even the hotel manager entered into the spirit of the occasion by wearing the clothes he reserved only for receiving royalty. "That night," Houdini recorded, "Mother and I were awake

1

all night, talking over the affair, and, if happiness ever entered my life to the fullest, it was in sharing Mother's wonderful excitement at playing queen for a day. The next morning, after having lived two ecstatically happy days, I escorted the Fairy Queen en route to America." [2] To capture the full flavor of this tasty vignette, it needs to be pointed out that not only was Houdini married at this time but his twenty-four-year-old wife, Bess, was a member of the happy party.

Whatever response this little play of make-believe may evoke in the casual reader, to the psychoanalytically schooled observer it contains compelling allusions to those fantasies known as Family Romances— imagined reshapings of one's past that serve to replace a humble and pedestrian origin with the glittering trappings of a rich and illustrious heritage. In its most common form, the term reflects the notion that the child is not the offspring of his alleged parents, but has been adopted or kidnaped as a baby from his real parents who are persons of royalty or other lofty station. As enacted by Houdini, the fantasy was modified to read: This lady is my real mother, but she is no unknown or obscure woman; she is a real Queen, for I am a conjurer, and whatever I wish is true.

Inasmuch as fantasies of the Family Romance are characteristically most active during childhood, it is difficult to restrain a sense of surprise that a grown man might engage in such unabashed play-acting. What is arresting about the mock levee arranged by Houdini in the Palm Gardens is not that, like so many others, he entertained the fantasy that his simple mother was a royal personage, but that, at nearly twenty-seven years of age, he experienced so little difficulty in translating that fantasy into a public spectacle. No less remarkable— or revealing—is the realization that his mother apparently offered no strenuous objection to participating in this childlike charade and that she, no less than her son, was more than willing to be cast in the role of "queen for a day." Together they enacted a Family Romance à deux.

It will come as no surprise, then, to learn that in fashioning the Houdini myth his mother was more than a passive collaborator; concerning the circumstances of his birth as well as the events preceding it, she was the perfect mentor for this future illusionist, for she tinkered with truth and fiddled with facts in a manner that bespoke a rich and fertile imagination. Like her son, she was able to erase with ease the thin line separating daydreams from reality. And as might be expected from her willingness to participate in her son's queen-for-a-day playlet, she played an active role in promoting other distortions of reality that were in time destined to become major tenets in the history of his life.

Her complicity in fostering his illusions began even before his birth, for it was evidently she who was responsible for falsifying the true facts of his origins. Ostensibly to provide him with the emotional security implicit in being of American birth, she let it be believed that, like his brothers Theodore and Leopold who followed him, he had been born in Appleton, Wisconsin. But it was not so. Ehrich— for such was Houdini's given name—was born in Budapest, like his older brothers Nathan and William, the first two sons of Rabbi Mayer Samuel Weiss and his wife, Cecilia. From a previous marriage the rabbi had a son, Herman, whose mother had died at his birth in 1863. Ehrich was born in 1874 on March 24, not on April 6 as his mother later asserted.[3] Theodore, who became the magician Hardeen, was born on February 29, 1876; Leopold, who was destined to become an eminent physician, was born on September 2, 1879. Gladys, the only girl among these children, was born many years later, on January 22, 1891, in New York.*

Although in later years Houdini invariably claimed he had been born in Wisconsin—he even attested to that fact in filling out an insurance application in November 1916—it seems doubtful that he was unaware of the real truth. It is known that his brother Theodore knew that Houdini had been born in Hungary, and it is most unlikely that Theodore would have kept this information to himself. Houdini recognized, moreover, that there was some confusion about his true birthday. "Re the birthdays," he wrote to Theodore on November 22, 1913, "I shall celebrate mine always April 6th. It hurts me to think I can't talk it over with Darling Mother, and, as SHE always wrote me on April 6th, that will be *my adopted birthdate*" [4] (italics added). It is noteworthy, in view of his admission of uncertainty, that in the insurance application mentioned above he gave the date of his birth as April 6.

Nor were the alleged circumstances surrounding his uncertain birthdate lacking in the luster and drama appropriate to Family Ro-

---

* Even these "facts" cannot be accepted without reservation. On page 222 of the November 1953 issue of the magic magazine *M-U-M*, a writer, William Frazee, claimed that the research department of Paramount Studios had discovered that Houdini and Hardeen were half-brothers, a fact which Frazee asserted had been common knowledge to the "old timers" in magic. Since both men had the same mother, the writer continued, "What was Houdini's right name?" Further complications are introduced by an entry in the 1880 census of Appleton stating that Theodore had been born in Hungary.

mance fantasies, for around the time of the event, it was said, his father engaged in a duel with a nobleman who had slandered him and his religion. In the ensuing combat his adversary was killed and the rabbi was forced to flee the country to escape arrest and the vengeance of the dead man's family. He ultimately arrived in Appleton, where he was reunited with his family and became the leader of a small synagogue. (Figure 2)

Despite the admittedly romantic appeal of this tale of derring-do, it imposes something of a strain on one's credulity. Not only does the image of a smoking pistol in the hand of a rabbi seem out of character with that profession, but the notion that a member of the aristocracy would have deigned to duel with an obscure rabbi in an affair of honor seems quite alien to Hungarian customs of the day. It should be added that according to a history of Hungarian duels, with the exception of some conducted by soldiers and other professionals, none were reported during those years.

Nor was the apocryphal duel the only instance in which Houdini's father was depicted as a heroic conqueror, for he was said to have been no less successful a combatant when vying for a woman's love. According to the accepted account, not long after the death of his first wife, Rabbi Weiss fell in love with twenty-two-year-old Cecilia Steiner while he was seeking her hand in marriage on behalf of a younger— and evidently more diffident—suitor. She preferred the rabbi, however, and in contrast to the fate of Miles Standish, the older man [5] was urged to speak for himself. When he did so he won the day, and his younger rival was dismissed.

Many years later, in a letter to Bess, Houdini's sister Gladys contributed her own embellishments to the family saga by asserting that so great had been the rabbi's fame in Budapest that the Kaiserin Josephine used to stop at his home when she was on one of her frequent visits to a nearby orphan asylum to pay her respects to the distinguished man. The fact that there was no Kaiserin Josephine, and that under any other name it is doubtful that her Royal Highness, traveling from Vienna, would have bestowed such favors on an obscure Hungarian rabbi, merely attests to the infinite reaches of Gladys's imagination. Nor did it stop there.

Presumably seeking to establish proof of Houdini's American birth, her letter went on to claim that he had been named for another baby Ehrich, who was born in Budapest and died suddenly after a fall. Brokenhearted, the parents agreed that if ever they should be blessed with another son, he was to be named after the dead infant.

It was for this reason, she explained, that the first of the Weiss boys to be born in Appleton was named Ehrich. "You know, Bess," she continued, "in the Hebraic custom, newborn children are named for the departed." [6]

In this, however, she was somewhat inaccurate, for while it is customary to name a Jewish child after a deceased family member, the latter applies only to adults, notably to grandparents, not to dead children. On the contrary, to name a new baby after a deceased sibling runs counter to Jewish tradition, a fact that was undoubtedly familiar to Rabbi Weiss. Aside from Gladys's letter, there is no other evidence to support her story of an earlier Ehrich, which must be dismissed, together with her account of the pilgrimage of the apocryphal Kaiserin, as a figment of her imagination.

Nor did this document exhaust the rich lode of her fantasy. At the time of Gladys's final illness in January 1959 her hospital record contained the information—presumably supplied at her dictation—that her profession was ghost-writer (!), and that her mother had been born in France. Contrary to the statement that she was "self-employed," for years she had been supported by her brother Leopold.

Nurtured in a forcing-bed so fertile in falsehoods and rich in fabrications, it is no wonder that as young Ehrich matured he developed a wavering sense of reality and a strong disposition toward fantasy and illusion. Such influences contributed not only to his interest in magic but also to his susceptibility to the comforting satisfactions of the Family Romance, that revision of his personal past made all the more urgent by the unhappy realities of his childhood.

Despite the inclusion of real or imagined exploits in Rabbi Weiss's history, biographies of Houdini depict his father not as an invincible hero, not as a victorious combatant on the field of honor, nor as an object of reverence by an empress, but as a depressed and ineffectual man—especially after his emigration to America, where he apparently failed to adapt to his new life. In fact, there is reason to question the significance of his title "rabbi" altogether.

Mayer Samuel Weiss came to Budapest from western Hungary with the intention of becoming a lawyer. Lacking the necessary academic credits to pursue that career, he became a teacher of religion and "read rabbinical commentaries on Judaic tradition and devoted himself to the Torah." [7] There is no evidence, however, that he attended a rabbinical seminary or that he was ever ordained. An investigation undertaken by the American Jewish Historical Society failed to find any evidence that Houdini's father was actually a rabbi. Like many other learned Jews he may have acquired that title simply on the basis of scholarly attainments.*

Although initially he obtained a small congregation in Appleton —at an annual salary of $750—in time, perhaps because his teachings were considered old-fashioned and because he failed to learn English, the "Miles Standish" pattern was reversed and Rabbi Weiss lost his position to a younger and more "progressive" leader. Beset by professional frustration and economic woes, he gave way to a mood of gloom and to thoughts of his own death. "Such hardships became our lot," Houdini later recalled, "that the less said on the matter the better." [8]

The family then moved to Milwaukee, where, presumably to keep ahead of the rent collector, they had at least five different addresses during the years 1883–1887. Toward the close of 1885, an additional blow befell them when Herman, the rabbi's twenty-two-year-old son from his first marriage, was stricken with a rapidly advancing pulmonary tuberculosis and died in New York where he had been living. Perhaps because of this misfortune, Rabbi Weiss began to entertain morbid thoughts about his own death, for a few months later, on the occasion of Ehrich's twelfth birthday, he supposedly summoned the boy to his side and made him promise to look after his mother as long as she lived.

Once again it is difficult to accept a biographical detail at face value, for it seems strange that, among his five living sons, two of whom were older than Ehrich, the father would have singled out the latter to assume the sole burden of this heavy responsibility. In view of Houdini's penchant for seeking the position of the favorite, it seems more likely that his recollection of the scene was spiced by wishful thinking, enabling him to forget that his father may have exacted a similar promise from *all* the children.

Whatever the truth may have been, there is little doubt that emotionally it was a difficult time for Ehrich. Whether it was the recent illness and death of his half-brother, the gloomy forebodings of his father, or the generally miserable conditions of his life, he was evidently troubled and restless. On the day after his twelfth birthday in 1886, he ran away from home, announcing by postcard that he was bound for Texas and would be back in a year. Significantly, in light

---

* In his book, *World of Our Fathers,* Irving Howe relates that when one such "rabbi" was asked who had given him the title "Chief Rabbi of America," he had replied, "the sign painter."

of the promise he had ostensibly just given his father, the message was addressed "Dear Ma" and signed "Your truant son." [9]

The real reason for the boy's flight is problematical. Although some of his biographers have liked to view it as a brave gesture signifying his determination to make the fortune that would enable him to fulfill the pledge to look after his mother, a less romantic but more probable explanation is that he was having trouble in school, as he suggested in using the word "truant" in his farewell message.

In support of this suspicion is the evidence that throughout his life Houdini was afflicted by a vexing difficulty in spelling, manifested notably by transpositions of letters and syllables: e.g., Balsoma for Balsamo, Cagalistro for Cagliostro, Periora for Peoria. Some of his errors resulted in changing the gender of names—a possible reflection of confusion over his own sexual identity.

Such errors must not be ascribed to an intellectual deficit nor to a lack of adequate formal schooling, however, for Houdini was a self-educated man, whose excellent mind enabled him to amass considerable knowledge over the years. Despite his meager education he was fluent in both English and German. In his adult years he undertook the study of French, and as late as the last year of his life he was planning to enroll in Columbia University to take courses in English.

Moreover, the broad range of his intellectual interests is conveyed by the perceptive and sensitive comments he wrote about the museums he visited, and by his vast collections of books and letters. Houdini owned what is reputed to be one of the largest private collections of Lincoln's letters, and in his will he bequeathed his sizeable and varied collection of books—there were 5200 on magic alone—to the Library of Congress in Washington.

His troubles in spelling resemble those reversals, like "saw" for "was," which are typical of children afflicted by inborn learning difficulties, and which tend to be especially severe in the early school grades. In some instances, in fact, Houdini's transpositions involved not only single letters but entire words, as in a letter to his brother William, which he closed with the garbled phrase, "Love you to all from Bess and myself."

His errors often consisted of the gratuitous inclusion of superfluous letters: e.g., nerveous, asyleum. In 1916, despite twenty-two years of marriage, he inscribed a book of poetry to his wife: instead of Wilhelmina (her actual name), he wrote Wilheminia. It might be supposed that the problem was aggravated by his steady exposure to German at home, as when he wrote Carnavelt for Carnavalet, or Rooseveldt for Roosevelt, but at times his German spelling was equally faulty: in an entry in his diary for December 11, 1907, quoting a remark made by his mother, he wrote, "Wo bist du, mein *kindt?*" (italics added).

The fact that these errors persisted throughout Houdini's life suggests that they had been even more troublesome during his grade-school years and had interfered seriously with his progress in formal education. Not only may this have been the major reason for his running away from home, but in the form of an overcompensation, it may account for the particular satisfaction he gained in later life in lecturing before audiences of college and university students. It may have been responsible, too, for the canard printed in a souvenir-program biography stating that Houdini had once "taught a Junior class in his father's college [sic], thereby gaining a knowledge of human nature." Finally, it seems quite plausible that his extensive book collecting and fondness for literary mementoes in his later years may have been determined in some measure as a reaction to his early difficulties in reading and writing.

Whatever may have been the true cause of his running away, young Ehrich apparently never got as far as Texas, and there is no evidence that he ever returned to Wisconsin either. Indeed, his precise movements during those critical days of his early adolescence are shrouded in obscurity. Not only is there no indication that the rabbi's son became Bar Mitzvah, but, ironically, it was at the approximate age when such a ceremony would have taken place that he acquired a bullet in the palm of his right hand, which remained there for the rest of his life, prompting Christopher to refer to it as "a reminder of his runaway days." [10] The next recorded account of his whereabouts places him in New York, where at the age of fourteen he obtained a position as an assistant cutter in a necktie factory.

Whether his decampment should be viewed as a foretaste of those escape acts that one day would make him famous is conjectural, but surely it was a prophetic gesture, indicative of an urgent need to detach himself from an impoverished, grubby life, and to seek in its stead a world in which wishes could readily be transmuted into truth, and where magic stood triumphant over reality. If it had also been intended as a means of shaking off his family, he failed, for in New York he was joined by his father and not long thereafter by the rest of the family, which surprisingly was once again augmented in January 1891 by the birth of Gladys.

The economic hardships confronting this large family, as well as other considerations, make it doubtful that Gladys's conception was consciously intended. To her father, over sixty years of age, and her mother, nearing fifty, no child had been born for more than eleven years. Since it is well known that change-of-life babies are often conceived as a last-ditch affirmation of life by couples who feel threatened by the approach of advancing years or by signs of disease or imminent death, it is noteworthy that less than two years after Gladys's birth, on October 5, 1892, the rabbi died, apparently of cancer, which may indeed have manifested itself even before the child's conception. Not long before his death, moreover, Rabbi Weiss is once again said to have summoned young Ehrich to his side and made him promise to look after his mother, just as he had six years earlier.

Whatever truth may reside in these conjectures, it is beyond question that neither the rabbi's preoccupation with dying nor his death served to lend any credibility to the heroic images that had been bestowed upon him through anecdote and rumor. What were these when measured against the broken man who had foresaken his eminent position as the leader of a Jewish congregation and a Talmudic scholar to share the bench of his fourteen-year-old boy in a necktie factory? [11] Confronted by such an example of humiliation and failure, and surrounded by a family given to fanciful rewritings of its own history, it is no wonder that the son became easy prey to fantasies of the Family Romance, and embarked early upon what proved to become an endless quest for a heroic model of a father.

Once during his Wisconsin days, as he was shining the shoes of a well-dressed gentleman, he chanced to look up and recognized his customer as the governor of the state. Some forty years later, while waiting for his act to begin on a stage in Albany, New York, he peeked through the curtain, hoping to catch a glimpse of Governor Al Smith, who was said to be in the audience. His insatiable craving to hold communion with great and famous men seemed bound by neither time nor space. When he bought a family burial plot in the Machpelah Cemetery in Long Island, he did not fail to take satisfaction in the discovery that a famous magician, Antonio Blitz, who had once performed for President Lincoln, was buried but a few hundred yards away. On board ship in 1914, he succeeded in having his picture taken with Theodore Roosevelt and several other people. By dint of some adroit cropping of the photo he managed to eliminate these others and produced a picture which he then sent to his brother with the comment: "The enclosed will show that T. Rooseveldt [sic] and your brother are pals."

An indefatigable collector, his prized possessions included a writing desk that had belonged to Edgar Allan Poe and the heel from a shoe of the celebrated British magician Robert Heller. Just as a dress designed for a queen might confer regal attributes upon his mother, so it seemed that Houdini sought to acquire a new and glorious self by surrounding his person and embellishing his history with the presence, the trappings, and the memorabilia of both real and figurative kings. Such a one was Jean Eugène Robert-Houdin, the celebrated French King of Conjurers, who was to provide young Weiss not only with a new birth but with a new name.

Robert-Houdin, Hero and Guide

For you, in my respect, are all the world.
Then how can it be said, I am alone,
When all the world is here to look on me?

—A MIDSUMMER NIGHT'S DREAM

In the face of the generous mixture of fact and fancy that fills out his personal narrative, it is difficult to trace accurately the genesis of young Ehrich's involvement with magic and show business. What he later termed his "professional debut" was a performance on a trapeze rigged up in a neighbor's backyard where the boy was featured, not surprisingly, as The Prince of the Air. Houdini later embroidered his recollection of the occasion, claiming that even at the early age of nine he had learned to pick up needles with his eyelids, and had negotiated a successful escape after being tied up in a rope.[1]

Although in later years Rabbi Weiss was said to be disappointed that his son was seeking to become a magician, it was he who had originally introduced the boy to this unsavory world by taking him to the theater in Milwaukee to see a traveling magician named Dr. Lynn. According to his billing, the doctor cut up a man at every performance, a feat which made a lasting impression on young Ehrich. "I really believed that the man's arm, leg, and head were cut off," he confided to his diary many years later (June 11, 1914). It is not difficult to imagine the boy's horror as he saw the diabolical conjurer brandishing a butcher's knife and hacking away at his helpless victim, nor his immense relief when the man reappeared, as if by a miracle, with all his appendages intact.

Some forty years after this spine-chilling experience, the playbill of the National Theater in New York announcing the program to be presented by Houdini—"The Greatest Necromancer of this Age— Perhaps of All Times," the *Literary Digest* called him—included one stunt entitled "Paligenesia or Taking a Living Man To Pieces and Restoring Him by Installment," an invention of a celebrated Dr. Lynn, which had been performed by him "all over the civilized world." To be sure, Dr. Lynn's vast itinerary had included Milwaukee, Wisconsin, where one day during the 1880s the audience had contained a wide-eyed boy, named Ehrich Weiss, and his father.

The sequence of events noted here became a regular pattern in Houdini's life and an infallible formula for his mastery of intolerable anxiety: namely *the active repetition, under his own guidance and control, of a frightening experience to which he had originally been subjected as a passive and helpless onlooker.* Traces of the anxiety stirred up by Dr. Lynn's display of feigned slaughter can be discerned in Houdini's lifelong preoccupation with the themes of decapitation and mutilation. Undoubtedly, one method of coping with that anxiety had been to become a magician himself, the active perpetrator of these dreadful deeds.

Despite the lasting impression created by Dr. Lynn's butchery and repair, it is doubtful that it led young Ehrich to an immediate decision to become a magician. His initial steps in that direction apparently began somewhat later when, during his adolescence, his brother Theodore taught him his first coin trick. Soon he began to try his hand with other tricks, to learn some of the mysteries of locks and keys, and to study the methods and techniques of other magicians. It was in this setting that the decisive influence on his future burst upon him. In his late teens he chanced to discover a secondhand copy of an English translation of *The Memoirs of Robert-Houdin.* The excitement resulting from this encounter between the work of the renowned conjurer and the young novice was electric. "From the moment I began to study the art," Houdini would write later, "he became my guide and my hero. I asked nothing more of life than to become in my profession like Robert-Houdin." In pursuit of that cherished goal nothing could have been more logical than to follow the advice of a friend to appropriate the great man's surname, which he erroneously took to be Houdin, and to add an "i" to it.[2]

From now on there was to be no further question about either his vocation or his identity. At the age of seventeen Ehrich Weiss, the rabbi's son, discarded his name and gave up his job in the necktie factory. He had his eye on greater things, and under the bright banner emblazoned with the name Harry Houdini,* he stepped boldly into the profession of conjuring.

It is unnecessary to provide here a detailed account of the painful and frustrating early years of his new career—the difficulty of getting engagements, the hopes and disappointments, the failures, the paltry pay, and the lack of recognition. Rather than repeat the already recorded descriptions of degrading appearances in cheap "dime museums" and traveling circuses, or of his impersonating the medium in phony spiritualist seances, it will suffice to state that after seven years of struggling, he was so far from success that he began to toy with the idea of giving up his thus far fruitless dreams of glory and contenting himself with a steady job in the prosaic world of commerce.

And then, slowly at first, mainly through his ingenious escape stunts, Harry Houdini began to attract attention. Intuitively aware of the strategic uses of publicity, he visited numerous police stations and jails, challenging the officials to devise restraints that could contain him. By the summer of 1899, the once obscure magician was drawing such huge and enthusiastic crowds by his spectacular and daring escapes from handcuffs, leg irons, strait-jackets and other apparatus, that he found himself engaged by the Orpheum Theater in San Francisco for the amazing fee of $175 a week. Now decked out in the glittering titles of The Undisputed King of Handcuffs, Monarch of Leg Shackles, and Champion Jail Breaker, this virtuoso of escapology found his foot planted securely in the stirrup of fame. On May 30, 1900, he embarked for England and the Continent, where he was soon destined to become a sensation.

It was during the following spring that the mock coronation of his mother took place in Budapest. Not long thereafter, while he was in Paris, Houdini visited the Théâtre Robert-Houdin, and then went on a pilgrimage to Blois to place a wreath on his hero's grave. All in all it had been little more than ten years since the course of his life had been decisively and permanently altered by the chance discovery of the great Frenchman's *Memoirs,* a work which he had "read and reread until [he] could recite passage after passage from memory."

---

* The origin of Houdini's assumed first name, Harry, is in dispute. Some hold that it was taken from Harry Kellar, a foremost American magician of the day. Houdini's brother Theodore claimed that it was derived from Erie, a nickname for Ehrich, but this seems unlikely in light of Houdini's consistent efforts to dissociate himself from the Hungarian immigrant Ehrich Weiss. In time to come he dropped the name Harry altogether. "I would rather be called just 'Houdini,'" he wrote to Will Goldston on March 5, 1920. "It sounds better, looks better, and is better."

Yet a perusal of the book (published originally in 1858 as *Confidences d'un Prestidigitateur*) causes one to wonder whether its great appeal to young Ehrich Weiss arose entirely from its presentation of the history and practice of the art of magic. On the contrary, there is reason to suspect that its major emotional impact originated in those autobiographical sections which, in an almost uncanny way, seem to have anticipated analogous details in the life and thoughts of his future disciple, notably in the presentation of a number of episodes that are characteristic of fantasies of the Family Romance.

Like his later namesake, Robert-Houdin ascribed the main stimulus of his choice of the career of conjuring to the chance discovery of a book. An apprentice watchmaker, young Robert-Houdin—or, more accurately, Robert, for such was his original name—was seeking to buy a treatise on clockmaking, when through a clerk's error he obtained two volumes of an encyclopedia on magic and, anticipating Houdini, wrote: "Fascinated . . . I devoured the mysterious pages, and the further my reading advanced, the more I saw laid bare before me the secrets of an art for which I was unconsciously predestined. . . . This discovery caused me the greatest joy I had ever experienced. At this moment a secret presentiment warned me that success, perhaps glory, would one day accrue to me in the apparent realization of the marvelous and impossible." Like Houdini many years later, his fate appeared to have been dictated by accident: "The resemblance between two books, and the hurry of a bookseller, were the commonplace causes of the most important event in my life." Like Houdini, he too became obsessed with his find and committed it to memory: "Unable to sleep or rest, I went continually over the passages which had most struck me, and the interest they inspired only excited me the more." [3]

Meanwhile, young Robert continued in his profession, and in the course of time left his native Blois to pursue his apprenticeship as an assistant to a watchmaker in Tours. It was during this period that once again an accident of fate radically altered the course of his life. As a result of his eating contaminated food he was seized with violent abdominal pains, and he became critically ill. Haunted by the seeming certainty of imminent death, he was gripped by an overwhelming desire to return to his family. Against the doctor's orders, he left his bed, stole from the house and secretly embarked on the stagecoach for Blois. Once in the carriage, however, his suffering became worse than ever. "The journey was a horrible martyrdom to me," he wrote. "I was devoured by a burning fever, and my head seemed to burst asunder by every jolt of the vehicle. . . . Unable to endure it any longer, I opened the door . . . and leaped . . . on the high road, where I fell in a state of insensibility." * [4] After several days of forgetfulness and hallucinations, he regained his consciousness, and discovered that he had been rescued by a man and his servant, who had found him lying on the road. Soon thereafter his benefactor revealed himself to be the celebrated magician Torrini, who further explained that it had been the extraordinary resemblance between his own lately deceased son and young M. Robert that had prompted his act of mercy. Even more startling was Torrini's subsequent confession that it was he who had been responsible for his own son's death. Together they had been performing an act entitled "The Son of William Tell," when somehow a real bullet got mixed up with the blanks and the boy was shot dead by his own father. "His murderer stands before you!" Torrini cried out to the astonished young Robert.[5]

Presented with the opportunity to restore Robert to health, and thus make amends for his lamentable deed, Torrini's spirits began to improve. Treating the youth as his protégé, he taught him many secrets in the art of magic. In time he unfolded more of his own history, confiding that in reality he was not an Italian but a French nobleman, Count Edmond de Grisy by name, who had fled to Italy during the French Revolution. Nor had the count always been a magician; in 1796, he had obtained a medical degree in the city of Florence, where he began to practice. Circumstances, however, caused him to move to Naples, an action that was to have far-reaching consequences, for it was in that city where the count first saw and fell under the spell of the great Italian conjurer, Giovanni Giuseppe Pinetti. In a short time, yielding to the irresistible fascination of the art of necromancy, de Grisy forsook the practice of medicine and became a magician, soon finding himself a formidable rival of Pinetti. Appareled in a new name, Torrini, the erstwhile physician quickly eclipsed the famed Italian, and went on to ever greater triumphs, capped by performances before princes, cardinals, and even the Pope.

Romance, too, entered Torrini's life. In Rome he made the acquaintance of an opera singer named Antonio, "a charming lad of eighteen [with] a feminine face, small waist and timid demeanor . . . [who] looked like a boarding school miss in man's clothes." [6] Antonio

---

* Whatever the nature of Robert's illness may have been, there is reason to suspect that it was aggravated by motion sickness and claustrophobia. In the single allusion to ocean travel mentioned in his *Memoirs,* it is clear that he was susceptible to seasickness, a condition, incidentally, which would prove to be a cause of intense suffering to Houdini. Evidence will be presented later suggesting that Houdini was also a victim of a hidden claustrophobia.

fortunately had a twin sister, Antonia, who greatly resembled him and with whom de Grisy/Torrini fell in love. In time they married, but after the tragic death of their child in the "William Tell" disaster, Antonia died of a broken heart, leaving her brother Antonio as the sole companion of her guilt-ridden and bereaved husband. It was while the two men were traveling on the high road to Blois that they came upon the unconscious young Robert.

Having been restored to health and initiated into the mysteries of the art of magic by his savior, the time arrived for young Robert to leave his benefactor and return to his native Blois. Here he met a Mademoiselle Houdin, the daughter of a watchmaker, whom he subsequently married, and whose name coupled with his own resulted in his becoming known as Robert-Houdin. It was not until he was nearing the age of forty that he began the public career as a magician that was to confer upon him immortality in the world of conjurers.

Little difficulty stands in the way of discerning typical features of the Family Romance and related fantasies in the foregoing narrative. The Torrini chapter of the life of Robert-Houdin is a dramatic depiction of the rescue of a stricken youth by a personage of noble lineage who treats his protégé like a son, whom indeed the young man resembles. Here, too, is the presentation of a variant of that fantasy that has proved to be a characteristic ingredient in the early history of the creative artist. Citing the reputed discovery of the unknown shepherd boy Giotto by the great Cimabue as an example, Ernst Kris pointed out that this chance discovery of an obscure but talented youth by an established master, who becomes the young man's mentor, is a recurring and characteristic formula in the biography of many artists—even those whose well-recorded histories exclude the possibility of such an incident.[7]

A variant on this theme is found in an episode in Robert-Houdin's *Memoirs:* because of a bookseller's error resulting in his accidental encounter with a treatise on conjuring written by an established master, Robert-Houdin was inadvertently initiated into the wonderful world of magic. This episode is in itself a remarkable anticipation of the chance discovery of the *Memoirs of Robert-Houdin* by the young amateur magician Ehrich Weiss, who was soon to transform the great French conjurer into his hero, his guide, and, indeed, his demigod.

Not only did Ehrich Weiss adopt the Frenchman's name,* choose his profession, and copy his tricks, but even in fashioning the details of

* It is interesting to note that in a story about Houdini printed in the *Boston Post* on February 6, 1900, for some reason he was called *Robert* Houdini.

his life, he seemed to often be treading in the very footsteps of the master. This may be one reason for the fact that, despite strong doubts about their authenticity, certain articles in the Houdini saga persist, like the account of the initial meeting between Houdini and his future wife, Bess Rahner. The most reliable report of that encounter was supplied by Houdini's brother Theodore, who claimed that he had introduced them when she was a member of a song-and-dance team known as The Floral Sisters. According to an obviously more appealing version, however, the pretty eighteen-year-old girl first set eyes on the handsome young Houdini when she was sitting with her mother in the front row, watching him give a magic show at a school in Brooklyn.

Nor did this conclude the narrative of this romantic vignette. In the course of performing a wine-and-water trick, Houdini supposedly made an awkward movement that upset a glass on his table, causing the liquid to spill on her white dress and staining it "beyond redemption." Authentic or not, the episode invites a fairly self-evident interpretation. Full of apologies, eager to make amends and to appease the mother, who was outraged by this figurative defilement of her daughter, Houdini took Bess's measurements and gave them to his own mother, who immediately went to work. Within a week a new dress was finished, and when Houdini brought it to Bess, in the best fairy tale tradition, it fit her perfectly. That same day, June 22, 1894, they stole away to Coney Island, and when Bess got panicky lest her mother punish her for staying out too late, they suddenly decided to get married. One biographer, who challenged the authenticity of the story, pointed out that the judge who supposedly performed the ceremony was at that very time serving a prison sentence! [8]

This undoubtedly apocryphal story is strongly reminiscent of the account given in the *Memoirs* of Robert-Houdin's initial meeting with his future wife. In Chapter VIII the author recalls that he was engaged in performing in some amateur theatricals when he found himself the object of the rapt attention of a seventeen-year-old young lady. "A man is always delighted to find an attentive listener," he wrote, "more especially when it is a pretty young girl. A conversation ensued and became so interesting that we had a great deal still to say to each other when the hour came for separation." Like the accidental spilling of the magic fluid on Bess Rahner's dress, it was "this simple event," continued the *Memoirs,* which became the cause of M. Robert's marriage to Mlle. Houdin. [9]

There were other facets of the career of the famous French conjuror that, for one reason or another, were less readily copied, and demanded of Houdini a different style of imitation. Keen on duplicating the European and British triumphs of his namesake, he and Bess—The Houdinis—billed themselves as Monsieur and Mademoiselle Houdini, and in a playbill of 1894 announced that they had already played in London, Oxford, Cambridge, and Paris, although up until then they had never been abroad. By the time he had actually established a reputation in England, although it was impossible for him to repeat the several brilliant performances of Robert-Houdin before Queen Victoria, the resourceful Houdini, undeterred by Her Majesty's demise, contrived by means of the previously mentioned playlet to "allow [his] little mother to be Queen Victoria for a few fleeting hours." [10]

Even Houdini's funerary monument, which, though dedicated to his parents, is crowned by his own sculpted head, seems to have been inspired, in part at least, by an example associated with the memory of Robert-Houdin. On December 6, 1905, the French Society of Magicians celebrated the one-hundredth anniversary of the birth of Robert-Houdin at the Théâtre Robert-Houdin in Paris. Among other events, a poem in honor of the master was read, at the close of which a bust of Robert-Houdin, which stood upon the stage, was crowned with a wreath of laurel. Kneeling below Houdini's bust in the Machpelah Cemetery is a Pietà-like figure, holding in her hand a chiseled laurel wreath. It should occasion no surprise to learn that among the vast collection of books on magic that Houdini would bequeath to the Library of Congress in Washington, there are at least twenty-five volumes —many of them duplicates or translations—by Robert-Houdin.

In light of his fanatical devotion and worshipful reverence toward the Frenchman, and the display of the plagiarism which is said to represent the highest form of flattery, it is startling to discover that a time would come when, riding high on the crest of his ever-growing fame, Ehrich Weiss, now known as The Great Houdini, would lash out at his former idol and namesake, and showing neither mercy nor justice, would seek to topple him from his lofty throne and cast him disdainfully into the mud.

The Sin of Ham

Thy wish was father, Harry, to that thought:
I stay too long by thee, I weary thee.
Dost thou so hunger for mine empty chair,
That thou wilt needs invest thee with mine honours
Before thy hour be ripe? O foolish youth!
Thou seek'st the greatness that will overwhelm thee.

—HENRY IV, PART II

Neither the cause nor the moment of Houdini's violent about-face toward his revered spiritual father, Robert-Houdin, can be stated with certainty. According to one view, it was the result of a series of disappointments he experienced while seeking to pay homage to his idol during his visit to France in 1901.

Houdini's long anticipated visit to the Théâtre Robert-Houdin on the Boulevard des Italiens in Paris turned out to be the beginning of a parade of misadventures and disillusionments, for the place where the master had once held sway had lately been converted into a motion picture house, in which little of its glittering past remained save for its anachronistic name. Nor did Houdini fare any better when he subsequently sought to establish contact with other traces of his hero. When he learned that the widow of Robert-Houdin's son Emile was still alive, he sent her a letter, requesting her permission to place a wreath on the tomb of her illustrious father-in-law in Blois, and asking her at the same time to grant him an interview. Aside from learning that the lady had been ill for some time and did not wish to be disturbed, he received no reply. Undeterred, he took the train to Blois, the birthplace of Robert-Houdin, where he discovered that the great Frenchman's daughter Rosalie, a sculptress, was living with her husband. She also rejected Houdini's approaches, claiming she was working and did not wish to be interrupted. When he found out that no one would object to his visiting the grave, he ordered a wreath which bore the words, "Honor and Respect to Robert-Houdin, from the Magicians of

America," and proceeded to the cemetery. Here, alone except for a photographer who took his picture, he placed the wreath on the monument and then stood bareheaded before it for a full thirty minutes.*

Houdini reacted to these alleged rebuffs with an angry outburst in English garnished with Yiddish. "The nerve of those stuck-up fakers!" he supposedly screamed. "I'll fix 'em. I'll do 'em something. They won't forget Houdini. They want to play dirty, so I'll play dirty!" When it was suggested that Madame Robert-Houdin lived a secluded life and was entitled to respect, he supposedly shouted, "He stole other men's inventions. The Great Robert-Houdin! He was nothing more than a common thief! The old *gonif* (crook) never invented nothing and I can prove it. I'll write a book exposing the old fraud, the old *mumzer* (bastard)! His book is full of lies!" [1]

Since no witnesses are mentioned nor sources cited, there is good reason to question the literal authenticity of this scene. Not only is it doubtful that Houdini uncorked a flow of Yiddish at the conclusion of his thwarted pilgrimage, but there is no evidence that the full force of the repudiation of his hero emerged so swiftly, or that he decided to write his exposé on the spur of the moment. In fact, five years were to elapse before anything appeared in print indicating that Houdini had undergone a change of heart toward his idol.

In the September 15, 1906, issue of *The Conjurers Monthly*—a magazine of which he was both publisher and editor—Houdini discharged the first salvo of his disenchantment in an article in which he complained of his once having been treated "most discourteously" by the widow of Robert-Houdin's son. Ignoring reports he had received about her poor health, he chided the lady—whom he insisted on calling "Mrs. E. R. Houdin"—for her failure to show "a little common courtesy to the memory of Robert Houdin [*sic*], especially as she is now living in her old age on the proceeds of his endeavors, as she received 35,000 francs several years ago for the Théâtre Robert Houdin [*sic*], etc."

Just how the old lady's reluctance to greet an unknown American

* In support of his contention that Houdini was "the greatest publicity agent that ever lived," Sir Arthur Conan Doyle claimed that whenever Houdini laid flowers on graves—by no means an uncommon practice of his—it was in the pre-arranged presence of local photographers. Houdini evidently placed considerable store on the duration of his expressions of piety. His diary for May 20, 1916, records that he had visited the house from which "we buried dear old father. I had not been there for many years," he wrote, and "stood there in silent meditation for half an hour, in my mind's eye."

magician, whose name bore but a faint resemblance to her late distinguished father-in-law, or the fact that she was beholden to the latter for her financial support, constituted a breach of filial respect, was not elucidated. On the contrary, one may suspect that in this initial denunciation Houdini sought to disguise his personal pique by distorting the real issues and posing as a champion of lofty morality. Rationalization, the substitution of "good" reasons for real reasons, was a device that Houdini would employ at other times, notably, as on this occasion, when he felt repulsed.

Endowed with an immense vanity that brooked no rivals and tolerated no frustrations, Houdini was an unblushing egomaniac whose photograph adorned his stationery and his bank checks, who likened himself to Alexander the Great, and who, like Napoleon, signed his name imperially with a single word. (Figure 6) Flushed with his growing success, it is by no means unlikely that he believed his star was visible to all, that everyone had heard of him, and that the whole world would rise to its feet and cheer as he passed by. Most particularly, he would have expected to be received with open arms by his "adopted" family, the survivors of his childhood hero, and that they would celebrate his "return" by killing a fatted calf amid general rejoicing. Alas, if these were his secret expectations, he must have been profoundly crushed when virtually no one in his hero's family paid him the slightest attention. Surely this was more than he could bear and served only to fan the fires of revenge.

For a while these were but glowing embers that burned in Houdini's heart. It would not be until two years after the publication of the dimly smoldering article in the *Conjurers Monthly* magazine that the full fury of his wrath would finally erupt in the abusive diatribe, *The Unmasking of Robert-Houdin*. Making no pretense to contain his blistering rage, he ripped into the Frenchman, denouncing his "supreme egotism and utter disregard for the truth," his "farcical," "flagrant," and "unscrupulous" allegations and his "purloining tricks and laying claims to have invented tricks long the property of mountebanks as well as reputable magicians." [2] "Today," Houdini wrote, "after a century and a half of neglect, the laurel wreath has been lifted from the brow of Robert-Houdin where it never should have been placed and has been laid on the graves of the real inventors." [3]

Anticipating his later crusade against spiritualism and mind reading, Houdini advertised his book as if it were holy writ. During a theatrical engagement in Boston in May 1908, he promoted his book by having handbills distributed in the streets and in the theatre lobby, reading:

"I want every Bostonian who has seen my performance . . . to read my new book, *The Unmasking of Robert-Houdin.* First, because the truth about magic was never told until this book was written. I have proved to Boston that my stage challenges are genuine. I now challenge the reading public to find one misrepresentation in *The Unmasking of Robert-Houdin,* or, in all the literature of magic, one book that can compare with mine."

No less pretentious is the tone of the book itself and especially its ornate finale:

"So ends the true history of Robert-Houdin. The master magician, unmasked, stands forth in all the hideous nakedness of historical proof, the prince of pilferers. That he might bask for a few hours in public adulation he purloined the ideas of magicians long dead and buried, and proclaimed these as the fruits of his own inventive genius. That he might be known to posterity as the king of conjurers, he sold his birthright of manhood and honor for a mere mess of pottage,* his 'Memoirs' written by the hand of another man, who at his instigation belittled his contemporaries, and juggled facts and truth to further his egotistical jealous ambitions.

"But the day of reckoning is come. Upon the history of magic as promulgated by Robert-Houdin the searchlight of modern investigation has been turned. Credit has been given where it belongs, to those magicians who preceded Robert-Houdin and upon whose abilities and achievements Robert-Houdin built his unearned, unmerited fame. The dust of years has been swept from names long forgotten, which should forever shine in the annals of magic.

"Thus, end also my researches, covering almost two decades of time, researches in which my veneration for old-time magicians grew with each newly discovered bit of history, researches during which my respect for the profession of magic has grown by leaps and bounds; and the fruits of these researches I now lay before the only true jury, the great reading public. My task is finished." 4

Despite these far-flung, florid claims, the book not only failed to achieve its purpose but actually boomeranged both by adding luster to the fame of its intended victim and by leaving the author open to the charge of committing many errors of fact and reasoning. It is noteworthy that some thirty years after Houdini's allegedly earth-shaking

* A possible explanation for this strangely inappropriate Biblical allusion will be offered at a later point.

"unmasking," magicians were still alluding to Robert-Houdin as "The Great Master of Legerdemain," to whom "all of us owe our start."

Indeed, far from his having been carefully and systematically unmasked in a scholarly work drawn "from the very fountain head of information," as Houdini claimed, Robert-Houdin had been subjected to a wild and undisciplined assault that violated the most elementary principles of biographic methodology. Often the work has the shrill and disorganized language that is observed clinically in the disordered thinking and defective judgment of paranoid individuals. Some of the sentences are virtually meaningless; elsewhere the writing smacks of purple gradiosity. "It is a book that will live long after we are all dead," he boasted, and "will stand as a monument of years of diligent research and endeavor, and will bring me back to the minds of the public when I am long forgotten as a public performer." His certainty that the book would assure his immortality prompted him to compare it to the work of Sir Christopher Wren and the achievements of Alexander the Great. In a memorandum to Oscar Teale, his literary editor, Houdini wrote: "Like Alexander . . . who wept because he had no more worlds to conquer, Houdini sought for other worlds to enter, and has now augmented his stupendous library with historical Drama items. . . . He may not be able to compete with the Huntingdon, Wendell or Shaw collections as yet . . . but if his plans go right, who knows but that he will not have a famous library, even as his magical library is the greatest collection . . . in the world."

Consistent with the paranoid nature of Houdini's assault on his erstwhile hero is the realization that, like the pot calling the kettle black—clinically known as "projection"—Houdini was himself guilty of committing many of the very sins he laid at the door of Robert-Houdin. Thus, a few years after denouncing the latter for "robbing dead and gone magicians of all credit for their inventions," Houdini was advertising his "Crystal Casket Act" as "seen for the first time on any stage," although Christopher has pointed out that, far from being a Houdini original, the act was a replica of an invention of none other than Robert-Houdin himself.

Nor was this the only instance of Houdini's helping himself to the ingenious conceptions of Robert-Houdin and neglecting to acknowledge their sources. He evidently claimed to have invented a variation of the traditional trick of sawing a woman in half by "sawing a woman into twins," [5] but an earlier depiction of this same idea can be found in Robert-Houdin's *Memoirs*. In Chapter 6 of that book, in which Torrini narrates the story of his life to young Robert, the great magician explains how he performed the trick of sawing a person into twins by using the astonishing resemblance of Antonio and Antonia to create the illusion.

Houdini also displayed his employment of the psychological mechanism of projection when he accused Robert-Houdin of "supreme egotism" and an "utter unwillingness to admit any ability in his rivals." [6] Not only was this most unfair to Robert-Houdin—as anyone who reads his *Memoirs* can prove for himself—but it was strikingly applicable to Houdini, to whom most other magicians were anathema. He was especially antagonistic to other escapologists, and once, when he was introduced to the Maryland Escape King, he stated that he recognized no other escape kings, and haughtily walked away.[7] Even in the privacy of his diary he exhibited his supreme narcissism. On one title page he wrote:

HARRY HOUDINI
THE FAMOUS JAIL-BREAKER AND MYSTERIARCH.

Houdini's allegation that Robert-Houdin was a thief and a plagiarist was similarly far more applicable to himself than to the Frenchman. In an article in the *Conjurers Monthly* magazine, he expressed his suspicion that some beautiful clocks he had seen marked "Robert-Houdin" had probably been bought by the French magician, who subsequently had his own name engraved on them. (Apparently Houdini had forgotten that Robert-Houdin had been a professional watch and clockmaker before becoming a conjurer.)

Curiously, this is almost exactly what Houdini did with a book, *Elliott's Last Legacy,* written by a magician named Clinton Burgess. When the author asked Houdini to help him finance the publication of the book, Houdini agreed, but he did so at the price of virtually eclipsing the true author's identity. Houdini had his own name printed in large letters on the cover and spine and prominently on the title page, beneath which, in small type and eccentrically located, was printed: "Compiled by Clinton Burgess." [8] Facing the title page are a number of photographs of past presidents of the Society of American Magicians, all of which are dwarfed by the much larger picture of Houdini.

His penchant for plagiarism attained even more impressive proportions in the October 1907 issue of *Conjurers Monthly* in a paragraph on skeleton keys, which was lifted virtually bodily from an article on locks by A. B. Chatwood in the eleventh edition of the *Encyclopaedia Britannica:*

Houdini	*Britannica*
It is always possible to find the shape of the wards, by merely putting in a blank key covered with wax and pressing it against them. When this was done, it was by no means necessary to cut out the key in the complicated form of ward as shown here, etc.	But it was always possible to find the shape of the wards by merely putting in a blank key covered with wax, and pressing it against them; and when this had been done it was unnecessary to cut out the key into the complicated form of the wards (such as Fig. 3) etc.

Even the accompanying illustrations are identical. And a few years later the same plagiarized paragraph appeared in Houdini's book, *Handcuff Secrets*.

Finally, in answer to the charge that the celebrated *Memoirs* of Robert-Houdin had been written "by the hand of another man," it should be observed that, true or false, the accusation was certainly applicable to a number of Houdini's writings. Much of his book *The Right Way To Do Wrong*, Christopher has observed, was written by a promoter and newspaperman named Whitman Osgood. In fact, Maurice Sardina, a French historian of magic, has presented persuasive evidence that *The Unmasking of Robert-Houdin* was itself ghost-written. When Houdini remarked in reference to Robert-Houdin that "the truth was not in him," Sardina wrote, "he must have been looking in a mirror." [9]

Unquestionably the most compelling feature of Houdini's attempted literary assassination of his deposed idol, Robert-Houdin, is not the recording of a catalogue of baseless charges, which often prove to be childish projections of Houdini's personal misdeeds and private vices, but his failure to recognize a glaring flaw in the *Memoirs*, namely that the entire Torrini story, occupying more than a fifth of the book, was a complete fabrication, a fantasy of the author. According to Christopher, a meticulous search among the annals of conjuring has failed to uncover any evidence of the existence of a magician named Torrini, or of a French Count de Grisy.[10]

Under the circumstances it is remarkable that Houdini, who boasted of having turned the "searchlight of modern investigation . . . upon the history of magic as promulgated by Robert-Houdin," never troubled himself to undertake a similar inquiry. On the contrary, so convinced was he of the authenticity of the fictional Torrini that he chided Robert-Houdin for behaving badly toward him!

Moreover, Houdini exhibited a puzzling and uncharacteristic inattention to detail in reading this section of the *Memoirs* he knew so

well, for at one point he asserted that Torrini was an Italian. His unusual carelessness is further emphasized by his failure to detect a
number of patent incongruities in the Torrini story that should have
aroused his suspicions. According to the author, it was in the summer
of 1828 when, as young Monsieur Robert, he was picked up unconscious on the roadside by Torrini and his companion, Antonio. Soon
he learned that his benefactor had not always been a magician, for
"about twenty years before" [11] he had been practicing medicine in
Florence. "I was not a conjurer in those days," sighed Torrini. "Would
to heaven I had never become so!" [12]

At this point the attentive reader is bound to be perplexed by a
few inconsistencies in the matter of chronology, for Torrini's statement would indicate that as late as 1808 [13] he was still practicing medicine in Florence, while Pinetti, his supposed model, adversary, and
victim, died in 1800.

Yet elsewhere Torrini explained that in 1796 circumstances had
obliged him to move to Naples, where in the same year he first became
seriously interested in magic after seeing Pinetti perform at the carni-
val. "As I was madly attached to this sort of spectacle," he said, "I
spent every evening at the theatre, trying to guess the chevalier's
secrets, and, unfortunately for myself, I discovered the key to many of
them. . . . At length I could perform all Pinetti's tricks. The chevalier
was eclipsed." [14]

But now new difficulties arise, for 1796 was also given as the year
in which de Grisy/Torrini obtained his medical degree in Florence.
Hence the reader is asked to believe that he obtained his license, practiced medicine both in Florence and Naples (where he soon took his
place "among the best physicians"), fell under the spell of the great
Pinetti, forsook the practice of medicine for the art of magic, and in
an incredibly short time succeeded in surpassing his mentor and rival
—all in one year!

The fact that, in unleashing his literary haymaker, Houdini overlooked these inconsistencies and unaccountably spared the one obviously vulnerable target in his victim's armor suggests that, despite his
professed antagonism, he was secretly motivated to believe the romantic Torrini story. The reason for his gullibility may be uncovered
by noting the main theme of this fictitious tale.

Like Jack and the Beanstalk, the story of the overnight success of
Torrini, the aspiring young magician, capped by the defeat and dethronement of Pinetti, the reigning monarch of his craft, represents a
figurative depiction of the oedipal ascendance of a youth over his

father. Interwoven into this tale of symbolic parricide is the grim "William Tell" episode, which portrays the victorious Torrini as the accidental killer of his own son. Counterpoised against this mournful song, Robert-Houdin finally transposed his work into a cheerful major key as he recounted the happy miracle of his own rescue and his subsequent initiation into the secrets of necromancy by his repentant benefactor.

Lacking any trustworthy knowledge of the psychological makeup of Robert-Houdin, it can be only a matter of conjecture why he sought to embellish his *Memoirs* with this fictitious interlude. Surely the suggestion that the Torrini section was nothing more than "a literary device which [he] conjured up to make his early years more interesting" [15] is hardly an adequate explanation, for even if this was his conscious intention, it would hardly account for its content.

Whether the latter was a covert confession by Robert-Houdin of his own Family Romance fantasies as well as his oedipal conflicts cannot be stated, but there can be no doubt that his dramatic presentation of the virtually universal and highly charged interactions between fathers and sons, ranging from murderous rivalry and filicide to acts of compassionate rescue, must have struck a sympathetic chord— especially among those readers who, wrestling with kindred emotional issues, were strongly tempted to accept the Torrini myth as unimpeachable truth.

Such a one, it may be suspected, was Houdini, who, caught in a ceaseless identification with Robert-Houdin, blinded himself to the spuriousness of the tale, and like a bombardier flying over his enemy-held native village, was too fond of it to attack it. Not only might he have seen reflections of his own Family Romance fantasies in the Torrini story, but in its depiction of the alleged dethronement of Pinetti by young Torrini, he may have recognized a facsimile of his own wish to eclipse his erstwhile master, Robert-Houdin.

Surely it was no accident that the first signs of the repudiation of his idol coincided with the beginnings of his European success. Standing on the threshold of personal glory, in the full gaze of his adoring mother and exulting in the drama of her "enthronement," Houdini must have believed that at last his hour had come: the "son" had become the equal of the "father," and the moment had arrived when he might uncoil and strike.

In seeking to account for this *volte-face,* it should be noted that the publication of *The Unmasking of Robert-Houdin* was not to be the only blast he would fire at someone he had once loved or esteemed.

Some ten years after the publication of this work, he was to repeat that performance in the treatment of his youngest brother, Dr. Leopold Weiss, who, allegedly for having married the divorced wife of an older brother, became the hated object of Houdini's undying wrath, and was ostracized not only from Houdini's world in life but also from his own placement in the Machpelah Cemetery plot in death.

A similar pattern was to appear in Houdini's relationship with Sir Arthur Conan Doyle some years later. Once cherished as a "sacred treasure" in Houdini's life, like other bright stars in the magician's firmament, Sir Arthur was destined to come crashing down to earth, an object of scorn and ridicule. Indeed, still smarting from Houdini's ill treatment of himself and Lady Doyle, Sir Arthur did not fail to recognize that they had become victims of a personality trait that Houdini had displayed before. "It was the same queer mental twist," wrote Doyle, "which caused him first to take the name of the great Frenchman (Robert-Houdin) and then write a whole book . . . to prove that he was a fraud." [16] In Houdini's diaries, too, epithets like "hypocrites" and "dirty liars" are commonly aimed at persons once regarded as trusted friends.

Although from these examples it might appear that Houdini's affectionate sentiments often teetered nervously on the brink of belligerence, it was characteristic of his ambivalence that a protracted incubation period usually preceded the full germination of his hostility. Nearly seven years elapsed between the alleged rebuff he suffered from the relatives of Robert-Houdin and the publication of *The Unmasking,* and his expulsion of his errant brother and his cursed consort from the Machpelah Cemetery did not occur at the time of their apparent turpitude, but long after the guilty pair had tasted the forbidden fruit. By the same token, his denunciation of Doyle did not take place until a good six months after the alleged pretext for his change of heart.

The fact that Houdini apparently needed time to mull things over before he could bring himself to renounce an old position or denounce an old friendship attests to the strength of those attachments and to the reluctance with which he abandoned them. This undoubtedly accounts for the vehemence of his aggression; like an apostate from the true faith or a reformed revolutionary, he was forced to buttress his new allegiances with the bombast and slogans that would protect him from sliding back into the comforting safety of the old. The swollen torrent of his abuse of Robert-Houdin, it may be suspected, was unleashed not by any rebuff he fancied he had suffered, nor by the great discoveries he had made by means of the "searchlight of modern investigation," but by his urgent and desperate efforts to come to grips with the "father" of his Family Romance.

Psychoanalytic explorations of the fantasy of the Family Romance have shown that it usually arises as a consequence of the disillusionment felt by growing children in their parents, who were endowed in the early years with attributes of omnipotence and perfection, but are later discovered to possess feet of clay. On a deeper level of thought, the adoption of a glamorous, aristocratic surrogate parent may answer a nostalgic longing for the past, for the "happy vanished days," wrote Freud, when the child's father "seemed to him the noblest and strongest of men, and his mother the dearest and loveliest of women."

Such efforts to reshape one's heritage may be in vain, for the adopted parent of the Family Romance may be subjected to the same ambivalence of sentiment originally directed at the real parent he was chosen to replace. Not only the affection but the hostile rivalry, once directed toward the real father, may be deflected upon his substitute. Seen in this light, Houdini's repudiation of Robert-Houdin represents the son's ascendance over the father. It is not surprising that a fellow magician accused Houdini of committing the sin of Ham. In writing *The Unmasking of Robert-Houdin,* this author continued, "Houdini publicly mocked at his spiritual father's nakedness, and tried to show him up as not much different from other vainglorious members of the craft." [17]

To be sure, Houdini was careful to envelop his "parricidal" deed in a mantle of righteousness. When he announced, in the April 1908 issue of *Conjurers Monthly* magazine, that the price of his book had been reduced from $2 to $1, he sought to give the impression that these bargain rates had been motivated solely by lofty sentiments. *The Unmasking of Robert-Houdin,* read the announcement, was "a book with a mission, and the author felt it was his sacred duty to revise the history of his craft, to uncrown the French conjurer, Robert-Houdin, long acclaimed as the king of magicians, etc."

Ironically, some of the sheen that had been reflected from the bright image of his spiritual father, Robert-Houdin, now appeared to enrich the person of the real one. Houdini inscribed in his parricidal book:

This book is affectionately dedicated to the Memory of my father,
Rev. M.S. Weiss, PhD, LLD,
Who instilled in me love of study and patience in research.

Here, to be sure, was a touching display of filial piety, but it contained a concealed petard, for there is no known evidence that Houdini's father possessed either of these impressive degrees, or any other, for that matter. Neither in Hungary nor in America is there any indication that he engaged in studies—either in law or in religion—that might earn him the degree of Ph.D.; as far as the reputed L.L.D. is concerned, this is an honorary degree for which he was in no way qualified.[18] Astride the seesaw of his ambivalence, at the very moment when Houdini was casting his spiritual father into the mire, poetic and psychological justice bade him rescue his true father and raise him to a lofty station, decked out with titles and embellishments he had never won.

What once again commands attention in the Family Romance fantasies of Houdini is not that, like so many others, he harbored daydreams of being descended from illustrious forebears, but that he possessed an unblushing willingness to accept and to display his reveries as realities. Whether it concerned the coronation of his mother or the assignment of high academic rank to his father, it is evident that for this grown man the line separating fact from fancy was composed of the same magical fluidity that divides wishes from reality in the mind of a very little child. Like a child, too, he was not burdened by the demands of consistency; for all of his ultimate professed hostility toward Robert-Houdin, he apparently saw enough of himself in that celebrated Frenchman to make him want to believe blindly in every detail of his romantic history. (How closely he identified with his erstwhile hero is suggested by a slip of the typewriter in which he referred to his book as "Robert *Houdini* Unmasked.")

Something of his original feelings was evidently indestructible, for in time the seesaw of his sentiments tilted in the opposite direction. Supposedly he confessed that he had come to regret writing *The Unmasking of Robert-Houdin,* and when he heard in 1919 that the latter's tomb was in a state of neglect, Houdini wrote to the mayor of Blois, offering to assume the cost of restoring the monument.[19]

The Mark of Cain

Next, it imports no reason
That with such vehemency he should pursue
Faults proper to himself: if he had so offended
He would have weigh'd thy brother by himself,
And not have cut him off.

—MEASURE FOR MEASURE

The ambivalence that cast an occasional shadow upon his sentiments for his father was seemingly absent from Houdini's feelings toward his mother. In the composition of his Family Romance daydreams there was no visible surrogate for her, no discernible counterpart, say, of a Robert-Houdin to compensate for her deficiencies, for in the eyes of her adoring son she had none. Like some divine creature she was the embodiment of perfection, prompting him to write one day, "If God in His infinite wisdom ever sent an angel upon earth in human form, it was my Mother." [1] What need might such a son conceivably have had for the idealized mother of the Family Romance?

Despite her human form, Houdini spared no pains to dissociate this angel from all earthly attributes and worldly appetites, notably in the sphere of sexuality. Regardless of her many children and other evidence to the contrary, in the inscription he composed for her memorial in the Machpelah Cemetary, he did not hesitate to proclaim her chastity:

> Here in Eternal Peace Slumbers our Darling Mother,
> Cecilia Weiss, née Steiner,
> who entered her everlasting sleep July 17, 1913,
> as pure and as sweet as the day she was born, June 16, 1841.

She was no ordinary mortal, this "sainted mother," but a personage from a child's storybook, a good fairy who bestowed upon all adversity a happy ending. With her unfailing compliance in his world of make-believe, it was inevitable that Houdini's relationship with her bore the complexion of a fairy tale.

When his earnings first reached the amazing figure of a thousand dollars a week, Houdini impulsively asked to be paid in gold. As soon as this unusual request was granted, he ran off with the heavy bag of coins, and dashing into his mother's room, bade her hold out her apron, while he poured the gold "in a glittering stream" into her lap. It was this event, he would later assert, that gave him the greatest thrill of his life, a comment which differed very little from what he had said about her "coronation."

To be sure, he was quite unconscious of any symbolic meaning that might be attached to his thrilling gesture. It is most unlikely that the truant son of Rabbi Weiss was familiar with the Greek legend of the imprisoned Danae who, after a visit from Zeus, disguised in a shower of gold, gave birth to the hero Perseus. Nor was he probably aware of the brothel scene in Shakespeare's *Pericles,* in which the proprietor bids the virtuous heroine to serve the appetite of a prosperous client. "Pray you," he cries, "without any more virginal fencing, will you use him kindly. He will line your apron with gold."

Lest this shining moment in Houdini's life be tarnished by any hint of impropriety, it should be noted that in time it would be provided with a setting that furnished it with the seal of paternal sanction. According to this amended version of the event, it had all been foretold many years before when, as the family gathered about the bedside of the dying father, the latter, in a barely audible voice, reassured his grief-stricken wife, "Don't worry, Mama. Harry will pour gold into your apron one day." [2]

Such innocent intimacies between mother and son were a common occurrence, and Houdini's wife characteristically played no role in them. In later years, when his affluence enabled him to own his own home, he acquired a grandfather clock, which it was his custom to wind, but when he was away on tour the task was assigned not to Bess but to his mother. Such was the order of priorities in the Houdini household.

On his return, not only would he resume his role in the clock-winding ceremony but he would dress himself in the clothes his mother had given them because, he explained, it would please her and give her some happiness. No less gratifying was the habit this grown man had of laying his head on his mother's breast—in order to hear her heart beat, he said. It was just one of those "little peculiarities," he noted, "that mean so much to a mother and son when they love each other as we did." [3] How they loved each other is quite clear. In his wearing the clothes that she had selected for him, he was re-enacting the days of childhood when she used to dress him; and when he lay his head on her breast, she was indulging him in that playful sensuality that seductive mothers sometimes foster in their sons, even when they are approaching middle age. It was consistent with the pattern of their relationship that on the occasion of his first leap into New York Bay, he noted in his diary that his mother was there to watch him. "I wanted to have her with me, it being my first jump manacled. I thought something might happen. . . . Ma saw me jump!" he exulted. Despite his obvious pleasure in her being there, the dark hint of another sentiment is suggested by his comment that "something might happen." Was he alluding to the cruel idea that he had invited her to witness a disaster?

Later in the same year, an entry in his diary mentioned a telephone call to her, which he noted with his customary attention to the expense. "Gee, it was worth all that," he added, "just to hear Mother say wo bist du denn mein kindt?" [sic].

Shattering the playful atmosphere of this world of make-believe, it is no wonder that Cecilia Weiss's sudden and unforeseen death at the age of seventy-two came to him as a terrible shock. He was performing in Copenhagen at the time, and when someone handed him the cablegram bearing the fateful news, he supposedly fell unconscious to the floor. When he regained consciousness, he promptly canceled the remainder of his engagement and returned to New York where, at his request, the funeral had been delayed so that he might have a final glimpse of her. In her coffin he placed some woolen slippers he had bought for her in Europe. Later that night he stopped the grandfather clock, as if to signify that with her death time, too, had come to an end.

For some time he made daily trips to his mother's grave; at night his wife often heard him call out his mother's name, and often in the years to come he continued to talk to her. Sometimes when he visited her grave he would lie face down on it and speak to her, telling her of his work and plans. In his wife's opinion, he was never quite the same after his mother's death: "Something of the youthful quality went out of him, something of his earlier joyousness." [4] Along Broadway it was rumored that grief had driven him insane.

Although by September 1913 he was back at work in Europe, Houdini was moody and distracted and spent a good deal of time composing encomiums for his mother. To his diary he confided his melancholy and his loneliness. The morbid direction of his thoughts is reflected in an entry for December, in which he gave a detailed description of a visit to the Suicides' Graveyard in Monte Carlo. "Suicides are buried for seven years," he explained, "then, dug up, placed in boxes, and saved in this manner for future reference in case relatives wish to take the bodies away." Toying perhaps with the idea of joining his mother in death, he remarked upon the grave of a man and his wife who committed suicide together. From a pitiful letter written some time later it is clear this enactment of a *Liebestod* drama reflected Houdini's own thoughts of a reunion and a fusion with his mother's body in death. "I feel like a child who has been taken to the railroad station by mother," he wrote. "Train rushes in, mother manages to get aboard, and before my very eyes away goes the train and mother on board. Here I am left alone on the station, bewildered and not knowing when the next train comes along *so that I can join mother;* and wait I must until the Great Train Despatcher ordains my train time" (italics added).[5]

Among the allusions to his loss nothing is more poignant than this scene of an unsuspecting child abandoned by his mother in the frenetic atmosphere of a railroad station. In the eyes of a psychoanalyst the vividness of the picture suggests that it may have derived from a real experience, although there is no known account of such an occurrence in Houdini's childhood.

In time, as the depression over his mother's death lifted, he began to ruminate over the circumstances surrounding that unhappy event, and presently his sorrow gave way to questions about death-bed secrets, and later to suspicions of foul play. Factually what had happened was that in mid-July 1913 Houdini's mother went on a vacation to Asbury Park, New Jersey, where her son Theodore, the magician who called himself Hardeen, was performing. On the night of the fourteenth, without any warning, she suffered a stroke which left her unable to speak. Two nights later, when he approached her bedside after his return from the theater, Theodore believed she was trying to tell him something but was unable to get the words out. A few minutes later, at a quarter past midnight, she was dead.

Predictably, in the atmosphere of drama which Houdini invariably generated, the mystery of his mother's unspoken words, the "blocked message," became an overriding obsession. By November he became convinced that with it his mother had been trying to reach him and to shield him from some painful knowledge. Yet he must have obtained this knowledge from some other source, for he wrote to Hardeen, "Time heals all wounds, but a long time will have to pass before it will heal the terrible blow which MOTHER tried to save me from knowing." Although in his letter he did not specify the nature of this "terrible blow," ostensibly it concerned a family scandal: Sadie Weiss, the wife of Nathan, the oldest of the Weiss brothers, had left her husband, and after obtaining a divorce, was to marry Leopold, the doctor. Supposedly the "blocked message" contained the word *Forgive!*, an instruction to the hasty-tempered Houdini to exercise charity and understanding in dealing with this allegedly reprehensible conduct. (Figure 3)

Over the ensuing years Houdini would attend numerous spiritualist seances, hoping to hear the cherished word, and after each disappointment he would return to his mother's grave and complain, "Well, Mama, I have not heard!" [6] He was still waiting for it nine years after her death when he participated in a spirit-writing seance with Sir Arthur Conan Doyle and Lady Doyle in Atlantic City.

Despite the general acceptance of this account of the blocked message, it presents a number of troublesome inconsistencies. Since Leopold and Sadie did not get married until 1917, nearly four years after Cecilia's death, their marriage could hardly have been the blow from which she supposedly was seeking to shield Houdini. It is clear from his letter to Hardeen, moreover, that by November, if not earlier, he had already learned the nature of the "terrible blow"; but if it concerned some improper conduct on the part of Leopold, it did not seem to disturb his relations with Houdini, which continued to be friendly for at least two years after their mother's death. As late as July 16, 1915, on the second anniversary of that event, Houdini's diary discloses that they went together with Hardeen to Asbury Park to visit the place where she had died. In fact, no clear evidence of any hostility between the brothers appeared until after Leopold's marriage, early in 1917.

From this moment on, through some tortured reasoning, Houdini had arrived at the strange conclusion that Leopold's unseemly behavior had somehow contributed to his mother's death.

Despite the lack of logic in his thinking, as a fit punishment for Leopold's alleged villainy, Houdini decided to give his younger brother the axe. In his self-appointed role as executioner, Houdini seized an old family photograph, made in 1909, showing Bess, Leopold, and himself with their mothers, and with a pair of scissors, amputated his brother's head. (Figure 4) On the reverse was written in longhand,

"This is the picture from which Houdini later cut off his brother's picture, because he thot [*sic*] that an act of the brother had hastened his mother's death."

But the beheading of his brother in effigy was not the sole manifestation of Houdini's vengeance. Figurative excisions of Leopold were effected in several sections of Houdini's last will and testament, dated July 20, 1924. And as a final repudiation, clause nineteen pointedly omitted Leopold's name from the list of those he permitted to be buried in the family plot in the Machpelah Cemetery.

Leopold and his guilty consort, Sadie, were not the only victims of Houdini's will. Like Bonaparte assigning the thrones of Europe to privileged relatives and loyal favorites, Houdini ruled the Machpelah plot as if it were a personal fief or an exclusive club, admission to which waited on his pleasure. After naming his wife, his Hungarian-born brothers, Nathan and William, and his American-born siblings, Theodore and Gladys, as eligible for burial in this exalted piece of ground—while pointedly omitting Leopold and Sadie—the will expressly set out to separate *all* his married brothers from their wives, for it clearly stipulated that "no member of the respective families of my said brothers and sisters, nor any other person or persons whatsoever, shall be buried in the said plot."

In seeking to account for this arbitrary dictate it should be noted that, aside from Sadie, it could apply only to the wives of his brothers William and Theodore. Religion was certainly not the issue, for although these sisters-in-law were Christian, Houdini had specified that his Catholic wife Bess was eligible for burial in the family plot. Indeed the only credible motive for excluding the wives of William and Theodore was malice, a spiteful reflection of a life-long antagonism toward "outsiders."

Even in his pitiless punishment of the "adulterous" couple, spelled out in clause after clause of the will, the major focus of Houdini's wrath fell quite clearly upon the scarlet-lettered Sadie. "It is my express desire, intention and direction," reads paragraph eighteen, "that no part of either the principal or income of my Estate shall ever directly or indirectly go to Sadie Glantz Weiss, the divorced wife of my brother Nathan Joseph Weiss and the present wife of my brother Doctor Leopold David Weiss, and I direct that she shall receive no benefit directly or indirectly out of either the principal or income of my Estate or any part of it." Nor did he make any secret of his eager anticipation of her death and of the advantages to Leopold that would follow that hoped-for event: Leopold was to receive nothing of Houdini's legacy, states section seventeen, "unless his present wife, the divorced wife of my brother Nathan . . . shall have died."

These not very veiled death wishes aimed at his sister-in-law, coupled with clear indications that, once fulfilled, Leopold would be forgiven and reinstated in Houdini's good graces, throw grave doubts on the truth of the commonly held belief that his punitive condemnation of the supposedly guilty pair was motivated by high moral principle. Taking a cue from other samples of his vindictive aggression, notably the publication of *The Unmasking of Robert-Houdin,* makes it seem more probable that, though clothed in a mantle of righteousness, his merciless assault was fundamentally a trumped-up device designed to conceal a secret resentment, mainly against Sadie Weiss. These sentiments certainly did not result from her divorce from Nathan, which had taken place many years earlier and had failed to draw any evident disapproval from Houdini at the time. On the contrary, in a letter to Hardeen, written on January 19, 1914, alluding to Nathan, Houdini said, "I hope he gets divorced." [7] Indeed, his diary contains numerous indications of his disdain for her ex-husband:

February 17, 1907: Nat . . . did not know what he was talking about.

August 16, 1907: Nat refuses to come in the morning to have family foto taken. Pleads pressure of business.

August 6, 1911: (re a family photograph) Nat as usual is teasing Mother, and as usual I am sore at him. That is why I look so cheerful.

January 4, 1913: Nat came (to Bess's birthday party) after his cafe was closed, and had as usual his share to say.

January 23, 1915: Nat on a visit to us. I paid Nat's bill.

Counterpoised against these expressions of derision, the same diary indicates that at one time Houdini had felt warmly disposed toward Sadie. There is even a hint of flirtatiousness in his notation on June 2, 1908, that it was her birthday, and that he had "chipped in" with his brother Leopold to buy her flowers. That these two brothers may have been vying for her favor is further suggested by another entry in the diary describing an outing that these three had made together to visit her daughter Constance, an apparently retarded child, who was living away from home. If Houdini had secretly harbored tender feelings toward his sister-in-law, her ultimate marriage to Leopold might have unleashed the fury of a person scorned.

If it is argued that these speculations rest on tenuous evidence, they possess more than an element of plausibility when viewed against the broad canvas of Houdini's history, for in all aspects of his life he displayed a limitless megalomania that made it virtually impossible for him to endure the success of anyone else without extreme resentment. The sources of this craving for omnipotence may be discovered in the perilous and threatening circumstances of his childhood: the mysterious exodus from Hungary in his infancy, the separation from the father, the instability of life during the long voyage to America, the uncertainty of existence in that foreign land, the sounds of an unfamiliar tongue, the birth of two younger brothers, and the parade of domestic crises that beset this uprooted and impoverished household.

Although there are no reliable accounts of Houdini's memories of those anxiety-ridden early years, it is certain that they were punctuated by the sight of perplexing pregnancies, frightening obstetrical crises and terrifying bloody rituals performed on his little brothers when they were but a week old. In the eyes of a small child, the horror of circumcision and its association with cannibalism would be inevitably reinforced by the sight of the *metsutsa,* the sucking up of blood by the lips of one of the older and respected celebrants.* All of these disturbing happenings took place, in all likelihood, within the cramped confines of a series of different homes.

That these same domestic conditions subjected little Ehrich to other no less disturbing nocturnal events seems probable, and may have contributed to a lifetime of unusual sleeping habits. When he was an infant his mother worried because he seemed to sleep so little; whenever she bent over his crib, she asserted, day or night his eyes were always open. Perhaps he dared not close them, lest his parents, believing he was asleep, would engage in frightening sexual acts. Support for this conjecture may be discovered in what is evidently the only reported dream of Houdini. In a letter to Hardeen, dated January 19, 1914, Houdini related a recent dream in which he had seen his parents drinking coffee together under the trees in the park in Appleton. He ran for the *camera,* stopping from time to time to "feast [his] eyes on our Parents so calmly drinking and chatting. . . . *I feared they would note by my actions that I was excited,* but you know how dreams are: only possibly visions of the brain's 'efforts' " (italics added).[8] Aside from expressing a wish to see his dead parents again, engaged in an innocuous pleasure, stripped of its censorship the dream suggests the excitement and the fear of being detected of a boy watching a far less innocent scene. The "oral" element may also refer to a mother nursing a child. In later years he continued to display the same apparent distrust of

* Whether this custom, now largely abandoned, was observed by Rabbi Weiss is not known.

the state of sleep, for he wore a black silk bandage over his eyes—ostensibly because "the least ray of light would waken him." [9]

Nor were his parents' sexual activities and the births of siblings the only threatening events in his early years. As noted earlier, in late December 1885 when he was not yet eleven years old, his twenty-two-year-old half-brother Herman died of tuberculosis, an occurrence which left a deep and lasting impression on Houdini, whose diary would continue to mark the anniversary of the event as late as thirty years after.

In this grim atmosphere, charged with frightening scenes, a succession of younger rivals, and filled with an awesome catalogue of the precariousness of life and limb, it is not strange that young Ehrich acquired a constellation of personality traits designed not only to ward off the threat of abandonment but also to insure his invulnerability and eternal survival.

Just as a lonely and fearful child may seek to rescue himself from the morass of anonymity and impotence by identifying himself with the heroes of fairy tales and fiction, so did Houdini, by inventing his own personal myth, cultivate a ruthless grandiosity that enveloped him as he scaled the peaks of fame, from whose lofty summits he might gaze down disdainfully on vanquished rivals. Nothing so succinctly epitomized the fulfillment of this dream of imperial station as his flamboyant design for the costly exedra he had constructed in the Machpelah Cemetery, supposedly in honor of his parents.* There, in its geometrical center, towering above the gravestones of his parents, his grandmother, his five brothers, his sister, and himself, he planned the placement of his marble bust, flanked on either side by a stone column dedicated to his parents. (Figure 5)

In this majestic semicircle he possessed a pediment that surely he had always coveted, a seat chiseled in imperishable stone, from which he might preside like the majestic sovereign he sought to be in life, unthreatened by the claims of competitors and impervious to the intrusion of outsiders.[10]

Like a child he sought to dramatize his mental conflicts through the medium of fiction. A depiction of the theme of fraternal rivalry can be discerned in a short story attributed to Houdini, "The Hoax of The Spirit Lover," which relates the discovery of fraud perpetrated by a

* Although dedicated to both parents, in a letter of April 3, 1920, to Sir Arthur Conan Doyle, he mentioned having constructed an exedra "for my beloved mother." The reverse side of the pedestal supporting his bust carries the inscription "Erected by Houdini 1916 in sacred memory of his Beloved Parents." The size of the letters spelling out his name is about twice that of the rest of the text.

man who tries to collect life insurance by impersonating a brother dying of tuberculosis. The latter, it will be recalled, was the "Great White Plague" that had killed Houdini's half-brother Herman, and his brother William many years later.

He returned to these themes in another short story, "The Magician's Christmas Eve," in which the protagonist, a famous magician known as The Marvelous Balsoma,* marries the wife of another showman. But in this tale there is no hint of immorality, for the wife, unlike Sadie Weiss, is not a divorcée, but the widow of a vaudeville performer who has died, predictably, of tuberculosis. (It is noteworthy that the given name of the protagonist in this "tuberculosis" story is William, and that the widow's maiden name—Roberts—is almost identical to the "maiden name" of Robert-Houdin.)

If these varied manifestations of rivalry were later derivatives of his original hostility to the birth of a brother, one is bound to ask why he singled out Leopold as the chief target for his wrath and spared his brother Theodore, who had surely been no less of a usurper of little Ehrich's position in the family. Indeed, the uneven injustice meted out by Houdini is particularly noteworthy in his far-fetched attempt to pin the blame for his mother's death on Leopold. In thus making a scapegoat of the doctor he was being not only unfair but illogical, for unlike Hardeen, Leopold was not even on the scene in Asbury Park when their mother was stricken. If anyone might have deserved to be censured for not saving the life of a seventy-two-year-old lady afflicted by a stroke, it would have been the magician. Yet there are no known letters or other indications of Houdini's disapproval of the fact that, although his mother had suffered a cerebral accident and had been placed on the critical list, her son Hardeen had continued his performance on the local stage, even on the very evening that she died.

Cognizant of Houdini's frequent recourse to projection, it is entirely possible that in exculpating Hardeen he was simultaneously relieving himself of any blame for not being present when she was stricken. Like Leopold, he himself had been far from the scene, much farther in fact, for he had been performing in Europe at the time, and perhaps during the ensuing months he chided himself for having been away. † Kellock's description of his departure from New York, on the *Kronprinzessin Cecile* (!) suggests that he behaved as if he had a premonition that he would never see her again:

* The significance of the pseudonym *Balsoma* will be mentioned later.
† Zolotow apparently entertained a similar suspicion, for when Balsamo, his fictional recreation of Houdini, hears of his mother's death, he exclaims, I'll never forgive myself. . . . Why was I playing in theatres when my mother was dying?"

"Persons at the pier . . . saw Houdini clinging to a little old woman in black silk, embracing and kissing her, saying goodbye and going up the gangplank, only to return to embrace her again. *'Ehrich, vielleicht wenn du zurück kommst bin ich nicht hier'* (perhaps when you come back I shall not be here) his mother had remarked as they reached the pier together." [11] Typical of the ways of magical thought, he may have reasoned that had he remained with her she would never have died.

Bearing in mind that as Hardeen the Magician Theodore was a far more obvious rival to Houdini than his doctor/brother, it is all the more remarkable that he seized upon the latter as his scapegoat. There may have been subtle psychological reasons, however, that dictated this bias.

Leopold, it will be recalled, was born when Ehrich was approaching the age of six, a period of particular vulnerability in a boy which often represents the peak of his oedipal attachment to his mother. That at such a time her attention was inevitably totally focused on the new baby must have inflicted a painful sense of abandonment on Ehrich and presumably mobilized intensely hostile feelings toward the little intruder. In time, to be sure, those feelings were repressed, and as far as one can determine, Houdini and Leopold enjoyed a friendly relationship for many years. His mother's death, however, could well have re-awakened the ancient pain of separation and, compounded by the marriage of Sadie to Leopold, an ancient grievance.

Theodore, in contrast, born when Ehrich was less than two years old, was clearly far more a childhood companion to Ehrich. Indeed, it is claimed that it was Theodore who had taught Ehrich his first magic trick. There were other facets in their relationship, moreover, that may have caused Houdini to feel beholden to Theodore, and perhaps somewhat guilty, too. It has been claimed that in marrying Bess Rahner after a whirlwind courtship, Houdini had taken his brother Theodore's girl, for presumably Theodore had been dating Bess until he introduced her to his more aggressive brother. For jilting him, Theodore supposedly bore a grudge against Bess for some time.

And now insult was added to injury, for after the marriage Bess replaced Theodore as her husband's professional partner, and what had been billed as The Brothers Houdini * became The Houdinis. Finally, it might be assumed that Houdini's competitive feelings to-

* A reporter writing up their act on June 22, 1894, referred to them, perhaps with snide intent, as the Hunyadi Brothers. Hunyadi was a popular mineral water known for its laxative properties.

ward Theodore were tempered by the indisputable evidence of his professional superiority. Sometimes, in fact, Houdini treated Hardeen as if he were his protégé.

Despite any outward show of fraternal and professional harmony, it would be a mistake to assume that their relationship was devoid of friction. At best it was not much better than an armed truce, broken periodically by bursts of hostility. Hardeen clearly sought to win fame by following almost slavishly in his famous brother's footsteps. In a thirty-two-page pamphlet bearing the title *Life and History of Hardeen,* the author explained that he had chosen his stage name (originally Harden)—"a name known throughout every country in the civilized world"—because he did not wish to "confuse the public by adopting the same name as his older brother."

Apparently Houdini did not see it quite that way, for in a letter berating another magician for using his name, he wrote, "Why, you have acted worse than my brother. He calls himself Hardeen, but not Harry Hardeen." Indeed, Houdini's resentment toward his brother's nom de guerre was not without foundation, for Hardeen's publicity was so regularly spiced with allusions to Houdini that it is difficult to avoid the conclusion that the creation of confusion between the two performers was in fact his very aim. A notice in a German newspaper, dated December 9, 1900, referred to "Theo Hardeen" as "genannt HOUDINI der Zweite." The name Houdini is printed in huge letters; "der Zweite" is barely visible.

How Houdini must have felt about this appropriation of his name may be judged by an incident that took place one day in New York in 1925. Ostensibly because his personal mail was being sent to a radio shop called "Houdina," Houdini stormed into the store, wrecked the chandelier and smashed a number of cabinets and office fittings. Although he was charged with disorderly conduct, the case was dropped when, for some obscure reason, the complainant failed to show up in court. On another occasion he tried to forbid an illustrator named Hugh Deeny from using his supposedly given name.

Houdini's resentment toward his brother was also undoubtedly directed toward Hardeen's publicity, which was virtually indistinguishable from his own:

"Hardeen, the wonderful performer, known throughout the civilized world as being able to escape from the strongest handcuffs and bonds devised by the police, has combined showmanship and ability, and presented to the theater-going public a performance which will be talked of by the grandchildren of those who have had the good fortune to have witnessed his act."

Like Houdini, Hardeen also specialized in escapes from handcuffs, prison cells, milk cans, etc. On September 26, 1907, five months after his mother had watched the manacled Houdini make his first big bridge jump, Hardeen, King of the Handcuffs, The Handcuff Wizard, leapt, handcuffed, from a bridge sixty feet above the Ohio River at Louisville. (It is not recorded that his mother saw him.) And although in a newspaper interview in 1907 Hardeen denied that he considered himself his brother's rival, the same article stated that Houdini had confronted his brother on his return from Europe to learn "of his brother's intentions."

Apparently time brought no abatement to this fraternal strife. Fifteen years later, on January 6, 1923, Houdini's diary reported: "[Theodore] arrives for a short visit. We had a scrap in New York and I think he recognizes my condition." Just what was meant by this remained unrecorded, but there can be little doubt that Houdini tolerated his brother's ambitions so long as the latter stayed out of his way and acknowledged who was the one and only king.

Closely scrutinized, Houdini's attitude toward Hardeen does not seem to have differed significantly from that accorded other competitors. During the many years he ruled over the Society of American Magicians, he scuttled whatever democratic principles he may have embraced elsewhere, and presided over the affairs of the Society like a hereditary monarch. On trumped-up charges, he succeeded in expelling such eminent confrères as Blackstone and Dunninger, and he threatened the careers of others. In the theatrical world, too, by wielding his considerable influence, he was able to prevent a number of magicians from performing those acts he judged too similar to his own. When it came to getting his own way, for all his stiff-necked professions of morality, he could be remarkably petty, and sometimes cruel.

Once, for example, on learning that his aged and trusted librarian, Alfred Becks, had his heart set on buying a collection of books that was coming up for auction, Houdini dispatched an agent to bid for them under an assumed name. When the crestfallen Becks returned from the auction complaining that some stranger had outbid him, Houdini hid his ill-gotten loot in the cellar. But when the faithful Becks died in 1925, another aspect of Houdini's capricious personality emerged. Overcome with remorse, he sent three different floral arrangements to the funeral to make it appear that Becks had not been altogether friendless. Yet such was the unpredictability of this most inconsistent man that in the midst of his weeping after the funeral, he suddenly straightened up and, bounding out of his chair, exclaimed, "Now I suppose I can get those books out of the cellar!" With this, he rushed downstairs to fetch them, then returned to his chair, where he started to weep all over again, crying, "Poor old Becks!" [12]

There were other occasions, however, like his attack on the Houdina radio shop, when, undeterred by any considerations of compassion, he seemed to relish opportunities to throw his weight around. His vicious attacks on Robert-Houdin and others, the slow, smoldering build-up of his aggression and its ultimate explosion after questionable provocation, the inconstancy of his friendships, his quick-tempered and capricious switch from affection to scorn, his contentious demeanor and his ruthless and often arbitrary treatment of his confrères; all suggest that ever since early childhood there lay within his troubled soul a deep, dark pool of aggression that threatened at some unguarded moment to overflow its brim. When circumstances persuaded him that his cause was just and that heaven judged him on the side of the angels, like a fanatical crusader, inflated with a bursting sense of holy righteousness, he could let loose a blistering, withering assault, which, if untamed, could become murderous.

Such a "heaven-sent" opportunity came his way in December 1915 while he was performing in Los Angeles. In the course of the performance he learned that Jess Willard, then heavyweight champion of the world, was in the theater audience. Suddenly, and without any preliminary briefing or introduction, Houdini called out to the unsuspecting boxer, inviting him to join him on the stage and to serve as one of the "committee" that was usually selected from the audience. When Willard, taken unawares and apparently suspicious and uncomfortable in the situation, refused, Houdini became nettled and proceeded to bait the fighter with bombast and high-flown phrases. According to the account of the affair which he wrote to his sister Gladys, he called out to Willard, "Look here, you. I don't care how big you are, or who you are . . . you have the right to refuse, but you have no right to slur my reputation. Now that you have thrown down the gauntlet [whatever that might have meant to Willard], I have the right to answer, and let me tell you one thing, and don't forget this, that I will be Harry Houdini when you are not the heavyweight champion of the world." [13] This oratorical haymaker apparently brought down the house. Possessing no defense against the verbal punches thrown by this slick showman, Willard muttered a few epithets, and amid the hoots of the spectators, crept out of the theater, a crestfallen and defeated man.*

By 1915 Houdini had evidently forgotten what he had published six years earlier in the introductory chapter of his work, *Handcuff Secrets:*

> In addressing your audience do not become bombastic or overbearing in demeanour, but speak as you would to critical friends, thereby gaining their confidence and sympathy and, no matter what may worry or trouble you, never let your audience detect any irritability or ill temper, but always display a bright and pleasing manner. Nothing is more offensive to an audience than a performer to appear surly and bad tempered. He is there to please the public, and to do so he must be on the best of terms with himself and, I may add, in the best of humour.

Houdini had clearly wandered apace from these irreproachable precepts in his contretemps with Willard, which in retrospect was hardly a noble spectacle, although to Houdini it seemed as if, armed with a modest slingshot, he had just felled a latter-day Goliath—a not inappropriate image for the encounter between the diminutive magician, five feet four inches tall, and the towering Kansan, who was over six feet six inches in height and weighed two hundred and fifty pounds.

Houdini also had the additional advantage of attacking a man who was not a particularly popular champion. Although some months earlier, as The Great White Hope, he had been hailed for restoring prestige to the Caucasian race by defeating the black champion Jack Johnson in round twenty-six of a forty-five-round fight in Havana, Willard lacked the charisma of a hero like Jack Dempsey or Joe Louis. Not surprisingly, to some observers he appeared simple-minded, a trait which hardly made him a match for the verbal blows unleashed by Houdini.

Needless to say, in describing his triumph in a letter to his sister, Houdini embellished freely, pulled out all the stops and opened wide the swells. "My dear sister Gladys," he began. "Well, at last I manage to sit down and relate to you how I defeated the World Champion

---

* Cognizant of Houdini's tendency to pattern his behavior on others, it seems plausible that he drew his inspiration for the Jess Willard affair from the fact that in 1885 the great Harry Kellar succeeded in inducing the then heavyweight champion, John L. Sullivan, to come up on the stage and participate in a magic stunt. After it was over, Sullivan, much impressed, exclaimed, "I'll be damned if Kellar isn't the strongest little man I ever saw." It was from Kellar, it will be recalled, that Houdini probably acquired the name Harry.

Heavyweight Pugilist, Mr. Jess Willard, and why the newspapers gave me the decision over him, which makes me the Newspaper Heavyweight Champion of the World."

Drunk on his own rhetoric, from time to time he appears to have lost his vantage point of observation, so that he described himself as if he were both subject and object of his own narrative:

"I walked right down to the footlights nearest his side, and thundered out at him, white with rage," and

"My reply to Mr. Jess Willard just set those twenty-three hundred human beings stark, raving mad. Instead of a place of entertainment, it was a seething, roaring furnace."

"Honest, Gladys," he continued, "I have received at least a million dollars' advertising space from this fray . . . you will smile to know that I am greeted on the streets as, 'Hello, Champion' and 'How is the Champion?' " [14]

To be sure, the public acclaim accorded the "Champion" was enhanced by his draping the entire spectacle within the folds of the Stars and Stripes. "I am an American," he told reporters on the pink-tinted *Los Angeles Record* for December 3, 1915, "and I am more proud of that fact than anything else. That's why it cut me so to realize that Jess Willard, whom I regard as our champion, would act as he did. I have perfomed for kings, czars, and princes in Europe," he continued, "but I value one little audience with President Wilson * more than I do all the honors that they heaped upon me. The day that our President sent for me was the one which I shall always treasure in my memory as the happiest of my life, for I love my country and respect its President more than the greatest princes of the earth.

"So that's what hurts me when Jess Willard, whom I regarded as a fellow American failed to live up to our ideals in public. An American is always a gentleman, in my opinion." Then, with debatable accuracy, he added that he would not have pressed Willard to serve on the committee if he had "intimated he didn't want to. Instead he called me a faker and a four-flusher, before an audience of 2000 persons, and no real man would stand by passively and submit to such treatment."

There was more to this flamboyant exhibition than a mere exercise in *machismo* accompanied by a fanfare of jingoistic flourishes. The event provided for Houdini a public rostrum from which his strident voice could proclaim his patriotism, while drowning out the secret

---

* This occurred during the first week of December, 1914. The *New York Telegraph* for December 10 reported that Mrs. Houdini and his brother, Doctor Leopold Weiss, went with him.

stigma of his foreign birth. No less welcome was his possession of a pulpit where, resounding with the harmonies of his Family Romance fantasies, he might intone his reverence for the President of the United States.

Constantly in quest of an idealized father, it is not surprising to discover his recurring susceptibility to the awesome aura surrounding that high eminence. As noted earlier, in selecting a cemetery plot for his family and himself, he had been heartened to discover that nearby was the tomb of a magician who had performed for President Lincoln. Whether he was cheered by the prospect of enjoying the future company of that magician's remains or by the association with Lincoln cannot be decided, but there is no reason to suppose that in the next world he would be any less eager to rub elbows with great and famous men than he had been in this. And now, thanks to his encounter with Jess Willard, he had been presented with another opportunity to render homage to a president.*

Inasmuch as Houdini utilized the Willard affair as a vehicle for the enunciation both of his patriotism and his filial devotion to the figurative Father of the Country, and in light of the fate of other objects of his Family Romance fantasies, it is logical to seek for evidence of contrary sentiments toward these father surrogates, namely, thoughts of regicide or parricide.

In support of these expectations it is noteworthy that on January 6, 1906, he effected a spectacular escape from the prison cell in Washington, D.C., where Charles J. Guiteau, the assassin of President Garfield, had been confined while awaiting execution. Lest it be supposed that this was just another stunt, possessing no psychological significance for Houdini, it should be observed that for some reason he was particularly interested in this crime, and even owned a book about it: *The Trial of Guiteau, The Assassin* by George R. Hebart, which is now in the Houdini Collection of the Library of Congress. In seeking to account for Houdini's unmistakable fascination with this historical event, and his apparent identification with it, in contrast, say, to the murder of President McKinley, which took place in 1901, it should be recognized that the former occurred when Ehrich Weiss was a child of 7, a most impressionable age for a boy struggling with his own oedipal conflicts to learn about real or figurative parricide.

* It may be suspected that his sentiments toward Wilson referred more to the office than to the man, for on one of the seemingly rare occasions when Houdini voted, in November 1920, he cast his ballot for Warren G. Harding, a man who had little in common with Wilson, either as a statesman or as a scholar, and whose contribution to American letters is recollected largely for his coinage of the word "normalcy."

Viewed against this larger background, his encounter with Willard assumes wider implications: Houdini emerges as the good and submissive son; Willard as the crude, uncouth, bad boy. To Houdini the matter predictably carried sexual overtones. "The worst feature of the case," he told reporters, "was the blasphemous language used by Willard. . . . Women, for a large area about him, heard his profane expletives." Under the circumstances, it is not surprising that women in Houdini's own family were to play a prominent role in this *cause célèbre*.

Why did Houdini take this occasion to write what has been pronounced as his longest letter and address it to his sister? It might be argued that he was reveling in the opportunity of showing off before her, which seems plausible enough except that he was not in the habit of writing to her, save for an occasional postcard. More likely is the suspicion that he was seeking to insure himself against her possible disapproval of his conduct, when she would read about it in the newspaper, for his letter makes it quite clear that he felt somewhat uneasy about his treatment of Willard. He was especially concerned about his wife's opinion on that score.

"Bess was in the wings," his letter to Gladys went on, "flaming red. I felt sure she was going to give me the dickens, and just think of it— there I was hurling defiance at the greatest fighter of the human race, and, when I beheld my beloved little helpmate, I was actually afraid.

"But she was with me. In fact, in all my fights, when she thinks I am right, she is alongside, helping me load the machine guns. So, when I noted that Bess was not angry with me, I did not give a rap about what Willard thought of me." [15]

Nothing within the broad proscenium of this flashy drama is more arresting or more revealing of the complexity of Houdini's character than these final passages of the letter to his sister. What sharper paradox can be imagined than the spectacle of this strutting peacock, crowing over his annihilation of the "greatest fighter of the human race" before a cheering crowd of over two thousand people and peering anxiously into the wings for traces of his wife's displeasure?

The stark incongruity of these two facets of his behavior soon fades as the immediate setting is ignored, the progression of time reversed, and the scene transported to the stage of his childhood. Played in the theater of the past, the drama now discloses Houdini as a guilty boy who, seeking to unseat his champion/father, seeks anxiously for the approval of his mother/wife for his oedipal victory. Perhaps, too, the grown Houdini saw in Willard a surrogate for an unwanted younger brother and feared the reproving glances of a mother who had caught him in a hostile act toward the little intruder. Whether in reality such a deed did occur or lay repressed within the depths of his unconscious thought, there can be little doubt that its potential remained alive. And when, at last, Leopold's behavior appeared to justify the emergence of this long pent-up aggression, Houdini turned again to his mother, from whose voice beyond the grave he sought a message bearing an answer to that ancient call of conscience: Am I my brother's keeper?

It was probably a reenactment of that moral conflict that prompted Houdini to fear the disapproval of his wife for his hectoring assault on Willard, for clearly she had become a representative of his mother, just as the boxer had become a scapegoat for the American-born Leopold.

Recent developments in the professional career of Dr. Weiss may have made the search for a scapegoat even more pressing, for as one of the pioneers in the new and growing field of X-ray medicine, he was well on the way to making quite a name for himself. In his well-appointed office adjoining the elegant Plaza Hotel on Central Park South, where he arrived in his chauffeur-driven Rolls Royce or Pierce Arrow—he owned both—he was being consulted by the cream of New York society: the Schiffs, the Vanderbilts, and other notables, whose distinguished names were music in the ears of his proud mother. In time he and his wife acquired a palatial estate in Connecticut where they spent their weekends.

Ironically, Leopold's brilliant success may have far outpaced the original intention of his magician brother, who was evidently responsible for promoting his medical career. Ostensibly in order to conform to a legal regulation that the type of show Houdini was mounting required the presence of a bona fide physician, and "to keep the graft in the family," Houdini financed his brother's education at New York University and Bellevue Medical College, from which Leopold received the degree of Doctor of Medicine on May 16, 1899. Aware of Houdini's burning need to be his mother's favorite, however, he was no doubt piqued by the unforeseen outcome of his plans and by the realization that his position was once again threatened as his mother swelled with pride over the estimable attainments of her son the doctor.[16]

Evidently, Houdini's attachment to his mother was compounded by an undercurrent of anxiety, a fear that once again, as she had seemingly done in his early years, she might abandon him or pierce him with the sharp glances of her displeasure. Determined to insure their eternal union, it is no wonder that he was shocked and shattered by her death, and that following that calamity he sought to immortalize her by transforming her earthly being into a divinity. Yet the panegyrics he composed in her memory seem devoid of true depth of feeling and convey no sense of her real identity:

> This Mother, to whom Eternity means no more than a fleeting, forgotten second of Time, when working or watching for her children, you must cherish while she is with you so that, when the pitiless Reaper brings from the Almighty the Mandate recalling Mother, you may receive from your ever-present Conscience the consolation coming from the knowledge that you tried to smooth, tried to remove the briars from the path which she trod through this Mortal Valley of the Shadow of Death. . . . The Poet who wrote, "God Himself could not be Everywhere so He made Mothers"—gives poetic utterance to my own sentiment.

More sentimental than sentiment, one is prompted to say, for his mawkish words recall the lavender language of commercial bereavement cards, composed by anonymous hack writers to help obscure real feelings behind a wall of platitudes. Rather than conveying a sense of spontaneous grief, his comments give the impression that he felt he was on trial and was expected to give a good account of himself. Thus in August of the year of his mother's death, he closed a letter: "Yours, bowed down with grief," and in the following month, as if he were reporting to some unseen critic, he wrote in his diary: "Many a bitter tear I am shedding." The sense of distance from his emotions is also produced by the meticulous attention to detail that accompanies his expressions of sorrow. Just as on other occasions he had calibrated his grief and quantified his piety by enumerating and timing his visits to various grave sites, so over the years his diary registered the anniversaries of his mother's birthday. Characteristically, however, these entries were accompanied by indications of an obsessional concern for duty and details. On June 16, 1908, for example, after noting that it was his mother's birthday, he admonished himself with the words: "Remember It!" Anticipating the same anniversary in 1915 (after her death), he wrote, "Square wreath with 72 lilies for My Beloved Mother's resting place," to which he added the resolution: "I will get up early tomorrow to take them out."

This apparent need to document his sentiments in writing can be discerned in items in his diary alluding to other relationships. Noting that his brother William was about to be married, on February 24, 1907, he wrote, "Wish 'em luck," and on another occasion, after he had made peace (once again) with Hardeen, he was moved to write, "Glad to see him and he knows it."

Like a blind man guiding his uncertain steps with the aid of a white cane, Houdini's recourse to such statements, with their overworked banalities and empty slogans, seemed designed to furnish him with a sense of psychological orientation in a desolate mental landscape. Caught in a network of emotional defenses, when he found himself faced by the challenges of maturity and the demands of adult relationships, it is evident that he exhibited many of the same artificialities that he had displayed in the life of make-believe he had established with his mother. This was especially noticeable in the sphere of love and marriage, where again, as if to ward off the nightmare of separation, he took refuge in the illusion of an unending childhood.

V

A Doll's House

. . . *she pin'd in thought:*
And with a green and yellow melancholy,
She sat like Patience on a monument,
Smiling at grief.

—TWELFTH NIGHT

Houdini's marriage, an impulsive and hasty act undertaken when he was scarcely twenty years of age, did little to weaken his intense attachment to his mother. As the years rolled on, although Bess often accompanied him on his tours and from time to time continued to perform with him on the stage, she must have remained painfully aware that neither in this life nor in the next could she reasonably hope to dislodge her husband's "sainted mother" from her secure throne in his heart.

After his mother's death, the florid show of unwavering affection and immoderate sentimentality in which Houdini had decked out his relationship with her was transferred to his wife. Because he composed a daily love letter to Bess, even when he was at home with her, he was considered a romantic lover; but despite the admitted appeal of such a characterization, his behavior toward Bess is more suggestive of the same childlike clinging that had characterized his relationship to his mother. Such an impression is supported by his teasing style of distributing these billets-doux: as if he were setting up a treasure hunt for a children's party, he hid them about the house, playfully inviting his wife to find them.[1]

Nor was this the only example of his childlike behavior toward Bess, who, like her mother-in-law before her, seems to have been a willing partner in his little foibles and games of make-believe. According to her account, during the thirty-three years of their married life she was obliged to wash his ears every day—because he had never

learned to do so, she said, although it seems more likely that he enjoyed being babied in this fashion, and took care not to display any
sign of the self-reliance that might put an end to it. Fastidiousness
was clearly not his forte, for Bess used to steal his underwear during
the night to be sure he wore fresh linen in the morning. Once when
she was unable to accompany him on a week-long performance engagement, she packed his luggage with six shirts, each of which bore
a label indicating which day he was to wear it. But on his return home
at the end of the week, she discovered that all lay untouched in the
same order in which she had packed them. He was, she asserted, the
most helpless man in the world.*

In this grown-up nursery there seemed to be no room for real
children, and indeed, despite Houdini's fondness for them, there were
none. To be sure, his reputation as a man who loved children was reinforced by some well-publicized scenes. Once, in Edinburgh, shocked
by the number of shoeless children he saw walking about on the cold
wintry streets, he bought three hundred pairs of shoes at a bootmaker
and then invited all the children to the theater to see his performance.
A week later, in Glasgow, he kept an audience waiting while he
stopped to mend the broken crutch of a crippled little girl. Yet, however bountiful such actions might have been, and however much he
enjoyed giving performances before children in hospitals and orphan-
ages, such generous behavior involved him in no onerous long-term
commitments. It would have been quite another matter for Houdini
to father or adopt a child, and to adjust to the far-ranging changes
that would necessarily follow. Judging by his craving to be the center
of all the attention about him, it is doubtful that he could have yielded
his position to a newcomer. He seems to have had enough of that in
his own childhood.

Hence, although nearly every time he returned from giving a show
at some orphanage he would tell his wife about some child he had
almost brought home to her, somehow he never did, and the household remained forever childless, enlivened only by birds and dogs and
rabbits. Many of the notations in his diary about these creatures concerned their deaths. "Charlie, our dog, dying," he wrote during the
summer of 1909. "Bess crying. I don't feel any too good." And once
when a canary died, he noted, "Poor birdy and poor Bess."

* During the hearings at the House of Representatives in Washington in 1926, when
Houdini was testifying in support of a bill banning fortune-telling in the District of
Columbia, he introduced his wife as a character witness. One of the questions the
fifty-two-year-old Houdini put to her was, "Am I a good boy?"

Houdini was no less conscious of his wife's fondness for her big dollhouse with its carpets and furniture and her many dolls. "Bess gave away a lot of dolls—'Houdini mascots,'" he wrote in December 1923. "She sure loves to dress dolls and give them away. It is her sweet nature . . . and also an index of her character." Despite his evident awareness of her emotional attachment to pets and dolls, there is little to suggest that he viewed them as an expression of unfulfilled maternal longings.

On that score, to be sure, there is reason for some uncertainty, for despite her known love of children, it is difficult to gauge the strength of her yearnings for motherhood. Like her husband, she seems to have been burdened by needs that took precedence over any desire she may have had to have children of her own. They were the same needs, it may be surmised, that reconciled her to the role she was destined to play in the Houdini household.

Following her husband's death in 1926, Bess came upon the last letter he had addressed to her:

> Sweetheart, when you read this I shall be dead. Dear Heart, do not grieve: I shall be at rest by the side of my beloved parents, and wait for you always—remember! I loved only two women in my life: my mother and my wife.
>
> Yours, in Life, Death, and Ever After [2]

Despite its tenderness, there is cause to wonder how comforting this message may have been to the grieving widow. Though intended as Houdini's final declaration of love to his wife, it served as a reminder that, as one of his "two sweethearts," Bess would continue, even after his death, to share her husband with his mother—who had been ironically awarded first place in the text of his valedictory.

Yet, to judge from her own assertions in later years, Bess never experienced any conflict with her mother-in-law, whose acceptance of her "was the more beautiful," she declared, "because Houdini's love for his mother had dominated his life completely. . . . As I look back at this," she continued, "I realize that the perfect smoothness of our relationship was largely due to the mother's fine sense of human values and rare generosity of spirit. She kept her son's devotion and she made me feel that her life was enriched by my affection for her and by his happiness with me." [3]

It is not unlikely that other considerations contributed to this atmosphere of seemingly close harmony. Because of her involvement in show business, Bess had been virtually disowned by her own mother, who on one occasion reprimanded another of her children (there were nine girls and one son) for pointing out the errant Bess's picture on a billboard. Following her marriage to Houdini, matters between Bess and her mother grew even worse, and during the next ten or twelve years, she was virtually barred from her childhood home. Even when her mother became somewhat reconciled to having a son-in-law who was both a magician and Jewish, she continued to view him with alarm and suspicion, as if he were an agent of the devil. After his visits to her home she used to sprinkle the pictures on the walls with holy water.* Under the circumstances, it may be that in Cecilia Weiss Bess found some of the approval and warm affection that was wanting in her own home.

However, despite the gratifications which Bess evidently experienced in her relationship with her mother-in-law, it is hardly possible to read her account of its "perfect smoothness" without a few twinges of skepticism. Consistent with the assertions of one biographer who alluded to "accounts which tell a slightly different story of the feeling between Mrs. Weiss and Bess," [4] it seems somewhat strange that a woman, endowed with reasonably healthy feminine aspirations and who had once sought a career in the competitive world of show business, could have tolerated so easily and so uncomplainingly the subordinate role imposed upon her by the all-encompassing and bizarre liaison between a husband and his mother. Not only was she often assigned to play second fiddle, but there were gala performances conducted by the maestro, like the "enthronement" of his mother, at which Bess was a mere spectator, excluded, as it were, from the entire orchestra. How she felt, gazing at this scene and learning that it represented the happiest moment in her husband's life, is not recorded.

Ironically, the death of her mother-in-law was not followed by Bess's promotion to the position of concertmistress. Whatever ambition she may have entertained in that direction was evidently not strong enough to oppose the next step in her married life, which, far from elevating her to the status of "first lady," subjected her once again to a subordinate role. In August 1914, approximately a year after his mother's death, Houdini and Bess left the home on 113th Street in New York where they had been living for more than ten years, and moved to Brooklyn, where they stayed with the Hardeens

---

* It is not unlikely that Houdini played a major role in effecting the reconciliation. Around Christmas, 1905, his diary mentions that he bought a piano for Bess's mother, and in 1909 he brought her and his own mother to England for a summer holiday. Once the two mothers met, they apparently got on well.

and their two young children for the next three years or so. It is not known how Bess took to this new—and reputedly often stormy—domestic arrangement, nor what prompted it. Perhaps living alone in the house on 113th Street without his mother had become intolerable to Houdini, and drove him to find solace in the bosom of his brother's family.

Despite the show of tranquility and playful amiability, there are hints that the emotional climate of the marriage itself was often turbulent and edgy. There is a distinctly hostile note to an account on February 6, 1900, in the *Boston Post* of a "near tragedy" that occurred while Houdini and Bess were performing the "Metamorphosis" stunt, or "Substitution Trunk Trick," which required an incredibly fast change between the performer who is locked inside the trunk and the one outside it. On this occasion Bess was unable to get out of the trunk in which she was locked because Houdini had carelessly left the keys in his dressing room. When she was finally released after beating her fists against the inside of the trunk, she was said to be hysterical and screamed at him, "So this is how you try to kill me, is it?"

Her irritability and fits of temper were also recorded in his diary: "Bess had a brain storm"; "Raised hell because I kidded on the phone to the operator"; "Bess very angry with me"; "Bess very mad." Other entries suggest he felt threatened by her moods: "Bess has been very sweet lately; hope she keeps it up"—a vain hope, it seems, for two weeks later he observed, "When I get home she is sore, and is sore for the night."

Whether these outbursts were oblique expressions of her resentment toward the intrusive presence of her mother-in-law in her private life, or were signs of a general state of irritability and frustration, it is clear that Houdini was intimidated by them. Reminiscent of his undisguised anxiety over her possible disapproval of his treatment of Jess Willard, he was evidently continually fearful of arousing her displeasure, as if she might leave him if he were not a good boy. Once when this seemed to be happening, he was completely undone.

Kellock related an incident at a party when, ostensibly to tease Houdini, who was momentarily absent from the room, Bess sat on the knee of an Army colonel, who put his arm about her waist. When Houdini returned, a look of "incredulous horror" came over his face. "His knees sagged as if he had received a knockout blow. Mrs. Houdini rushed to him and helped him to a chair. He could hardly speak. She helped him into a taxi and into their lodgings. None of her explanations could lift him from his utter prostration of spirit. He wept bitterly far into the night. For days he dragged himself about, brooding and dejected." [5] It was as though the nightmare of abandonment had come true.

Houdini, in turn, had a reputation for being a strict monogamist and strait-laced. The latter trait was especially vexing to the directors of the adventure films in which he acted, for when he was supposed to embrace the heroine, he did so as if he were submitting to a painful duty, all the while glancing anxiously at Bess, who was standing by. Ostensibly to relieve his conscience, Houdini insisted on giving her $5 for each kiss he bestowed on the "other woman" in the film. This exaggerated recoil from sensuality, even under the sanctioned auspices of movie acting, reinforces the impression that sexually Houdini was a severely inhibited man, who encountered almost insuperable difficulties in effecting a fusion between erotic and romantic love. Support for this impression may be found in his short story entitled "The Marvelous Adventures of Houdini," in which the heroine—whom Houdini considered a *femme fatale*—is virtually devoid of physical appeal. She is described as "a girlish woman, or rather a womanly girl, one whose affections would spring from a mental attraction, rather than from a physical or sex magnet."

A similar display of prim rectitude was evident in his well-known intolerance of risqué humor. As if to convince himself of the righteousness of his prudery, he recorded sober homilies in his diary:

> Inferiority is the Mother of Profanity.
> A man cursing is a man momentarily weaker than circumstance.
> Thwarted or harassed in the march to some immediate Canaan, we curse.

Nor were these aphorisms the only samples of the puritanism that found its way into his diary. Like an adolescent boy fresh out of Bible class, he denounced a person called X as "a bad woman," and on another occasion, after he had indignantly stormed out of a nightclub where he had seen a supposedly naughty act performed by two girls, he wrote in his diary that they "ought to be publicly horsewhipped."

Consistent with the observation that from time to time Houdini gave utterance to expressions of lofty indignation when he was seeking to conceal sentiments of a less noble nature, it may be justly wondered if he employed the same device in dealing with issues of personal morality. Whether there was any truth to the rumor that he engaged in "interesting sexual perversities," [6] there is some evidence that despite his elaborate show of fidelity, he at least "toyed" with extra-marital flirtations. After his death, his wife came upon a thick packet of love letters written to him by various women, as well as carbon copies of his letters to them, which the cautious Houdini had saved, presumably to protect himself against possible recriminations.

Of these "other women," Zolotow singled out a professional associate, whom he described as "a vivacious redhead, voluptuous and sexually wild," and with whom, supposedly, Houdini had had an affair. However, aside from asserting that it had long been a subject of gossip among magicians, Zolotow offered no proof of its existence, nor any evidence, if indeed it did occur, that it possessed the attributes of maturity with which he sought to endow it. Cognizant of the character of Houdini's marital life, which in some respects seems to have resembled the picture of a couple of childen playing house, Zolotow wrote, "I like to think that, finally, late in his life, Houdini, for the first time, had a genuine and emotionally rewarding relationship with a real woman." But his wishing does not makes it so, and from what can be deduced from Houdini's extreme narcissism and his questionable capacity for mature love, Zolotow's assumptions seem unwarranted.[7]

These are the same assumptions that prompted Zolotow to introduce a prominent erotic element in his fictional "life" of Houdini, *The Great Balsamo*. In that novel the author contrived to have his hero engage in a passionate love affair with his employer's young wife, who leaves her husband and two-year-old son and runs off with her lover.

The wife-stealing motif recurs in a dream of Balsamo's on the eve of his drowning in a sealed packing case submerged in the Boston harbor: *"He was in bed with the queen who was naked. Then he knew why the king hated him."* The final touch in this transparently oedipal drama takes place on the following morning when, on his way to his final and fateful performance, Balsamo passes by a political mass meeting where the speaker reminds him of his late father.

Despite modifications in some details of Houdini's personal history, it is clear that in fashioning the erotic aspect of his novel, Zolotow drew freely upon elements in Houdini's past. Like the latter's father, for example, Balsamo's cuckolded employer comes from Budapest. Again, like Rabbi Weiss, the employer is some eleven or twelve years older than his errant wife.

Whatever may have induced Zolotow to inject this bold oedipal theme in his narrative, psychologically speaking there is little reason to believe that it was applicable to Houdini. On the contrary, both his early history and his subsequent development suggest that he had never attained an appropriate mastery of his own childhood oedipal problems. As a consequence, as though afflicted with a sort of emotional vertigo, he careened between viewing his mother as a totally asexual being, and depicting overt erotic behavior between mother and son in his fictional writings. In his personal life he went out of his way to remove any hint of an oedipal flavor from his love life, choosing as his wife and sexual mate a woman who was the very antithesis of his Jewish mother. (Who could have been less like her than Bess Rahner, a Catholic and a showgirl?) And, as noted, in his vigilance to lop off the ugly head of incest wherever he fancied it had raised itself, Houdini had subjected his brother Leopold to figurative decapitation as fit punishment for his having committed the quasi-oedipal crime of marrying the divorced wife of his oldest brother. Seen in this light, Zolotow's notion that he could have embarked on an illicit affair with another man's wife—and a mother at that—seems distinctly out of character. For him to have done so would have found him living far beyond his psychological means.

For all Houdini's notorious fixation on his mother, his attachment to her served him more as a refuge from adult sexuality than as a prelude to it. He behaved toward her as if he were an indissoluble part of her, a being bereft of the separate and distinct identity that is necessary for the establishment of a mature and loving bond with another woman.

Seemingly trapped within this network of a mother/child oneness, Houdini behaved from time to time as if he were seeking to escape. Both his running away from home on the threshold of puberty and his early and impulsive marriage may be viewed in such a light. An attempt to establish a sense of distance and independence from her may also be discerned in his strange practice of signing letters to her, not with the intimate expression of filial affection, "Your loving son, Ehrich," that he might have used in earlier years, but with the single, stark and remote moniker: "Houdini."

Indeed, despite his much vaunted reverence for his "sainted" mother and despite the show of unwavering devotion he directed toward his wife, it is difficult to avoid the suspicion that beneath the richly ornate fabric of his devotion lay a lining of strong resentment toward the entire opposite sex. On one occasion when he participated—vicariously—in a symbolic act of violence, it might be concluded that he harbored hidden sentiments toward women that deserves an even harsher term.

During his European travels in 1909, Houdini became increasingly interested in art, and spent a good deal of both time and money in buying pictures. As a consequence of his admiration for the works of the English genre painter William P. Frith (1819–1909), he bought two portraits of women attributed to him, entitled *The Departure* and *The Return*. He then arranged to have an audience with the aged artist, during which the latter looked at the paintings but denied they had been done by him. At this point, Houdini wrote in his diary, "I allowed him to destroy them. He took out a knife and cut the lady's throat in each painting."

Although it might be argued that it was Frith and not Houdini who had committed this brutal deed, it is evident that it was done at the behest of Houdini, who was evidently more concerned with the matter of the authenticity of the paintings than with their intrinsic artistic appeal. Inasmuch as he had originally esteemed them enough to acquire them, in keeping with his penchant for destroying persons in effigy, he may have seized upon the issue of their authenticity as a pretext to promote this act of violence.

It is a major premise of this study that such ambivalent feelings, as well as the polarities of confinement and escape that seemingly characterized Houdini's relationship with his mother, invaded other aspects of his life as well. Although the most conspicuous manifestation of this conflict appeared in the genesis and evolution of his professional career as an escape artist, it was evidently no less characteristic of his personal relationships, most notably in the sphere of his love life.

Although the true facts concerning his erotic behavior may never come to light, it seems likely that Houdini approached the condition of adult sexuality with a comparable admixture of passive surrender and forceful aggression. To judge from clinical experience, it is possible that this psychological conflict gained expression either in his overt behavior or in the guise of fantasies, as sadomasochistic perversions.

Support for these conjectures may be discovered in his creative art, which, like dreams and reveries, may be interpreted as expressions of undisclosed impulses and suppressed imagination. Like a naughty boy driven to confess his evil deeds, both in his fictional writing and in his motion pictures Houdini left a well-lit trail of wickedness which may justly be regarded as revelations of secret fantasies of depravity and sexual deviations. Conspicuous among them are thinly veiled allusions to the well-known perversion, *bondage*.

VI

Of Human Bondage

Your hands nailed love to the tree
You stript him, and scourged him with rods,
And drowned him deep in the sea
That hides the dead and their gods.

— SWINBURNE

The asumption that Houdini's fiction may be regarded as revelations of his private fantasies and unconscious impulses may be challenged on the ground that his stories were ghost-written for him, and therefore were the creations of someone else. Speaking of the musical compositions of Frederick the Great, Voltaire warned that one should never criticize the music of a monarch, because one never knew who had written it.

Despite this caveat, there is ample justification for viewing Houdini's films and stories as valid self-portraiture. Although a number of the stories were actually written down by others, notably that prolific creator of horror tales, H. P. Lovecraft, it is fairly well established that their main themes and the plots on which they were based were suggested by Houdini.[1] This is not hard to believe, for the stories are filled with allusions to the adventures, the historical events, and even the proper names associated with his life. Even if he was not the author of every line or the creator of every descriptive passage, the essential narratives and the basic ideas bear the unmistakable imprint of Houdini's signature.

Houdini made at least five films, drafted several scenarios, and wrote innumerable short stories and serials. Of all these works, none is more psychologically revealing than a twelve-page "original story of Harry Houdini," entitled "Yar, the Primeval Man." Bearing a 1921 copyright, and evidently intended for motion picture production, this story purports to be an account of man's earliest beginnings. In a brief introduction the author explains that since these "primitive people" had no verbal language, they employed the sounds of animals to express words. It is noteworthy that all of the examples of emotion that are listed refer to the matter of combat and aggression: "the cry of defiance," "the squeal of fear," "the growl of rage," "the cry of the captured," etc. In contrast, no sounds are mentioned which might be used to convey feelings of affection or tenderness, which is hardly surprising in light of the outline of the plot:

> The Strange People are happy. They dance with glee for they have the better position. They squirm in and out of the great boulders, and with mighty pushes send huge rocks tumbling down on their enemies, the Little People. They soon tire, however, of watching the writhing wretches below, and turn to rest in their caves. Yar, chief of the Strange People, looks for his . . . mother . . . but she is nowhere to be found.
>
> Soon he discovers that she is hanging helplessly on the ragged edge of a cliff, but while he is attempting to rescue her, he is captured by the chief of the Little People, his enemies, and his mother is dragged off by the hair.
>
> A prisoner, Yar is then lashed to the branches of a tree by huge ferns, which causes all the Little People to rejoice, for they know that he is about to be killed by being hurled into a mighty cataract.*
>
> All look upon his seemingly hopeless plight "with savage joy"—all, that is, except for a young woman, the "Sun Girl," who falls in love with him although he is an enemy of her people. Then, as if by a miracle, Yar breaks his bonds, rescues his mother, and, followed by the girl, leads them both to safety. Many adventures follow, during which the hero saves the two women from a succession of perils, and in the end everything turns out happily and all three retire together into a cave.[2]

Despite its dubious literary merit and its simple-minded conception of anthropology, the work offers interesting insights into certain aspects of the mental life of the author.

A number of facets of the story carry the clear stamp of self-portraiture. Yar's relationship with his mother, for example, seems to be patterned on Houdini's attachment to his mother. Like Bess, Houdini's Catholic wife, Yar's mate comes from an alien people. Like Bess, too, who allegedly first set eyes on her future husband while he was

---

* This detail, as the reader will later discover, was related to Houdini's fascination with Niagara Falls. One of his projected stunts was to go over the Falls and come out alive.

performing magic, the Sun Girl first espies Yar and then falls in love with him when he is shackled to a tree, from which, in classical Houdini tradition, he soon performs an incredible escape.

Again, like Cecilia Weiss, Yar's mother becomes a prominent and intrusive presence in her son's romantic life, although it soon becomes clear that her relationship to her son's mate is distinctly wanting in that "perfect smoothness" that Bess Houdini later claimed existed between herself and her mother-in-law. In view of the reports of the generous altruism that flowed between these two, especially with respect to the matter of wearing apparel, it is noteworthy that in the story of Yar, not only are the two women angrily combative toward one another, but the chief issue over which they fight is clothing, specifically the ownership of an animal fur that Yar has obtained to keep them warm. Even after Yar's rudimentary brain has hit upon the happy solution of tearing the skin in two so that they can share it and thereby end their feud, the Sun Girl is far from satisfied, for she kicks and bites as she springs at her rival, trying to snatch the old woman's portion, too. To Yar, the girl "looks adorable in her rage," a comment that recalls some of Houdini's diary notations regarding Bess's temper. Indeed, the reader may justly wonder whether in this entire scene Houdini was revealing a glimpse of the hidden emotional climate that pervaded his domestic life.

Unquestionably, however, the most arresting features of the story are the allusions to acts of binding and escape, which are described in a manner that leaves little doubt of their erotic significance. Inspired, as it were, by the painful binding to which he has been subjected by his enemies, after he has gained his freedom Yar treats the beautiful Sun Girl to the very same experience. But now it possesses a different meaning: whereas the aim of the Little People in binding him was to torment him in these restraints before destroying him, the result of his subjecting the Sun Girl to binding is the creation of a state of sexual arousal. In a scene that is strongly reminiscent of several well-known literary depictions of fur fetishism * and other deviant sexual practices, Yar wraps her in a fur skin, in which she looks "very attractive," and then ties it on her by winding huge ferns about her body. (Here the reader may discern allusions to Houdini's strait-jackets, ropes, and chains.)

The response to Yar's act of binding is electric: "The touch of her

* E.g., von Sacher-Masoch's *Venus in Furs*, and Joseph Conrad's *The Arrow of Gold*.

flesh thrills him. He touches her again, each time more tenderly, and puts his arms around her. Slowly he crushes her to him. Some impulse [!] drives him to place his lips on hers, and then he kisses her. It is the first kiss."

The girl is hardly less excited, for she "dances with joy." Yar, evidently quite unfamiliar with such behavior, is "astonished at her pleasure and kisses her again and again. The people . . . look on in awe." Despite her new-found mounting ecstasy, it must not be supposed that the Sun Girl is willing to seek it out indiscriminately, for when another member of the group approaches her, signaling his deside to "try this new amusement," she "quickly stoops, picks up a stone and promptly crashes it upon [his] head."

It is soon apparent that Yar's mother has no intention of being left out of this atmosphere of newly discovered sexuality and passion, for she emerges from her cave, holding her half of the fur skin about her and indicating that she, too, wants her son to tie it on her, just as he has done for his mate. This Yar proceeds to do, arranging her robe "in the same way." He goes even a step further. "Remembering the kiss, he kisses his mother." This is apparently an unprecedented action, for "both are astonished."

So, it may be assumed, was the creator of this sexy scene, for now the plot was hovering perilously on the brink of incest. Never at a loss for getting out of tight situations, however, Houdini hastily escaped from his uncomfortable predicament by assigning a thoroughly different meaning to the kiss between Yar and his mother. "It was not like the kiss of the Sun Girl," he asserted, "but as if God had kissed them both. *It is sacred.*" (italics added). Fumigated by the odor of sanctity, "a look of joy overspreads the old woman's face and she places her arms about her son, swaying backward and forward with cries of joy. . . . She places her lips on Yar's brow. It is a sacred rite." [3]

It was also a narrow escape which the author had contrived by introducing some last-minute allusions to God and divine dispensation. However, in light of the total absence of instinctual inhibition that has hitherto characterized the behavior of these quasi-subhuman creatures, the reader is understandably somewhat taken aback by the sudden introduction of a moral dilemma, and by its equally unforeseen resolution. Up to this point there has been no intimation that these anthropoid folk possessed either a code of morality or a system of religious beliefs. On the contrary, the only reference to such matters has been an irrelevant and passing allusion to Thor, the god of fire, who, in any event, was hardly the sort of deity the author had in mind to bestow the seal of divine grace upon Yar's hanky-panky with his mother.

What had happened in the course of his writing, it would seem, is that while drifting heedlessly down the stream of his romantic narrative, Houdini suddenly awoke to discover the dangerous rapids that lay just ahead. Then, thanks to an adroit maneuvre, which consisted of invoking the moral values of his own far different culture, he managed to elude the hidden reefs of incest and to guide his literary craft into the safe, still waters of desexualized love.

The implied sequence in his thought processes is all the more remarkable, for it mirrors the course of the psychosexual progression in the life of the young child, in whom oedipal strivings and other forbidden impulses are generally repressed and sublimated, and succeeded by the development of conscience, or the superego. The observation that in the Yar story such a transition was depicted in so haphazard and belated a fashion invites the suspicion that, as a child, the author himself had encountered comparable difficulties in mastering his own primitive impulses and in replacing them by progressively mature standards of morality.

Similar conclusions are implied in those curious passages in the Yar story which demonstrate that tenderness toward children appears for the first time when these primitive people are provided with an example of maternal affection. In imitation of the "sacred" model of tender love exhibited by Yar and his mother, the other females in the community now begin to alter their behavior toward their children. They cease dragging the little ones about by the hair and begin to lift them lovingly in their arms. In response to their "wordless crooning . . . the children are rocked to sleep."

Indeed, no less striking than the close brush with incest residing in this strange tale is the lack of any natural loving impulse or physical demonstrativeness, be it between parent and child, or between adults. According to this conception, the reader is encouraged to conclude that all such attitudes are learned, for apparently the only natural and spontaneous impulses possessed by these people are varieties of hostile and cruel aggression.

Once again it is reasonable to conclude that such a view of the psychosexual makeup of primitive man was a projection of the author's own mental makeup and personal history. Not only does the story of Yar suggest that Houdini may have experienced serious deformations in the development of his superego, but that he was a constant prey to the sudden and ill-controlled emergence of his own untamed impulses. It would consequently explain why his affectionate sentiments seemed rarely free from the risk of contamination by violence.

In the Yar story, such a fusion of cruelty and love is reflected by the ease with which the theme of bondage is transformed from a prelude to slaughter into the foreplay of love. It is the similarity between these fictional details and Houdini's professional stunts which suggests that his performances of binding and escape were essentially desexualized enactments of sadomasochistic practices. Such a conjecture gains further support from another of his stories, "The Spirit Fakers of Herrmannstadt," which was published in 1924 in the magazine *Weird Tales*:

> Having just completed a theatrical engagement in Vienna, Houdini, the celebrated magician, is approached by an aristocratic Hungarian, a countess, who begs him to help save her and her sister Rosicka from ruin. The sister had fallen under the evil influence of a spiritualist medium who is trying to force her to sign a statement that will expose the "bestial behavior" of her dead father. Although the magician, Houdini, has been sworn to secrecy by the countess not to reveal the nature of the "unbelievable debaucheries" of her late father, there are ample hints that they consisted of luring innocent peasant girls into the dungeons of his castle where he subjected them to unspeakable and obscene abuses. In fact his own death was caused by poisoning inflicted by the bite of an insane girl he had kept shackled in one of his dungeons. In the course of his dangerous and exciting mission to save the sisters from the spiritualist demon, the hero undergoes a series of miraculous escapes from his evil adversary: he frees himself from handcuffs while swimming under water, escapes from dungeon cells—in short, he runs the entire gamut of the Houdini repertoire.

Not to be overlooked in this grim tale of binding and debauchery are several allusions to the author's personal history. The setting of the story is in his native Hungary, in Herrmannstadt, a name evoking the memory of his deceased half-brother. Also noteworthy is the name of the countess's sister, Rosicka, the diminutive of Rosa, which, according to some sources, was the name of the popular opera singer who—apparently erroneously—was reported to have been Rabbi Weiss's first wife and the mother of the same Herman.

Houdini's fascination with the themes of binding and romance gained pictorial expression in his motion picture *Haldane of the Secret Service* (originally entitled *Mysterious Mr. Yu or Haldane of the Secret Service*). In this film, the hero, bearing the not too undecipherable name *H*eath *H*aldane, is engaged in tracking down a band of counterfeiters who have murdered his father and are now menacing a girl with whom the hero is slated to fall in love. In the course of his avenging mission he gets trapped in a warehouse, dumped Houdini-fashion into a river, picked up by an ocean liner, and then fastened to a wheel and tortured. Miraculously, the man with the magical initials escapes from his bonds, rescues the girl (whose father turns out to be a drug addict), and marries her.

The recurring counterpoint of sexuality and torture unfolded in these and other literary and cinematic creations of Houdini, as well as the broad features of his escape stunts, are strongly reminiscent of the clinical condition known as bondage, a well-established category of deviant behavior that usually involves the attainment of erotic excitement by being bound and restrained. These similarities will become evident in the following excerpts from case reports that have been published in the medical literature. The practice of bondage, it should be noted in passing, is often dangerous, and sometimes fatal. It has been estimated that in the United States there are some fifty such deaths each year.

A fifty-year-old actor, whose death was certified as an accident, was found dead in a bathtub, strangled by a rope which was wound around his neck, looped over a door, and tied to his wrist and ankle. There was a ball in his mouth, with a gag tied over his mouth, a scarf over his eyes, and *hand-cuffs on both wrists.* His apartment contained common fetishistic articles, such as those made of leather and rubber, as well as chains, whips, and an elaborate library of sado-masochistic pornography composed of stories and pictures of men and women bound and gagged in bizarre positions. On the desk was a long list of such positions, e.g., Tied by the neck to a tree [compare Houdini's "Yar" story]; walk through the street tied and naked [compare Houdini's "Naked Tests" and photos of him in chains, naked, save for a jock strap].

Another man, a thirty-year-old transvestite, killed himself by hanging from a chain which had been looped around his neck and fastened with a padlock. The ends of the chain were brought down to his body where they were attached to a short length of rope which was looped around each leg at the crotch and attached to the ends of the chain by a small padlock on either side. A suicide note described his elaborate practice of transvestism and his intention of killing himself by setting fire to the female garments he would be wearing. [Houdini narrowly escaped being seriously burned when he allowed himself to be tied at the stake surrounded by a ring of burning faggots.]

Masochistic behavior in a twenty-six-year-old man consisted of his being beaten by whips, burned with cigarettes, and *locked in a small box* in which he could hardly move.[4]

Another young man attained sexual arousal by binding his ankles together with rope, which he then passed up between his thighs, beside his penis, and up to his buttocks. A modification consisted of his hanging by a strap from the hinge of a door, *bound and head downward*. [This is reminiscent of Houdini's stunt of hanging head downward, bound in a strait-jacket, from the cornices of tall buildings. In light of Houdini's own history, it is noteworthy that this subject was reported to have been strongly attached to his mother. Again, like Houdini, who engaged in the practice of fettering during his adolescence with his brother Theodore, this patient made his first attempts at binding, not on himself, but on a younger brother.] [5]

While the practice of bondage is often accompanied by other perversions, notably sadomasochism, fetishism, and transvestism, most of the subjects studied have apparently regarded themselves as male in gender, although strong unconscious feminine identifications are readily noted.

To what extent the latter applied to Houdini is conjectural, but, in any event, it is hardly possible to avoid the realization that he was immoderately concerned with the measure of his manliness. Whether, like several examples of impostors cited in psychoanalytic literature, he was afflicted by some undisclosed physical defect for which he strove to overcompensate with a show of "manly" aggression is not known. It is said he was too vain to wear eyeglasses, which suggests that he may have regarded them as a sign of physical inferiority. And he once told the magician John Mulholland that one should capitalize on one's native endowments. Houdini failed to understand why Mulholland never tried to find some way in which his "most generously proportioned ears" might serve him in his magic, like Houdini's great strength, enormous lung capacity, and bow legs.[6]

To be sure, Houdini was less than five feet five inches in height, which is decidedly short for any kind of king and must have been especially galling to this one, who was nearly a half-foot shorter than his rival kid brother Hardeen. Despite their disparity in size, however, there is a picture of the two of them standing on the far side of an automobile in which they seem to be of equal height. Knowing Houdini's penchant for doctoring photographs, it is not unlikely that he directed the pose, arranging for himself to stand on the running board and for Hardeen to stand on the ground. Like Napoleon the

First, John Paul Jones, and other diminutive historical figures, Houdini gave no indication that he regarded his small stature as a serious barrier to an aggressive pursuit of power or a show of masculinity.[7]

In addition to all the quasi-manly panoply of aggression and the thunder of abuse he promiscuously unleashed, there are recurring allusions to manliness sprinkled throughout his writings, notably in *The Unmasking of Robert-Houdin.* On page 293 he wrote:

> A man who has made a fortune in the world of magic . . . [should be] clever enough and *manly* enough. . . .
> That he might be known to posterity as the king of conjurers, he sold his birthright of *manhood* and honor [italics added]. . . .

In another passage, in denouncing a sideshow performer for biting off the head of a snake, he accused the man of having *"debauched his manhood* for a few paltry dollars" (italics added). That Houdini was revolted by this admittedly unappetizing spectacle is hardly remarkable, but the allusions to debauchery and manhood seem gratuitous unless one assumes that his revulsion was enhanced by an unwitting recognition of the sexual, and perhaps homosexual, significance of the performance. Indeed, both the act and the language denouncing it are reminiscent of the perversities practiced in Houdini's short story, "The Spirit Fakers of Herrmannstadt."

No less applicable to Houdini is the observation among clinical examples of bondage of "a stubborn streak of indomitable endurance, a challenge to death, and finally, an invitation and welcome to death." Even when it is carried out in privacy, indulgence in bondage is inevitably experienced as a spectacular, exhibitionistic, and theatrical affair, prompting one writer to assert that it represents "a creative and artistic effort" in which the "protagonist becomes the producer, director, author, and chief actor in his own dramatic construction." [8]

Nothing could more aptly describe Houdini, who, in bringing derivatives of the practice of bondage before the public and into the domain of the theater, was successfully divesting it of its manifest perversity and presenting it as good clean entertainment. Whether the public was equally oblivious of the fact that it was witnessing a desexualized presentation of a perversion is, of course, problematical, but the accounts of some popular reactions to his dramatic stunts border sufficiently on the hysterical to suggest that, on an unconscious plane at least, the deleted erotic component was somehow recognized. Following his escape from a strait-jacket, the *Philadelphia Press* of January 19, 1906, observed:

The audience was simply frenzied. Men and women stood upon their feet and simply cheered. Almost before Houdini could completely emerge from his leather prison, a dozen men upon the stage ran to him, and in wild enthusiasm swung him to their shoulders and carried him about. There was tumult of applause that lasted many minutes. A score or more of physicians connected with hospitals for the insane witnessed the performance and expressed wonderment at Houdini's marvelous feat.

Seen against this background of sadomasochism, it is not unreasonable to view his recommendation of a public horse-whipping for the naughty girl performers in a somewhat different light, namely as a pretext for the unleashing of his own repressed perverse impulses.*

Whether the practice of bondage eventuates in the mutilation or death of the self or of others, or whether the subject succeeds in escaping unharmed from his own dangerous and risky schemes, there can be no mistaking the element of violence it contains, hovering precariously on the boundary between sexuality and crime. This realization is especially relevant to an understanding of the personality of Houdini, who not only seemed susceptible to the perverse practice of bondage but also displayed an unmistakable kinship with the criminal.

* "Her flesh was lyrical and sweet to flog,
  For the whip blanched her blood
  Through every vein
  Flooded with hate shot a hot flow of pain
  And her screams were muffled by a
  Brackish fog."
  Donald Evans: "Loving Kindness" from *Sonnets from the Patagonian*

VII

A Virtuoso of Imposture

"And were you pleased?" they asked of Helen in Hell.
"Pleased?" answered she, "When all Troy's towers fell,
And dead were Priam's sons and lost his throne,
And such a war was fought as none had known,
And even the gods took part, and all because
Of me alone. Pleased? I should say I was!"
                                    —Lord Dunsany: THE INTERVIEW

Heralded as the world's foremost jail-breaker and the man who could free himself from a "burglar-proof safe," Houdini achieved fame, it should be emphasized, not as a skillful prestidigitator, but as a man who could escape from handcuffs, leg-irons, and other apparatus *designed for the restraint of criminals*. He created a sensation in England by walking out of the jail in Leicester that Oliver Cromwell had built to detain political prisoners. In Russia he effected a seemingly miraculous escape from a prison van used to transport criminals to exile in Siberia. It will be recalled that in Washington he broke out of the cell where the assassin of President Garfield had been confined, and when the celebrated eighteenth-century convict ship *Success* visited New York in 1913, Houdini managed to escape from one of its ancient teakwood cells with its six-inch-thick doors, despite the reputation of the ship that it had never lost a prisoner. Another of his stunts was an escape from a gallows.

To be sure, there is no reason to suppose that Houdini suspected that there was any hidden psychological significance in these exploits. When, in August 1910, he paid $6.50 at an auction and acquired the electric chair formerly used for executions at the Auburn State Prison, and, despite his wife's objections, insisted on installing it in their living room, he explained that it was done simply "for sentimental reasons." (!) No doubt he would have furnished a similar explanation to account for the annual Christmas Eve shows he performed for the inmates in Sing-Sing Prison. "It is my belief," says the narrator of

Lord Jim, "no man ever understands quite his own artful dodges to escape from the grim shadow of self-knowledge."

From what may be inferred about Houdini's character, it is exceedingly unlikely that that "grim shadow" ever seriously troubled him. Beyond question, he would have dismissed as absurdities not only the notion that his toying with prison cells and fraternizing with convicts implied a hidden kinship with the world of crime, but that these activities possessed any psychological significance whatever. Pressed for an explanation, he would have retorted: "Show Business!" and undoubtedly many would have agreed.

There were others, however, who, prompted in part by reports of petty household thefts during his childhood and an early fascination with locks and lockpicking, might have gained a different impression and arrived at the conclusion that deep within the recesses of his complex personality there lay a streak of hidden criminality. "Had he put his abilities to evil uses," wrote one of his biographers, "he would undoubtedly have been the gravest individual menace ever known to organized society. He could enter or leave any building or chamber at will, leaving no trace of breakage behind him, and he could open the strongest steel vault as easily as a skilled second-story man could pry loose a bedroom window. . . . Had he chosen the crooked path, society would have been compelled to have put him to death for its own protection, for nothing short of the capital penalty would have served." [1]

Houdini himself evidently sensed how near that crooked path he might have strayed. While describing a lock-picking gadget, marked "Houdini," which he always carried about with him, he acknowledged that with it he had "opened thousands of ward locks on doors," to which he added, "such an implement, if in the possession of a burglar . . . would be a very dangerous thing." [2] "I am a born lockpicker," he wrote in *Confessions of a Jail Breaker.* "This is a gift. It usually lands its beneficiary in jail, but I have domesticated it and refined it until it has landed me before applauding monarchs and paying audiences. It all depends on whose lock you pick." [3]

Other chroniclers of his life story were more explicit. Reflecting an intuitive suspicion of Houdini's psychological kinship with the criminal, Zolotow, in his fictional recreation of Houdini's life, depicted a period of overt crime, notably of thefts and robberies, in the early history of his hero Balsamo. Indeed, the very pseudonym assigned to his protagonist serves as a mirror of the author's conviction of the potential for lawlessness in the Balsamo/Houdini character, for

Balsamo was the original name of that notorious personage "Count" Cagliostro, the man whose name has become the hallmark of imposture and fraud. *The Cagliostro* is, in fact, the name of the sleek yacht owned by Zolotow's hero.

But the author of *The Great Balsamo* was not the only one to liken Houdini to the infamous Cagliostro.[4] Following Houdini's death a similar comparison was voiced by Sir Arthur Conan Doyle, while *The New Yorker* magazine of November 12, 1926, characterized Houdini as "Cagliostro *redivivus* with all the show and the deceit of the famous magician cast away." The most strikingly impressive example of a sense of kinship between these two personages was provided by Houdini himself, who, in a short story entitled "The Magician's Christmas Eve," dubbed his hero The Marvelous Balsoma.

Whether the reversal of the vowels in Balsoma was intentional, or, more probably, another manifestation of Houdini's notoriously careless spelling, the pseudonym he chose for his fictional "celebrated necromancer" is close enough to *Balsamo* to indicate just whom he had in mind in composing this patently autobiographical story. Houdini's fascination with the character of Cagliostro was unmistakable, and like his one-time reverence for Robert-Houdin, it bore the quality of an identification.

Prefiguring Houdini, the history of the notorious Count is richly embroidered with elements of the Family Romance. Although it has been generally accepted that Cagliostro was born of humble peasant stock in Sicily, in his testimony in Paris in 1786, when he was on trial for his alleged complicity in the celebrated "Affair of the Diamond Necklace," he claimed to be ignorant of the place of his birth, asserting that he was descended from Christian nobility, and that his parents had died when he was but three months old, leaving him in Medina in the care of the Great Mufti of Arabia. Here he was supposedly brought up in a luxurious palace, surrounded by numerous servants and guided by a devoted tutor. At twelve he left his home (again, like Houdini), and began his travels. In Mecca he was shown such attention and kindness from the Sheriff or Governor of that sacred city that he "oftentimes thought that personage was his father." [5]

Despite these extravagant claims, it was rumored that his real father had been "of Jewish extraction," a detail that may have exerted a special appeal upon Houdini. In light of the assertion, moreover, that Cagliostro's real mother was named Felicia, and that his wife's maiden name was said to be Feliciani, it may be significant that the heroine of Houdini's "resurrection" film, *The Man From Beyond,* was named Felice, as was her great-grandmother, with whom the hero had been in love prior to his imprisonment in ice one hundred years before.[6]

Additional evidence of Houdini's interest in Cagliostro is offered by an inventory of his library, which lists "a large collection of letters by and manuscript material about the famous and interesting character, Cagliastro [sic]—probably one or two hundred by estimation." It has been claimed that Houdini himself ranked as the single most valuable document in his vast library what he believed to be the only existing autographed letter of the famous imposter.

Houdini's effort to follow the footsteps of the notorious Count was clearly reminiscent of his dedication to the memory of Robert-Houdin. On December 11, 1913, his diary states: "Visited Cagaliostro's [sic] old Home; took a few snap shots." Later on the same day he paid a visit to the Théâtre Robert-Houdin, proof that, despite his noisy denunciation of the French conjurer five years earlier, he still responded to the magic of his name.

How closely these two celebrated men were linked in Houdini's mind is further emphasized by the fact that he devoted no less than four pages to the subject of Cagliostro and his wife in *The Unmasking of Robert-Houdin,* which also included reproductions of their portraits. The originals were said to be in the "Harry Houdini Collection."

In fact it seems probable that Houdini's interest in Cagliostro was at least partially determined by his own identification with Robert-Houdin, whose preoccupation with the Italian mountebank is evident to anyone who reads his *Memoirs.* Allusions to Cagliostro are especially frequent in the "Torrini" section of the work, in which the "count's" unhappy fate—he was condemned to perpetual imprisonment —is presented as a warning to those who incur the wrath of the Church. When Robert-Houdin later relates his own career as a conjurer, he mentions that a news leaflet issued to his patrons was called *Le Cagliostro.*

There is a pretty interweaving of these triple strands of identification—Cagliostro–Robert-Houdin–Houdini—beginning with a charming description in Robert-Houdin's *Memoirs* of the "Vanishing Handkerchief Trick," which the author performed before King Louis-Philippe at St. Cloud in 1846. In this trick, after six handkerchiefs belonging to the audience had mysteriously disappeared, as if by magic they were found in an iron chest that had been dug up in the garden. Also contained in the chest was a message, written on old parchment:

This Day, the sixth of June, 1786, this iron box, containing six handkerchiefs, was placed among the roots of an orange tree by me, Balsamo, Count of Cagliostro, to serve in performing an act of magic, which will be executed on the same day sixty years hence before Louis Philippe of Orleans and his Family.

It goes without saying that the entire performance created a most pleasing effect, not the least of which was produced by the imprint of Cagliostro's own seal on the packet containing the six missing handkerchiefs. The seal, the author explained, had been given him by Torrini, who had been an old friend of Cagliostro.

Discovered during his adolescent years, the account of this brilliant *tour de force* evidently made an equally memorable impression on young Ehrich Weiss, for when he, too, became an established conjurer, he repeated the very same trick at an entertainment in New York City, causing the vanished handkerchiefs to be miraculously retrieved from under the top step of the winding staircase in the Statue of Liberty in New York Harbor. Admittedly inspired by Robert-Houdin's performance at St. Cloud, Houdini's version, which he described in *The Unmasking of Robert-Houdin,* differed in one detail—it lacked the delightful prophetic message inscribed by a noted personage from a previous era.[7]

In light of Houdini's frequent misnaming of his French idol, his apparent misspelling of Balsamo, and the erratic spelling in his diary of Cagliostro—all the correct versions being readily available to him and set down properly in *The Unmasking of Robert-Houdin*—it is all the more remarkable that in that book he went to considerable lengths to rectify some supposed errors committed by others regarding the correct name of Cagliostro's wife. Noting that in the *Encyclopaedia Britannica* she was called Lorenzo, he pointed out that in reality her name was Seraphinia Feliciani. But here he erred again, for the *Encyclopaedia* gave her name as Lorenza, not Lorenzo, which is a masculine name, while his version of what he maintained was her true name should have been spelled Serafina, not Seraphina, and certainly not Seraphinia.*

Aside from the *Encyclopaedia Britannica,* in composing his biographical notes on Cagliostro, Pinetti and others with such unblushing assurance, Houdini evidently drew heavily on a work by Henry R. Evans, entitled *The Old and the New Magic.* As he had done on other

---

* The probable significance of his masculinizing the name Lorenza and femininizing Balsamo by altering their endings will be discussed in Chapter 14.

occasions, he repaid his debt to Evans by attacking him. In the *Conjurers' Monthly* magazine he denounced the very book that had proved so useful to him, asserting that it was "full of bad mistakes, misstatements, and a great deal of worthless material." However, inasmuch as the details in Evans's account of Cagliostro correspond fairly closely with the biographical information that was available at the time of Houdini's article, it is not clear what he was objecting to, unless it concerned the matter of the Countess's correct name.[8]

In any event, since Cagliostro changed his name with ease, styling himself variously the Marquis of Balsamo and the Marquis of Pellegrino (probably inspired by the name of the mountain overlooking his native Palermo) before settling on Count Alessandro de Cagliostro, which titles were accompanied by parallel variations in his wife's designation, Houdini's fretful insistence on what he claimed to be the authentic version of her name seems excessive. Indeed it is difficult to restrain the suspicion that his obsessive need to validate her pseudonym was a reflection of a kindred urgency to certify his own, and to lend iron-clad credibility to his own imposture.*

Although some may object to the imputation of charlatanry to Houdini the Handcuff King, arguing that as an escapologist he never claimed miraculous powers nor denied that his tricks were accomplished by gimmickry, or what he called "natural means," there had been a time, early in his career, when his performances left nothing to be desired in the catalogue of fraud and quackery. "The borderline between magic and occult charlatanism is a tenuous one at times," observed Gresham, "and many a magician has crossed it when broke." [10]

Broke Houdini surely was in his dime circus days, when, struggling desperately to keep body and soul together for himself and Bess, he often crossed that borderline by posing as a "spirit medium" in his performances in the American hinterland. In preparation for this imposture, it was his practice to visit local cemeteries and memorize the names, dates, and other information inscribed on tombstones. These facts, supplemented with rumor, gossip, and stories from old newspaper files, gave him a wealth of data concerning both the living and the dead.

Armed with this array of information, Houdini was ready to perform unbelievable and frightful miracles. Standing at the front of the stage, the master necromancer would close his eyes, and in a seeming

---

* Once, in a fit of pique when another magician referred to him as "Most Illustrious Ehrich Weiss," the latter jumped out of his chair and yelled, "The name is Houdini!" [9]

trance, summon strange spirits and strange presences from the dead, and tell dark secrets that struck terror into the credulous minds and guilty hearts of his superstitious listeners. Ironically, in light of his later fanatical campaign against spiritualists and mediums, in those impoverished early days he seemed to have no scruples about holding these phony seances. "I give Syscromatic and Clairvoyantic Readings [sic], telling you the Past, Present and Future," read his advertisement. "Do you believe in Spiritualism? If not, why not? If you want to give Manifestations and Slate Tests I can give you full instructions and make you a full-fledged medium." It was not without reason that he was called a "virtuoso of imposture," and that of the myriad titles bestowed upon this latter-day Cagliostro, the one that he was said to prefer above all others was: The Greatest Necromancer of the Age.[11]

Although Houdini's arrival at the pinnacle of success brought an end to these shady practices, he by no means became a model of moral rectitude, and there is evidence that some of his most publicized escapes were accomplished by unrevealed fraud. Guided by the principle: "Thou shalt not fret too much about how to get that top billing," he would denounce rival escapologists as imposters and charlatans who were seeking by foul means to deceive the public, when it was clear that his real grievance against them was the fact that they were copying his own crafty methods. His favorite magicians, it was said, were the dead ones—he had nothing to fear from them in competition.

Even toward the very end of his life he was tempted to stray from the path of virtue. "E.D. called and offered me a partnership if I would manage her and authenticate her 'seership,'" he wrote in his diary on October 20, 1925. "[She] said we could make $100,000 a year. I told her I'd think it over! What a fool," he added, "to even think I'd be crooked!" Yet, fool or not, he did think it over, and evidently his conscience troubled him enough to cause him to confess the whole unseemly business to his diary.

Like his attitude toward certain persons and issues, Houdini's approach to the subject of crime was clearly contradictory. Side by side with the fascination that drew him into the underworld of prison cells and shackles, and the temptation to engage in a life of fraud, was the beguiling attraction to enlist in the ranks of law and order. According to Minnie Mooser, a lady in her nineties who, with her sister Hattie, ran The Aladdin Studio Tiffin Room, a celebrated tea room in San Francisco during the Prohibition Era, Houdini once told her how he had been engaged by the U.S. Coast Guard in rounding up rum runners in those days. One night, she recalled, Houdini took her sister for a drive to Half Moon Bay and pointed out the places where he had done "underwater sleuthing for liquor caches and other little investigations for the Treasury Department." He had been asked to assist in this activity, he had explained, because he was such a good swimmer and had trained himself to withstand cold. Equipped with these unusual endowments, he "would swim out to a suspected rum runner's boat, look around, and report back to the authorities." [12]

Truth or fiction, the report reflects the same portrait of Houdini as the embodiment of law and virtue that he depicted in film and fiction. By assuming the role of an agent of the law he was able to extricate himself from the moral dilemma presented by the beguiling lure of criminality and at the same time assign his evil proclivities to real or invented villains—while retaining for himself the spotless image of a hero. (The criminal and the policeman, remarked Conrad in *The Secret Agent,* "both come from the same basket.") It was the same psychological device of splitting his ambivalence that would enable him to disavow his covert fascination with spiritualism and to pose as its arch enemy. The function of the magician, observed Edmund Wilson, "has characteristics in common with those of the criminal, of the actor and of the priest . . . and he enjoys special advantages impossible for these professions. Unlike the criminal, he has nothing to fear from the police; unlike the actor, he can always have the stage to himself; unlike the priest, he need not trouble about questions of faith. . . ." [13]

Yet in other instances it would appear that the position he adopted in ethical issues was determined less by considerations of right and wrong than by the prospects of satisfying his passion for notoriety and his quest for omnipotence. There may have been some exaggeration in the assertion that "he would murder his grandmother for publicity" (an opinion he cherished sufficiently to copy into his diary), but where personal aggrandizement was at stake, he allowed neither his father's teachings nor religious tradition to stand in his way. In seeming obedience to the injunction to honor his father and his mother he erected a monument to their memory, but simultaneously he violated another commandment and succeeded in upstaging them by crowning the entire exedra with his own graven image. Indeed, as an expression of that limitless effrontery known as *chutzpah,* and as an exercise in magical ingenuity, Houdini's success in negotiating the admission of his chiseled likeness into a Jewish graveyard after his death ranks with the most spectacular escapes he effected during his lifetime.

So conspicuous a defect in his superego development, and such an unremitting compulsion to perpetuate the fantasy of the Family Romance far beyond its usual restriction to the years of childhood are typical of the psychologic makeup of the imposter. Even more relevant to an understanding of the personality of Houdini is the realization that beneath the imposter's pursuit of an assumed persona is a profound disturbance in the sense of self. Certainly this describes Houdini and his life-long search for a heroic model.

Fashioned by bits and pieces borrowed from the likenesses of others, the image of Houdini emerges less like a coherent portrait than like the haphazard assembly of a collage. Confronted by so wavering a sense of a basic self, Houdini existed in a precarious state of psychological limbo in which the splintering of his contrived identity could be warded off only by a constant display of spectacular gestures. Supported by the reassuring plaudits of a cheering public, he sought to confirm the intactness of his inner being. Faced by the perpetual menace of psychic disintegration and threatened by the awful vision of death, he was driven to establish the illusion of his own immortality.

VIII

The Dance of Death

It strikes an awe
And terror on my aching sight; the tombs
And monumental caves of death look cold,
And shoot a chilliness to my trembling heart.
—Congreve

It must not be supposed that Houdini's interest in necrologies and burial grounds came to an end when he abandoned his career as a phony spiritualist medium, nor that his preoccupation with death began after the loss of his mother. Throughout his life he made endless trips to cemeteries which he recorded with photographs and memoranda. Often these visits assumed the nature of a pilgrimage, and the tombs became the shrines of men he had admired; on more than one occasion he undertook to rescue the grave of some departed confrère from neglect or oblivion.

His scrapbooks contain numerous photographs of graves, chiefly of fellow magicians or family members, in which Houdini himself is often visible, standing bareheaded alongside. It was this practice of making certain that whenever he laid flowers on graves it was in the prearranged presence of local photographers that prompted Sir Arthur Conan Doyle to label Houdini as "the greatest publicity agent that ever lived." However, another possible explanation for his lack of modesty in these graveyard scenes is that it constituted a counterphobic measure: standing erect among the tombstones gave proof that although death lay all about him, he was indisputably alive. Similar considerations may have prompted him to make annotations in the margins of old theater programs indicating which of the performers listed were no longer alive.

In time this interest predictably came to embrace the matter of his own death and the deaths of members of his family. The search for a family burial plot became an issue of major importance, prompting his wife to record the "somber pleasure" he seemed to experience while "shopping around" for a satisfactory site.[1] * At last, on August 15, 1904, Houdini found a suitable one in the Machpelah Cemetery in Queens, New York, and on the following day he bought it for $450. Two days later his diary records he had the bodies of his father and his half-brother Herman dug up and reburied in the new plot. Evidently he took a good look at the proceedings, for like a latter-day Hamlet, he wrote: "Saw all that was left of poor father and Herman: nothing but skull and bones." To which he added, with evidently greater care for dentition than devotion, "Herman's teeth were in splendid condition."

Scattered throughout his bulky diaries are countless allusions to deaths and their anniversaries: "Father died fifteen years ago today," be noted on October 5, 1907. "Sat through whole service, heard Rabbi Hecht preach. Said *Kaddish*." A year later he again noted the anniversary and announced his intention of saying *Kaddish*.

After the death of his mother such notations became more frequent:

November 21, 1914: sixteen months and five days since MOTHER died.

February 24, 1914: Brother Herman died twenty-nine years ago.

February 19, 1915: Wanted to take Aunt Sally out, but Doc [brother Leopold] says it will kill the old lady.

February 25, 1915: Aunt Sally passed away. Only outlived my beloved mother one year, seven months and nine days.

May 30, 1915: Trip to cemetery with Dash [Hardeen], Sam and Fanny G., etc. Sam's father died eighteen years ago today.

July 16, 1915: To Asbury Park with Doc, Dash, etc., and self to see where Mother died.†

Like his diaries, the clippings and news reports pasted in his scrapbooks reflected his strange preoccupation with death:

Oakland (California) *Post*, March 29, 1923: Seventy-nine Millionaires ended own lives in past year.

Tulsa (Oklahoma) *World*, December 7, 1923: Gridiron claims nineteen lives as toll during season of 1923, records disclose. [This item gave a brief account of each case, including one player who choked to death

* In the 1953 movie, *Houdini*, Bess speaks scornfully of the people "who pay a dollar to see a man in love with death."

† This entry shows that Houdini and his brother Leopold were on speaking terms at this time, two years after their mother's death.

on a plug of chewing tobacco, another who contracted blood poisoning after breaking his leg, etc.]

Another indication of his fascination with the macabre is a news story from *The New York World*, dated September 8, 1924, entitled "One Thousand Articles in Stomach," which told of a fifteen-year-old girl whose penchant for swallowing hardware, coins, and other objects was expected to prove fatal. He also saved an account of a man who had installed a radio in his coffin so that he would know what was going on in the world after his death, and another about a Polish couple who had confessed to committing fifty-one murders in the past few years. Others read: "Helped German slayer to get clothes of victims," "Woman Demon Kills Twenty," etc. Allusions to a sense of his own vulnerability are discernible in his collection of news accounts of anti-Semitic acts by Ku Klux Klansmen, pogroms in his native Hungary, and an item denying that the Jews had crucified Christ.

In seeking to account for this unrelieved tolling of the knell of disaster, the suspicion arises that Houdini was held in the grip of a deep and unremitting fear, resulting in part from some close brush with death at an exceptionally vulnerable moment in his childhood. Evidence in support of such a conjecture is provided by recently discovered hospital and cemetery records concerning the hitherto undisclosed fate of his half-brother, Herman.

At the age of twenty-two, on November 16, 1885, Herman Wise [*sic*] was admitted to Kings County Hospital, in Brooklyn, New York. Just short of six weeks later, on December 24, he died. The diagnosis was *asthenia et phthisis pulmonum*, or pulmonary tuberculosis. The scanty hospital records indicate that he was married and living in Brooklyn; his occupation was listed as "hostler." How long he had been living away from his family in Milwaukee and how long he had been in failing health is unknown.[2] Since considerable shame was attached to the diagnosis of consumption in those days, especially among Jewish people, it is not remarkable that there is no mention of Herman's condition in the available biographic material on Houdini. It may be safely assumed, however, that Herman had been ill for some time, quite possibly, in fact, while he was still living with his family in Milwaukee. The likely traumatic impact of his illness and death on his impressionable brother, Ehrich, may be judged by the fact that some three months later, on the threshold of puberty, as if fleeing from the fates (and from school, too), the twelve-year-old boy ran away from home.

Yet despite his flight, he does not seem ever to have rooted out the memory of Herman's illness and death. Many years later, alluding to a group photograph of his wife, his mother and himself, Houdini had written: "I hope not the last time together. Who knows? The old must die, and *the young can* [italics added]." Five days later, on January 8, 1907, after noting in his diary that he had been measured for a coffin for one of his escape stunts, he added, "I wonder how soon I'll be in one for fair."

But Herman was not the only member of the family to fall victim to tuberculosis. Houdini's diary of May 25, 1908, states that his older brother William was afflicted by "consumption of the throat." "May result fatal," he added, "if he does not take care of himself. He will have to go to the country." By July William was evidently better and able to talk. On the anniversary of his mother's death in 1920 he was apparently well enough to accompany Houdini, Hardeen, brother Nathan, and sister Gladys to visit her grave at the cemetery. Later he suffered a relapse, for on December 4, 1924, the diary indicates that he was a patient in the tuberculosis sanitarium in Saranac, New York.* "Visited Brother Bill in Saranac Lake," Houdini noted. "Bill very sick and suffering." One month later he was dead.

It is hardly surprising that the subject of tuberculosis played a pivotal role in several of Houdini's short stories, and that sickness proved to be among the topics most commonly mentioned in his diaries: "Nat reported dangerously ill"; "Bess operated on"; "Bess has not been well, think she does not take care of self"; "X injured in auto accident. May lose both legs. Poor fellow."

It was undoubtedly to escape such perils that Houdini adopted a style of life that was to cloak him in a mantle of immortality. From an early age he became a health fanatic, renouncing tobacco and alcohol and dedicating his energies to the perfection and invulnerability of his body. As a teenager he engaged in numerous athletic activities, and he became proficient enough in swimming and diving to try out for the U. S. Olympic Team. To keep himself in top physical shape he exercised every morning, and when training himself to leap from bridges into the chill waters below, he immersed himself daily in a tub of water filled with blocks of ice. His diary of January 9, 1907, states that he had bathed in water at a temperature of forty-seven degrees. One writer alluded to Houdini's "moral compulsion" to subject himself to "unremitting disciplines and sacrifice," like run-

* The despised Leopold was responsible for arranging for his admission to the sanitarium. Doctor Weiss also helped send William's son through medical school.

ning ever increasing distances or swimming for long periods in icy rushing streams, "in order to gain that muscular flexibility and *respiratory power* . . . without which his seemingly superhuman feats, such as his underwater escapes from packing cases, would have been impossible [italics added]." [3]

Not unexpectedly, in the face of injury or ill health, Houdini's behavior was characterized by an attitude of denial. During a "wet-sheet" escape act in November 1911 in Detroit—an ill-fated locality it would prove to be—he suffered an injury when his "opponents" strapped him down "with such force [that he] burst a blood vessel in [his] kidney." Although as a consequence he passed blood in his urine, he ignored the symptom for two weeks before consulting a doctor, who promptly ordered him to bed. By the first of December he resumed his performances—too soon, it would seem, for he continued to suffer considerable pain. "Maybe I should have laid off for another week," he admitted. [4]

Some years later, early in 1920, he displayed a similar attitude of denial when he began his British tour with a broken ankle. True to form he ignored it until it became so painful he could hardly walk. Only after doctors had warned him that he might become permanently disabled did he reluctantly interrupt his performances for a week.

He was to repeat this behavior in Albany, New York, in the fall of 1926, during the final weeks of his life, when he insisted that "the show must go on" despite indications that during the preparations for his immersion in the "Chinese Water Torture Cell" act he had suffered a fractured ankle.

Intent on attaining eternal youth, the arrival of Houdini's fiftieth birthday in 1924 came as something of a shock. "I am fifty years of age today," he wrote, "and can't believe it. But I am!! But not in body and far from it in mind. I believe if I live I'll be better in body and mind than ever before and more capable of making a living in my old age! But I must provide. *Now!*" It seems likely that these sentiments were partly inspired by a determination to avoid following in the footsteps of his impoverished and enfeebled father. Ironically, it would be his inflated sense of physical invulnerability that would ultimately prove to be his undoing.

Just as his personal habits were aimed at preserving his health and warding off the inexorable march of aging and death, so was his professional routine composed of a repertoire of acts which seemed designed to prove his indestructibility. His escape from prison cells that once held celebrated criminals awaiting execution not only reflected his sense of kinship with them, but, like his ability to sit with insouciance in the electric chair installed in his home, furnished proof that the lethal devices that signaled the approach of the dark shadow of death for ordinary men held neither terror nor threat for him. Like a boy brazenly exhibiting his indifference to highway traffic by shuffling across a busy thoroughfare, Houdini exposed himself to a varied catalogue of hazardous situations as if he, too, were proving his immunity to the menace of death. One characteristic of his death-defying stunts seemed designed—unconsciously perhaps—to demonstrate his invulnerability to the dread respiratory disease that had carried off Herman, and later struck down his brother William. Whether he broke free from a nailed box submerged in the icy waters of New York Bay or fought his way out of the stinking carcass of a strange sea monster, he was displaying a triumphant mastery of his lungs over the threat of suffocation, an unspoken defiance of the Great White Plague.

In May 1926, a twenty-six-year-old Egyptian Miracle Man named Rahman Bey created a sensation by going into a trance and immersing himself for an hour in a coffin lowered into the Hudson River. His manager challenged Houdini to duplicate the feat, and after a series of practice sessions in which he remained in a sealed box in the basement of his home, Houdini was ready. Just before the final test he declared, "I am going to prove that the copy book maxims are wrong when they say a man can live but three minutes without air, and I am not going to pretend to be in a cataleptic state either." [5] Later, after he had broken Rahman Bey's record by a half hour, Houdini explained that the secret of his success was to relax and to breathe rhythmically with short intakes of air.* He believed, furthermore, that his method might help save trapped coal miners and deep sea divers, enabling them to survive far longer than had been thought possible. "I trained for three weeks in water *to get my lungs to battle against air*," he explained [italics added].†

Despite his seeming triumph over death, there were times during

---

* After Houdini defeated Rahman Bey, the *Brooklyn Eagle* sent an Egyptian to interview him in his supposedly native tongue, "but the fakir did not understand the language."

† It is tempting to suspect that, in choosing to become a physician and, more particularly, a radiologist, Houdini's brother Leopold was also unconsciously seeking to combat the menace of consumption. But, while Houdini strove to ward off the dread fate of his brothers by cultivating the myth of personal invincibility, Leopold, armed with the magical eye of X-ray vision, fought with the weapons of medical science.

the performance of his *Danse Macabre* when he stumbled and nearly fell, like the time he arranged to be tied at the stake while surrounded by a ring of burning faggots. With reason, he had counted on getting free in less than two minutes; what he hadn't counted on was the imaginative illumination of the scene by some enterprising boys who, seeking to brighten things up, poured kerosene on the fire. Then matters began to take a serious turn, for the wind blew and sent flame and smoke into Houdini's face, and the two minutes seemed hardly enough. By the time he was free, his clothing was on fire.

"My chief task," he once said, "has been to conquer fear. When I am stripped and manacled, nailed securely within a weighted packing case and thrown into the sea . . . it is necessary to preserve absolute serenity of spirit. I have to work with great delicacy and lightning speed." And then in a prophetic vein, he added, "If something goes wrong, if there is some little accident or mishap, some slight miscalculation, I am lost." [6]

There came a time when, because of such a "slight miscalculation," something almost did go wrong, and nearly fatally, too: as if he were guided by the inspiration of Edgar Allan Poe, the muse of claustrophobia and the poet laureate of death, Houdini submitted himself to the experience of being buried alive.

The Premature Burial

*Your worm is your only emperor for diet: we fat all creatures else to fat us,
and we fat ourselves for maggots: your fat king and your lean beggar is but
variable service, two dishes, but to one table: that's the end.* —HAMLET

"It may be asserted without hesitation," wrote Poe in "The Premature
Burial,"

> that no event is so terribly well adapted to inspire the supremeness of
> bodily and of mental distress, as is burial before death. The unendurable
> oppression of the lungs—the stifling fumes of the damp earth—the cling-
> ing to the death garments—the rigid embrace of the narrow house—the
> blackness of the absolute Night—the silence like a sea that overwhelms—
> the unseen palpable presence of the Conqueror Worm . . . these con-
> siderations, I say, carry into the heart, which still palpates, a degree of
> appalling and intolerable horror from which the most daring imagination
> must recoil. We know of nothing so agonizing upon Earth.

Some seventy years after these lines were written, Houdini, always
ready to try novel publicity stunts, responded to a dare that he attempt
to escape after being buried under six feet of earth. Beginning with
shallow pits, he succeeded in breaking out of successively deeper
graves, encountering no difficulties until they were four or five feet
deep. By that time some of the onlookers suggested that matters had
gone far enough, but Houdini insisted on going ahead. Finally, when
a grave at a depth of six feet was prepared, he leaped in, stretched out
on his back and covered his face with his hands as the earth was shov-
eled in. Feeling the heavy pressure of the sod, he experienced a moment of panic as he awoke to the realization that he was in a real
grave, *buried alive* six feet below the surface. "All his life he had been
. . . preoccupied with speculations on the mystery of death," wrote

Kellock. "He had constantly visited graveyards, and now his thoughts on these things crowded up morbidly into his mind. Suppose he couldn't get out? If he choked to death there in the close darkness— then what?" [1]

"Despair—such as no other species of wretchedness ever calls into being," writes the narrator of "The Premature Burial," "despair alone urged me, after long irresolution, to uplift the heavy lids of my eyes. . . . It was dark—all dark."

"Suppose he blacked out, or suffocated," Houdini wondered. "He tried to call for help, but no one heard him." [2] "He tried to shout, merely wasting . . . precious breath and choking his mouth and nose with sand." [3]

"I endeavored to shriek," continued Poe's narrator,

> and my lips and my parched tongue moved convulsively together in the attempt—but no voice issued from the cavernous lungs, which, oppressed as if by the weight of some incumbent mountain, gasped and palpitated with the heart at every elaborate and struggling inspiration. . . . I writhed, and made spasmodic exertions . . . and then, too, there came suddenly to my nostrils the strong, peculiar odor of moist earth.

"The earth trickled in Houdini's mouth and clogged his nose. Desperately he began to dig his way up. He clawed, tore, ripped, forced, pushed, crawled. Finally, as he saw a patch of blue above, he collapsed." When his assistants pulled him from the grave, he was covered with grime and his fingers were raw. "I tried out Buried Alive in Hollywood and nearly (?) did it," he wrote. "Very dangerous; the weight of the earth is killing." [4]

It is said that during this terrible ordeal Houdini was beset by "gruesome fantasies [that] paralyzed his initiative." [5] Although they were not described, it may be safely assumed that, in submitting to this and to other strange trials, he was giving active expression to fantasies that had visited him for many years, perhaps for much of his lifetime. Moreover, just as his live burial stunt bears a striking similarity to Poe's "Premature Burial," so it is possible to discern a consistent kinship between others items in Houdini's repertoire and Poe's literary art. Houdini clearly recognized that kinship; on the threshold of his movie-making career he announced that "Edgar Allan Poe will furnish the first scenarios, as his tales contain the desired amount of mysticism, danger and opportunity for physical exertion." [6] It is significant that one of his most prized possessions was Poe's portable writing desk, and that among the very few pictures he retained of the graves of persons who were neither family members nor friends nor fellow magicians was a photograph of the tombstone in Baltimore of Edgar Allan Poe.

On the surface, to be sure, these two men were strikingly dissimilar. What could have offered a sharper contrast to the dissolute, debauched Virginian than the teetotaling and straitlaced rabbi's son? Despite these and other obvious differences, they shared a number of characteristics. Both were outspoken in their veneration for their mothers and expressed it in similar maudlin language. Poe wrote:

> Because I feel that in the Heavens above,
> The Angels, whispering to one another,
> Can find among their burning terms of love,
> None so devotional as that of Mother.*

while in his dedication to *A Magician Among the Spirits*, Houdini declared:

> If God in His Infinite Wisdom
> Ever set an angel upon earth in human
> Form, it was my Mother.

Fixated on their mothers or on mother surrogates, neither achieved a mature marital relationship and neither attained parenthood. Exposed from an early age to the spectacle of lethal illness, namely tuberculosis, both men grew older harboring an obsessional concern with death, which in one way or another became the leitmotif of their lives and art. Both harped on graves and epitaphs, and each sought in his own way to ward off the inexorable appetite of the "Conqueror Worm." Yet their individual style of doing so differed. As a literary artist Poe sought to conquer the specter of death through fiction and poetry; like an unrelieved pedal tone, the peal of death sounds the ground bass in many of the sad melodies he composed. Unendowed with comparable literary gifts, Houdini was preeminently a performer who danced to these melancholy strains upon the stage; he was the mime whose gestures illumined the other's words.

In his frantic zeal to deny its reality, Poe toyed with death as if it were an illusion, or better still, a mistake which gained expression through catalepsy and the nightmare of live burial. "Scarcely, in truth, is a graveyard ever encroached upon, for any purpose, to any great extent," he wrote in "The Premature Burial," "that skeletons are not found in postures which suggest the most fearful suspicions." In story after story—"The Narrative of A. Gordon Pym," "Loss of Breath,"

---

* This was written not to his dead mother but to Mrs. Clemm, his mother-in-law and paternal aunt.

"Berenice," "The Fall of the House of Usher," "The Tell-Tale Heart," and others—he returned to the theme of the premature burial, and in the story bearing that name, after providing a number of chilling examples, he depicted himself as a victim of the same horrible fate.

Although, in contrast, Houdini sought to dismiss Poe's ghoulish fantasies by demonstrating that he could survive in a sealed airless box and claw his way out of a living tomb, both strove to attain the same victory over death. Anticipating Houdini's involvement with spiritualism, his poignant attempts to communicate with his dead mother, and his alleged authorship of a movie scenario concerning the transmigration of the soul, entitled *Il Mistero di Osiris—a Mystery Tale of Old Egypt,* Poe wrote stories about metempsychosis and life after death. In one, "Some Words With a Mummy," he told of the return to life of an Egyptian, embalmed in a state of catalepsy five thousand years earlier. In view of its theme of triumphant resurrection, it is noteworthy that this work projects a mood of lightness and euphoria.

In sharp contrast in his "The Facts in the Case of M. Valdemar," a story which describes the ghastly result of hypnotizing a man who is on the point of dying—of consumption. Although M. Valdemar ultimately dies, his physical dissolution is suspended for seven months, during which interval "the dead man can merely move his hideous, black, swollen tongue and utter sounds as from the Beyond." When, at last, an attempt is made to waken him from his long trance, "his whole frame at once—within the space of a single minute, or less, shrunk—crumbled—absolutely *rotted* away. . . . Upon the bed . . . there lay a nearly liquid mass of loathsome—of detestable putrescence." *

Both of these stories anticipate the central theme of Houdini's first motion picture, *The Man From Beyond,* in which the hero is discovered frozen in a block of ice in which he has remained in a state of suspended animation for a hundred years. As he is chopped out of his cryogenic tomb by Arctic explorers he comes back to life, and recalling events of a century before, utters the name of his beloved.† Restored to civilization, he meets one of her descendants and soon falls in love with her. Later, in a hair-raising scene, he saves her life by swimming out into the Niagara River and seizing the canoe in which she has been drifting just as it is about to plunge over the Falls.

* Houdini was to deal with a similar theme of the interplay between hypnosis and death in "The Mania of Wangh Pagh," as will be noted later on.
† Present-day movie-goers may recognize here an anticipation of Woody Allen's film *Sleeper.*

This, it will be recalled, was the very fate awaiting Houdini's primeval man, Yar, whose enemies were preparing to fling him into a waterfall after they had bound him with ferns. No less striking is the realization that Houdini had devised a plan of going over Niagara Falls in a nailed box. Although this stunt was never carried out, it had been his intention that moments after his supposed annihilation at the foot of the Falls, and when the horrified spectators were convinced that, without a shadow of a doubt, he had been smashed to bits in the splintered wreckage, he would suddenly appear on the shore, smilingly acknowledging the thunderous applause of the incredulous crowd.[7]

This miraculous triumph over certain death, this magical resurrection, stands in stark contrast with the ominous fate that awaits the two brothers doomed to be sucked into a whirlpool in Poe's "Descent into the Maelstrom." Curiously, Poe's acount of their terrible destruction contains an allusion to the very site of Houdini's death-defying stunt: "Speeding dizzily round and round with a swaying and sweltering motion, and sending forth to the winds an appalling voice, half shriek, half roar, such as not even the mighty *cataract of Niagara* ever lifts up in its agony to Heaven" (italics added).

In the end, virtually all of Poe's invented characters suffer the same awful doom—exterminated by the plague known as the "Red Death," buried under the fresh plaster of a wall, cemented up in a wine cellar, dismembered and thence hidden in pieces beneath the floor boards, nailed into a casket, or bound at the bottom of a black prison pit, gnawed by rats and menaced by a descending pendulum swinging a deadly scythe—all are victims of an airless claustrum. These were the mournful ballets composed by Poe for which Houdini wrote a new choreography, seeking to replace the sad steps with brave leaps and bolder turns. No passive victim of a yawning maelstrom, Houdini leaped from high bridges into the icy waters below, escaped from his shackles and swam safely to the shore. No burial alive for him who proved he could survive in a submerged box or escape from a living tomb; no suffocation for him behind cemented walls; he ignored such material obstacles and earned the title The Man Who Walked Through Walls. As for dismemberment, as a boy he had seen it happen on the stage, and in later years he learned it was all an illusion. Neither coffins, prison cells nor iron vaults could contain him, for he was an escape artist, a virtuoso who made a mockery of claustrophobia and a jest of death.

Or so it seemed. Yet a close and searching look at Houdini's life and an informed inquiry into his mental makeup reveal slight but tell-tale evidence that these daring acts fulfilled the psychological purpose of warding off an underlying fear—the same claustrophobic terror that Poe sought to exorcise through his literary art. Once, relatively early in his career and after the Champion Jail Breaker had entered a telephone "closet" in the lobby of a Kansas City hotel, a prankster, passing by, turned the key and locked the door from the outside. When Houdini discovered that he couldn't get out, he broke into a terrifying rage, hammering with his fists on the door, kicking and screaming as if he were imprisoned for life. "What fool trick is this!" he shouted. From that time on, it is said, he never entered a telephone booth without placing his foot securely in the path of the door. As an added anticlaustrophobic measure, he always took care to carry in his pocket a little gimmick, about the size of a pocket knife, that contained a set of steel lock picks which could open most doors.

Despite these precautions, some years later he was caught again in the same trap when, at a magicians' banquet, a group of his confrères decided to shut up the World Famous Self-Liberator in a pay toilet. As on the previous occasion, Houdini obviously failed to find anything funny in the situation and unleashed a storm of fury at his would-be captors.

Another experience suggestive of claustrophobia occurred, as mentioned earlier, when he was sewn into the belly of the so-called sea monster in Boston in the fall of 1911. Ostensibly because the carcass had been sterilized with chemicals, after Houdini had been lowered into its dark interior he became "sick and dizzy" from the fumes, and in a panic started to kick at the enclosing walls. Despite the explanation for his symptoms, however, it should be noted that they were similar to those he habitually experienced within the belly of those leviathans fashioned by man—ocean liners.

Curiously, Houdini first became aware of his unusual susceptibility to seasickness not on the high seas, but on a coastal trip when he was traveling from St. John, New Brunswick, to Boston during the summer of 1896. Although the precise date of the voyage is unknown, an inquiry placed with the Eastern Steamship Company, which made the run, and with the Cunard Company, elicited the opinion that voyages undertaken in those waters during that season tend to encounter a mild sea. When Houdini, scheduled to take part in the evening's entertainment, finally made his appearance in the passenger lounge, he was said to be as white as a ghost and shaking as with a palsy. "In a weak, hollow voice he tried to start his explanatory speech, but the effort was too much for him. He lurched forward and nearly fell to the floor. Then he began bleeding at the nose. He reached the ship's rail just in time." [8]

From this time on seasickness became a source of intense suffering for Houdini. The mere act of buying tickets on dry land for his various sea voyages almost invariably brought on violent nausea. On his first trip to Europe in the late spring of 1900, even before the ship had left New York harbor, it was said his eyes began to roll and his color turned green. By the time the first ocean swells reached the ship, Houdini made for his cabin, threw himself on the berth and did not come out again until the ship reached Southampton. By the third day he was said to be "delirious," and his wife spent virtually the entire trip feeding him small amounts of ice and lemon juice. "She dared leave him only for meals," wrote Kellock, "and then she had to take her sheets and tie them firmly to the bed, carefully knotting the sheets underneath where he (the Escape King!) could not reach to untie them. At one time [she] kept a life preserver strapped about him for fear he would jump overboard in his delirium." [9] Curiously, the depiction strongly resembles the malady allegedly suffered by young Robert-Houdin on the stagecoach carrying him home to Blois. "The journey was a horrible martyrdom to me," Robert-Houdin had written. "Unable to endure it any longer, I opened the door . . . and leaped . . . on the high road, where I fell in a state of insensibility." [10] As was noted earlier, it is difficult to avoid the impression that motion sickness and claustrophobia contributed to the author's ordeal.

It goes without saying that a berth in a ship's cabin, to say nothing of the cabin or even the ship itself, is a claustrum par excellence. Indeed, in Poe's "The Premature Burial" it is the narrator's awakening at night in the narrow berth of the cabin of a small sloop lying at anchor on the James River that prompts the terrible fear that he has been nailed in a coffin and buried alive. Even in the less cramped quarters of the vessel—the salons and other public rooms—the realization that there is no escape, combined with the disturbance in equilibrium brought on by the tossing and rolling of the ship, confers upon susceptible individuals an intolerable sense of confinement and helplessness that expresses itself in uncontrollable nausea and vomiting.

It is indeed well-known that claustrophobia and related motion sickness are highly dependent upon the matter of control. Being closed in is not so oppressive if one feels that it is possible to break out; it only attains the proportions of panic if all avenues of escape are closed. Persons who are afraid of trains, boats, and airplanes state that it is the impossibility of getting out in case of emergency that is unbearable, and that they figuratively rescue themselves from one station to the next while traveling on the train. For this reason many claustrophobic persons will use a local train making frequent stops rather than an express, since the former permits them to escape periodically. In automobiles many such subjects feel anxiety only when someone else is doing the driving. "Why should I be afraid," asked one person, who habitually drove, "when I can stop the car at any time?" Hence, individuals who as passengers suffer severely from nausea are often magically cured as soon as they take the wheel. This occurrence is sometimes rationalized by the statement that the sufferer has no confidence in anyone's driving but his own.

Like such people, Houdini suffered no seasickness when he exchanged the passive role of passenger on an ocean liner for the active freedom of an aquatic athlete plunging boldly into the sea. There is reason to believe that his wife understood this well when she feared that in seeking to escape from his confined existence he might hurl himself over the side of the ship. Describing his own experiences with seasickness on a troop ship while traveling to England in dangerous waters during World War II, the psychiatrist Meerloo affirmed that the best remedy was being forced to help others. "I got over my seasickness when I had to encourage others and assure them that they would get better." [11] "In our activity alone," wrote Conrad in *Nostromo*, "do we find the sustaining illusion of an independent existence as against the whole scheme of things of which we form a helpless part."

Nothing in Houdini's life so well fulfilled this aim as did his brief, intense and passionate fling with aviation.

A Modern Icarus

Oh! I have slipped the surly bonds of Earth
And danced the skies on laughter-silvered wings . . .
—John Magee: HIGH FLIGHT

Houdini's interest in flying began in the year 1909, a year that was marked by a particularly strong upsurge in enthusiasm for aviation. In July of the previous year the celebrated Wilbur Wright had come to France to set up shop at Le Mans. His subsequent flights created a sensation as he promptly shattered all established flying records. In October 1908 he kept a plane aloft for over an hour. Shortly before Christmas he succeeded in covering ninety-nine kilometers in one hour and fifty-three minutes, climbing to a height of 460 feet. These records were soon eclipsed by others. The air race was on.

Toward the beginning of November 1909, while playing in Hamburg, Houdini went out to the race track and saw his first flight. He was beside himself with excitement, and when the plane landed safely after a brief and erratic spin, Houdini rushed up to the pilot and besieged him with questions. He demanded to know how he might learn to fly and how he might acquire a plane for himself.

Within a week the second problem was solved, for he became the owner of a French Voisin plane, and he rented a wooden house in which to store it. From now on the plane was his obsession; virtually all other subjects disappeared from his diary. "Everything was flying," wrote Kellock. "Each morning early he dashed out to his new toy." [1]

But although he had the word HOUDINI painted in large letters on the sides of the plane and had his picture taken standing beside it —with his cap on backwards, in proper aviator fashion—some weeks would elapse before he could take off. Day after day high winds kept him on the ground and he had to cool his impatience while he received instructions about the engine and the controls. Finally, after two weeks of waiting, the wind died down, and not long after daybreak Houdini attempted his first flight. But hardly had he left the ground when he crashed. His diary recorded his misfortune with a single sentence: "I smashed machine; broke propeller all to hell."

Undaunted, some weeks later, on November 26, after the plane had been repaired, he tried again and, using the parade grounds outside Hamburg, made his first successful flight. Permission to use this location had been granted him on condition that he teach the local regiment the art of flying. Perceiving an additional source of publicity in this assignment, he had many pictures taken of himself seated in the plane, surrounded by German army officers.*

Throughout the rest of his engagement in Hamburg, which lasted until the end of December, he spent virtually all his spare time with his machine, and when he left Marseilles on January 7, 1910, for Melbourne, Australia, the crated aircraft was carried along in the hold of the ship. His flying instructor, a French mechanic, accompanied him. "Hope all will be well with me and my machine," he wrote in his diary. But as far as his stomach was concerned all was far from well, for except for a quiet passage through the Suez Canal, the twenty-nine-day voyage was an uninterrupted nightmare of seasickness. During the entire trip he had only fourteen meals, and by the time it was over he had lost twenty-eight pounds.

Flying was very much in its infancy in those days, and up to the time Houdini arrived in Melbourne with his plane (early in 1910), no one had yet made a successful flight in Australia. When Houdini discovered that he had a chance to be the first to do so, he could think of little else. Every night after his show he left Melbourne to spend the night with the Voisin at Digger's Rest, a field some twenty miles away. There is no indication that Bess accompanied him on these nightly assignations.

Once again his eagerness to fly was hindered by bad weather. This was especially vexing because a local man who had acquired a Wright machine was also trying to become the first successful aeronaut in

---

* When the United States entered the war he tried to destroy these pictures, saying, "I taught those fellows to fly, and they may have killed Americans." Aside from illustrating his grandiosity, the episode is noteworthy for once again demonstrating his penchant for destroying people in effigy by mutilating their photographs.

Australia. People were betting between the two rivals. Meanwhile Houdini was giving nightly theatrical performances, and on February 18 a huge crowd saw him leap manacled from Queen's Bridge. It was reported that shortly after he entered the muddy waters of the Yarra River a corpse floated to the surface, causing some of the spectators to believe it was the body of the great magician. When Houdini rose to the surface and saw this strange apparition, he was said to be so startled that he could not swim away and had to be hauled into a boat by his attendants.

Finally, after three weeks of anxious waiting, during which his competitor had not succeeded in taking to the air, Houdini's mechanic gave his approval for the test. And so it was that on March 16, 1910, at five in the morning, Houdini took off in his Voisin, circled the field and, amid a wildly cheering crowd, made a perfect landing, thereby becoming the first person to fly a plane in Australia. On that day he made three trips, on one occasion staying in the air for nearly five minutes; all in all he covered an estimated seven miles, flying at an altitude of one hundred feet.

When his show opened in Sydney on March 28, he obtained a new flying field there, and, as before, he would get up as early as 2:00 A.M. to be with the plane. He made four flights in Sydney before his plane crashed on April 22, and although he was unhurt, the landing gear was seriously damaged. The mishap was attributed to a heavy crosswind, but it is hardly possible to discount the contribution of the human factor to this accident. Suffice it to say that by the time his Australian engagement was over, at the beginning of May, Houdini was described as "a wreck," a designation that he himself endorsed when he acknowledged that he had not had much sleep for two months. "I now seem to have lost the habit," he added.

He also seemed to have lost much of his frantic zest for flying, for although his plane was packed in the hold of the ship that was to take him to Vancouver, he never flew again. With his departure on May 11, a brief but fervent chapter in his life had come to a close. Nothing could have expressed more succinctly the abrupt and precipitous fall in his spirits than his remark made shortly before embarking: "I am certain that I will break all records for being seasick on this trip. I saw the steamer . . . and am sick already." [2]

In contrast it is noteworthy that the accounts of his adventure as a flyer contain no hint of motion sickness—hardly surprising in light of what has been said about the influence of action in warding off that condition. How he might have tolerated being a passenger enclosed within the claustrum of modern air travel is of course not known, but a fair guess is: not well.

The hypothesis that Houdini's interest in flying was determined in part by hidden mental forces may be challenged on several counts. Some will assert, and with justice, that like so many others he was caught up in the general flying fever of the day; others may claim, with equal plausibility, that he discerned in it a rich opportunity for expanding his reputation and gaining invaluable publicity, as was demonstrated by the large crowds that gathered at the airfields and by the generous press coverage he received. It cannot be denied that he squeezed out every available drop of advertising from this adventure.

Despite the validity of these observations, they fail to account for either the immoderate intensity of his preoccupation with flying or its sudden abatement. The character of his brief and intoxicating career as a pilot bears the unnatural, almost manic tone of a person caught in the grip of an infatuation. That he also recognized the all-consuming quality of his dedication to flying, and perhaps its potential danger was reflected in his comment, "It is time I had the biplane packed, or it would have given me nervous prostration." In this he was probably right, for from the reports of the pace he had been pursuing, it is difficult to see how long he might have continued to maintain his psychological, let alone his aeronautical, balance.

These considerations lend support to the belief that Houdini's venture into aviation served not only as a source of pleasure and publicity but as a psychological defense against concealed mental conflicts. If this opinion is valid the possibility remains that he was faced by the danger that sooner or later that defense might fail. Some "slight miscalculation" might have allowed those same conflicts to break through, causing him, like Icarus, to fly to his own destruction.

The ancient myth of the escape of Icarus and his father Daedalus from the labyrinth of King Minos is not the only literary allusion to the relationship between flying and claustrophobia. Herman Melville's *Typee,* a novel replete with the themes of captivity and enclosures, provides an especially clear example. Seeking to escape from the dense thickets that surround them in their island prison, the narrator and his companion Toby seem to be hopelessly trapped and oppressed for want of air. "Alas! The farther we advanced, the thicker and taller, and apparently the more interminable, the reeds became. I began to think we were fairly snared, and had almost made up my mind that *without a pair of wings* we should never be able to escape from the toils. . . . [italics added]"

But even more appropriate is the pronounced emphasis on air travel in the writings of Poe. No less than four of his tales are concerned with balloon flight, all of which are virtually devoid of the grim and morbid mood of his "claustrophobic" stories. Indeed, the antidotal nature of these stories of flying is emphasized in "The Unparalleled Adventure of One Hans Pfaall," [3] in which the narrator explains that he had undertaken his aerial voyage *as an alternative to committing suicide.* "It was not that to life itself I had any positive disgust, but that I was harassed beyond endurance by the adventitious miseries attending my situation. . . . I determined to depart, yet live—to leave the world, yet continue to exist—in short . . . I resolved . . . to force passage, if I could, to the *moon.*"

One incident in the story is curiously relevant to Houdini. In the course of a severe storm Hans finds himself hurled over the rim of the balloon car, and only because he has been lucky enough to catch his foot in a piece of rope, which causes him to dangle head downward in space, is he saved from plunging to earth from the great height. His position—depicted in other tales of Poe as well—is identical to that contrived by Houdini in one of his most publicized stunts—hanging head downward by a rope attached to his feet from the top of a tall building. The possible psychological significance of this will be mentioned later.

It is noteworthy that a visitor to Poe at the time he was writing this story found him in "that exalted condition which alternated with periods of depression. Speaking of the story on which he was at work ("Hans Pfaall"), the author himself seemed to be traveling to the moon and gesticulated, clapped his hands, stamped his foot, and almost leaped into the air." Poe's other balloon stories also possess this elated and even manic quality, as if, lifted from the confines of the dreaded claustrum, his art acquired a lighter-than-air euphoria. (Despite the attempt at humor, these stories are not very funny, regardless of the altitude. Poe's humor, wrote psychoanalyst Marie Bonaparte, ever wears a "gruesome grin.") [4]

Besides serving as an antidote both to claustrophobia and to depression, there is a further psychological significance to flying that should not be overlooked. The fashioning of winged phalli in the sculpture of antiquity bears witness to an ancient symbolic association between creatures that fly and a bodily organ which is mysteriously endowed with the power of defying gravity. Hence in many cultures birds and bats are common symbols of the penis, which is commonly known by such vulgar names as *cock* and *pecker*. By the same token anything that flies may carry a symbolic phallic meaning, as is evident from the following old joke:

> Small boy, pointing to the sky: "Ma, is that a mail plane?"
> Mother: "No, son. Those are just the wheels."

A more poetic animation of the airplane can be discovered in the writings of Antoine de Saint-Exupéry, the French flier and writer, who referred in a letter to his mother to the Spad-Herbemont planes as "the real kings, besides which no other plane exists." In a burst of enthusiasm he spoke of their "evil look, with the profile of an eagle frowning. . . . It's a terrifying plane. That's the one I want passionately to fly." [5] That he sought to acquire this power by becoming a pilot is clear. Later, in the novel *Vol de Nuit,* he would speak of this union between flier and plane—"of the mystery of metal turned into living flesh." When the doomed hero Fabien touched the steel rib he felt the "stream of life flowing into it . . . it was alive."

Paradoxically, emasculation or figurative castration may also be expressed in terms referrable to birds. The term applied to the husband of an unfaithful wife is *cuckold* in English, *cocu* in French and *Hahnrei* (from *Hahn,* cock) in German. The transformation of a man into a bird as a symbolic depiction of his castration is dramatically illumined in the motion picture *The Blue Angel.* In this film, as a consequence of his infatuation with a voluptuous music-hall tart, a pompous Prussian schoolmaster forfeits his respectable position and is reduced to the ignominy of appearing on the stage as a ridiculous crowing rooster. His degradation becomes complete when he is forced to perform before an audience composed of hooting and jeering former students. A preview of what lies in store for him takes place in an early scene in which the professor discovers that his beloved pet bird is dead. Anticipating the later behavior of his inamorata, his housekeeper removes the dead bird from its cage and without a vestige of either pity or regret callously throws the small corpse into the fire.

In view of the generally accepted impression of a disturbance in Poe's erotic life, it would seem likely that the emphasis on aerial travel in his writing was determined not only by a reaction to his phobias and to his recurring mental depression, but as a denial of sexual inadequacies as well. It may not be irrelevant to point out that the subject of the famous poem which established his reputation on both sides of the Atlantic in 1845 was a bird (a raven).

It was surely not without significance, then, that Kellock referred to Houdini's plane as his "toy" and "pet," for like a child he embraced it with a single-minded obsession. In leaving his wife after every stage performance in Australia to spend the rest of the night with his Voisin (or should it have been called his Voisine?), he made it abundantly clear that he had endowed it with an intensely personal significance, as if it were a living thing.* Indeed, his devotion to the machine recalls his behavior toward his mother both during her lifetime, when he would lie with his heart upon her breast, and after her death, when he would lie upon her grave. The comparison is not without precedence: "Suckled by the plane," wrote Saint-Exupéry, "I feel a sort of filial affection for it. The affection of a nursling." [6]

Such sentiments anticipate observations made about Air Force pilots during World War II by Major Douglas D. Bond, psychiatric consultant to the Eighth Air Force. Remarking on the priority accorded the plane in the emotional life of many fliers, Bond cited such comments as: "After flying, my wife comes first"; "No woman will ever come between me and flying"; "Airplanes always tooks the place of girls for me. . . . Mother used to try to get me to put up my planes and go to dances, but I never wanted to. I wanted only to stay with my planes." Some men described their attachments to the plane as "almost a sexual feeling."

The symbolic meaning of aircraft, wrote Bond, "affords insight into the love of flying, for clearly such love is not that for another person or object, but rather the narcissistic love for one's own body." As might be expected, he continued, such men are commonly affected by sexual disturbances. Owing to their difficulty in loving any other object besides themselves, the marriages of many devoted fliers are "notoriously casual." [7]

The relevance of these observations to Houdini scarcely needs emphasis. Like Bond's fliers, his devotion to his plane—and to his mother—was a quasi-symbiotic attachment that constituted a serious barrier against the establishment of adult relationships. Moreover, if the claim of a psychological kinship between Houdini and Poe is justi-

---

* Excluded from these intimacies, it may be that Bess felt like the wife of Charles Gould in Conrad's *Nostromo*, who, recognizing her husband's total preoccupation with his silver mine, realized that he was "in the grip of a cold and overmastering passion which she dreaded more than if it were an infatuation for another woman."

fied, it would seem logical to ascribe Houdini's sudden and intense involvement in flying to psychological motives and conflicts similar to those of Poe.[8] Specifically, aside from providing him with the gratification that often arises from a new and exciting venture, flying served Houdini as a defense against both claustrophobia and a hidden melancholy and pointed toward a concealed sexual problem.

"You have no idea," Saint-Exupéry once told his mother, "of the calm, the solitude that one finds in a tête-à-tête with one's engine at an altitude of four thousand meters." But like Icarus, who flew too near the sun, Saint-Exupéry met his death while flying. It was a fate which Houdini, still leading a charmed life, somehow managed to escape.

Figure 1. Cecilia Weiss, Houdini's mother, in "Queen Victoria" dress. Essen, Germany, 1901. (PHOTO COURTESY MARGUERITE ELLIOTT)

Figure 2. Rabbi Mayer Samuel Weiss, Houdini's father. Appleton, Wisconsin, ca. 1876. (PHOTO COURTESY MARGUERITE ELLIOTT)

*Figure 3. Dr. Leopold Weiss and his mother viewing his medical diploma. New York ca. May, 1899. (*PHOTO COURTESY MARGUERITE ELLIOTT)

Figure 4. Dr. Leopold Weiss (decapitated by Houdini ca. 1917), Houdini, Bess, and their mothers, 1909. (PHOTO COURTESY RICHARD ERNST)

Figure 5. Exedra in Weiss plot in Machpelah Cemetery, Cypress Hills, Queens, New York, showing "Pietà" figure in foreground.

(PHOTO COURTESY DEENA RUBINSTEIN)

Figure 6. Personal bank check of Houdini.

Figure 7. Decapitated Chinese pirates from Houdini's scrapbook.
(PHOTO COURTESY RICHARD ERNST)

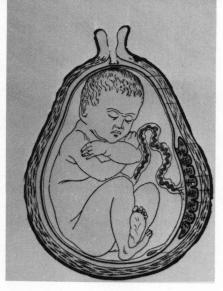

Figure 8a. Sketch of intrauterine fetus. (FROM L. B. AREY's Developmental Anatomy, W. B. SAUNDERS CO.) *8b. Poster for Houdini's water-can stunt.* (PHOTO COURTESY HOUDINI MUSEUM, NIAGARA FALLS)

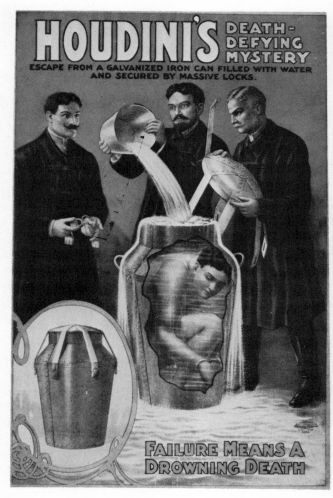

Figure 9. Houdini's crucifixion stunt, posed with model. (PHOTO COURTESY HOUDINI MUSEUM, NIAGARA FALLS)

Figure 10a. The Chevalier d'Eon, the celebrated transvestite, as a woman. 10b. As a man. (PHOTOS COURTESY FREDERICK A. STOKES CO.)

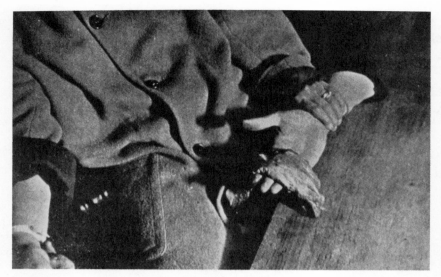

Figure 11. "Ectoplasm" issuing from genitals of Margery, the Boston medium. (PHOTO COURTESY PROCEEDINGS OF THE AMERICAN SOCIETY FOR PSYCHICAL RESEARCH)

Figure 12. Exedra in Machpelah Cemetery after Houdini's bust had been smashed in April 1975. (PHOTO COURTESY RICHARD BELLER)

XI

Claustrophobia

"Ahem" said the mouse with an important air. "Are you all ready? This is the driest thing I know."　　　　—ALICE'S ADVENTURES IN WONDERLAND

The belief that many features of Houdini's professional repertoire, as well as his behavior, were unconsciously designed to cope with a latent claustrophobia merits an excursion into the nature and genesis of that strange phenomenon—the unreasoning fear of being caught within an enclosure or crushed by its encircling walls.

For sheer melodrama it is doubtful whether any claustrophobic situation can vie with the condition known as *penis captivus*. A common topic for debate in the locker rooms and corridors of junior high schools, it denotes the inability of copulating couples to uncouple because of the sudden clamping action of the vaginal muscles. The fact that the medical literature contains no bona fide reports of this harrowing experience has not discouraged belief in its existence nor has it dimmed the lurid setting in which it is said to be staged. A classic example of *flagrante delicto,* this poignant drama allegedly occurs when the sudden and unforeseen arrival of a third person triggers a spasm of the female genitals. Envisaged no doubt as a fitting retribution for illicit behavior, the grisly picture of the unsuspecting penis ensnared in an unyielding vaginal trap derives from the recollection or the rumor of scenes of animals stuck during coitus, and requiring a dousing by a bucket of water to effect their separation. This failing, more drastic measures—some too awful to contemplate—might have to be considered.

Although in authentic instances of claustrophobia sexuality and the threat of genital mutilation often play a conspicuous role, the fear confronting the claustrophobe is basically irrational and the setting

111

in which it usually takes place is far more mundane than in the example of the apocryphal *penis captivus.*

Like Houdini's "telephone closet," the circumstances conducive to claustrophobia are generally devoid of true danger and they include the ordinary trappings of everyday living: the barber's chair, the hair-drying apparatus in beauty salons, restaurants, self-service elevators, and the like. While it is true that elevators are known to get stuck between floors and that trains and cars are occasionally stalled in tunnels or on bridges, reports of such occurrences do not account for the phobia—they merely lend it a modicum of plausibility, for like all phobias, the fear of enclosed spaces is a displacement of an inner (unconscious) mental conflict upon an external situation.

An awareness of the absence of real danger, however, does nothing to allay the terror. On the contrary, unless one has experienced this irrational dread or has observed in others the show of impending suffocation, the gasping for air, the desperate attempts to release the confining collar and constricting clothes, it is difficult to appreciate the magnitude of the claustrophobe's distress and his total imperviousness to reassurance or logical argument. The "appalling and intolerable horror" to which Poe alluded in "The Premature Burial" impels the victim toward a single aim—*to get out* even if it means rushing into real danger, as Bess Houdini feared her husband might do by leaping over the ship's rail in a frantic effort to escape the agony of his seasickness and probable claustrophobia.

It is difficult to supply a simple answer to the question, Of what is the claustrophobe afraid? Some persons afflicted with barber-shop anxiety may fear that in a moment of madness the barber will suddenly slit their throats from ear to ear, a symbolic derivative of the fear of castration. Castration of the son by the father, personified by Father Time, has been read into Poe's "The Pit and the Pendulum," in which a double swinging axe—"a crescent of glittering steel"—affixed to the base of a weighty rod of brass, slowly descends from the ceiling of a dark prison cell and foretells its victim's inevitable doom.[1]

Poe returned to this theme in "The Predicament," a purportedly light-hearted work that may be viewed as a comic antidote to this harrowing tale of Time the mutilator. In "The Predicament" the protagonist is not a male prisoner, lying in solitary confinement in a subterranean dungeon cell, but the Signora Psyche Zenobia, a cheerful lady who, seeking to gain a good view of the city, climbs to the top of the cathedral belfry and pokes her head through an aperture in the wall. Little does she realize that her head now lies in the direct path of the scimitar-like minute hand of the cathedral clock. Before she has time to withdraw her head, the sharp edge of the minute hand proceeds to cut through her neck. As her head is slowly being amputated she is "amused" by the sound of the ticking of the clock's machinery (Father Time again). She also regards with merriment the loss of each of her eyes as they pop out of her head, "winking and blinking" at her. When her head finally falls off and plunges into the street below, her sensations are of "entire happiness." In light of earlier observations concerning Poe's use of physical ascension as a setting for a mood of elation, it is not surprising that the action for this "funny" story of physical dismemberment takes place high in the air, at the lofty top of the belfry (where the bats are, for sure).

Another depiction of figurative castration in a claustrophobic setting can be found in "The Adventure of the Engineer's Thumb" by Houdini's one-time friend, Sir Arthur Conan Doyle:

A young and impecunious engineer is lured into the country in the dead of night, ostensibly to inspect and repair a defective hydraulic press that is being used for some undisclosed purpose. When he arrives at the job, which is located in "a *labyrinth* 2 of an old house," he is met by a beautiful woman who begs him to leave before it is too late, but he needs the generous fee he has been promised and decides to stay. When he discovers that the press is being used for counterfeiting silver coins his employer becomes enraged and, deaf to the entreaties of his lady accomplice, pushes the engineer into the room-size press, slams the door and turns on the machinery, which causes the entire ceiling, like the flat end of a piston, to descend on the trapped man. At the last minute, by smashing through a thin side wall, he escapes, and guided by the woman, enters the bedroom, where he hangs by the window sill preparing to drop into the garden. Before he can relax his hold, however, his crazed employer rushes into the room and hacks off his thumb with a butcher's cleaver.

The oedipal flavor of this story, in which a young man suffers the amputation of a member as he is being shielded by a compassionate woman from a grown man's murderous rage, is reminiscent of the story of "Jack and the Beanstalk," which contains no explicit allusion, however, to either claustrophobia or castration. On the contrary, the dread fate awaiting Jack is not the loss of his thumb or penis, but the crunching of his entire body by the ravenous jaws of the giant, who keeps muttering:

Fee-Fi-Fo-Fum,
I smell the blood of an Englishman;

Be he alive or be he dead,
I'll grind his bones to make my bread.

Read closely, Doyle's story contains a similar theme, for the engineer, like Jack, comes close to having his bones ground to a pulp—not by a giant's powerful teeth, but by the massive jaws of a hydraulic press. The very fact that in the course of his miraculous escape from the jaws of death the engineer's thumb is amputated by a meat cleaver emphasizes the point that beneath the theme of castration this story concerns the fear of being eaten alive.[3]

Eating—notably in public places—is in fact a common stimulus for claustrophobic anxiety, which often assumes the fear of "passing out" or fainting. Although the subject may attribute his mounting discomfort to a lack of air or the inaccessibility of exits, these are invariably rationalizations to conceal unconscious fantasies related to cannibalistic impulses or the morbid dread of being eaten. The myth of Cronus (Time), who ate his own children, the story of Jonah and the Whale, Little Red Riding Hood, Hansel and Gretel, and numerous other fairy tales contain unmistakable allusions to those fears of being devoured that occupy a prominent position in the mental lives of children.

Indeed, in these stories and fairy tales, the transformation from a loving mother who tells her child he is so sweet she'll eat him up into a frightful witch who periodically pinches a caged boy to find out whether he's fat enough to eat, parallels in "oral" terms the contrast between a mother's warm embrace and the terrifying anxiety of smothering claustrophobia. Thus may the innocent wish to return to the imagined security of the womb be distorted into the horror of being shut up in an airless cavern, whose opening is guarded by fearful teeth—the *vagina dentata*—whose interior sizzles with the blistering heat of an inferno, and where the victim is faced by the prospect of being burned or buried or eaten alive.* Paradise, a word of Persian origin, once signified a walled enclosure.

Clinical experience shows that what brings about this radical change are alterations or disruptions in the mother-child relationship, often occasioned by new pregnancies and new children. Confronted by the ever-swelling evidence of a prospective rival, some children, especially those afflicted with a wavering sense of emotional security, dis-

---

* How early in life the psychological mechanism of projection may come into play is illustrated by an observation attributed to Ernest Jones: a boy of three or four, watching his mother nurse her new baby, pointed to her breasts and remarked, "Those are the things that used to bite me."

play an unmistakable outrage. Wild rages, accompanied by the biting or clawing of anything and everything, are not uncommon and convey a wish to attack the mother's body and to destroy the unborn child within. (The innocence of children, observed St. Augustine, is caused less by the purity of their thoughts than by the weakness of their limbs.)

Such a chain of events was illustrated by a young married woman who, during her *second* pregnancy, harbored the notion that for no particular reason an anonymous passerby would suddenly kick her viciously in the abdomen. She also entertained the strange idea that the fetus was attacking her from inside and digging its fingernails into her liver.

The first of several children, when she was three years old her position of only child was placed in jeopardy by her mother's second pregnancy. Although many years later she recalled having kicked the new baby—a girl—in the "stomach," it seemed probable that she had used this "memory" as a screen to conceal real or fantasied attacks on her pregnant mother. Matters became even worse when she was seven, for at that time her mother gave birth to a long-awaited son, whose superior genital equipment inevitably added to her jealousy. Vestiges of that envy later warped her own sexual life and caused her to become somewhat wanting in feminine tenderness. At one time, in fact, she found herself entertaining the idea that her vagina, infrequently visited by her spouse, was the repository of a collection of razor blades, an image that may be said to have crowned the condition of *penis captivus* with figurative decapitation. Surely it was more than caprice that caused the lethal machine employed during the French Revolution to be known familiarly as *Madame* Guillotine.

The fact that claustrophobic anxiety is so often rooted in distant memories of pregnancies and births accounts for the claustrophobe's preoccupation with questions about intrauterine life, and particularly, how the unborn baby breathes when it lies immersed in water within the mother's body. A thirty-year-old claustrophobic patient developed the theory that it all worked like an old-fashioned toilet tank: when the mother urinated, the water level dropped, permitting the baby, like the bell-float, to come up for air. After inhaling a few breaths of air the baby is again immersed as the water level gradually rises.[4] A similar idea was voiced by another patient, who in addition had frightening dreams of being under water and unable to come to the surface because his head was constantly hitting the bottom of a boat or some other obstacle.

The similarity between these dreams and the apocryphal story of

Houdini's entrapment under the ice following his plunge into the Detroit River needs little emphasis. His encounter with a corpse in the muddy Yarra River in Melbourne, in 1910, is similarly reminiscent of another claustrophobic patient who had a dread of swimming under water lest he look up and see the round bottoms of boats and debris floating above him in the water.[5] Associations to these images suggested that they referred not only to unwanted siblings, but to the patient, who might be sucked like feces and dirty bath water into the gurgling drain and flushed away.

It is evident, then, that what the claustrophobe fears is not merely castration, but his total annihilation—whether by being passively chewed up, abandoned, or thrown away. But on a deeper level of mental functioning, a major role in the genesis of claustrophobia must be assigned to a hidden *claustrophilia*—a longing to return to that maternal haven that is unencumbered by new pregnancies or new babies.

Paradoxically, the victim's intentional or unconsciously motivated exposure to the claustrophobic situation often serves as an attempt at mastery. This device, aimed at transforming what has been passively endured into an experience over which the subject has active control, is regularly observed among children who often discover pleasure and comfort in repeating in play what has frightened them in reality. The same psychological sequence determines the repetitive dreams of persons who have been exposed to severe psychic trauma. In such dreams, the subject orders a "replay" of the traumatic event, but with the significant difference that now, instead of being its passive victim, he has become the active creator of its reenactment. Similar strategies play an important role in many aspects of everyday life, such as the choice of a vocation and the selection of hobbies. A morbid dread of illness in childhood has often led to a medical career, just as a fear of heights has prompted others to engage in mountain climbing and a masked claustrophobia has induced a mania for spelunking.

Impressive examples of such "counterphobic" measures appear in the realm of art. Like the dreamer who tries to master a frightening memory by becoming its recreator, the artist often seeks to attain power over what he fears by pursuing it and depicting it in a variety of ways. This, to be sure, was a major determinant in the reiterated thematic material narrated by Poe, whose writings served not only to disclose the nature and the intensity of his morbid fears of entrapment, but to establish a sense of mastery over them.[6]

In all likelihood, the same counterphobic device was responsible for

Houdini's unending dedication to the drama of escape. Such a transformation of claustrophobic anxiety into mastery by means of active
repetition is illustrated by the evolution of his strait-jacket escape.

During an engagement in Nova Scotia in 1896 Houdini made the
acquaintance of a Doctor Steeves, who invited the magician to accompany him on his rounds at a local mental hospital. Fascinated,
Houdini watched as hospital attendants strove to subdue a violently
disturbed patient by wrapping him in wet sheets and then tying him
to a cot. He also saw a patient "struggling on the canvas-padded floor,
rolling about and straining each and every muscle" as he tried to free
himself from a strait-jacket. The spectacle so impressed Houdini that
he was hardly able to sleep that night. "In such moments as I slept,"
he wrote, "I saw nothing but strait-jackets, maniacs, and padded cells!"
In the wakeful hours of the night, however, he wondered what the effect might be upon an audience to see a man placed in a strait-jacket
and watch him force himself free.

The next morning, having begun to master his sensations, he received permission to try to escape from a strait-jacket. For one entire
week, using an old one given him by Doctor Steeves, he practiced
steadily and finally perfected the act that he would present upon the
stage. This, it may be surmised, was a paradigm of the counterphobic
origin of many of his escape stunts, as well as the device that enabled
him to master his childhood anxiety aroused while watching the famous mutilation act of Doctor Lynn in Milwaukee.

There is no assurance, however, that the adoption of such counterphobic measures provides a lasting protection against morbid fears.
On the contrary, it is characteristic of such psychological defenses that
they demand constant renewal, for the original forbidden childhood
impulses, as well as the reactions erected against them that have resulted in the phobia, press repeatedly for discharge. The physician
who hopes to discover in the letters MD attached to his name an amulet
guaranteed to ward off the threat of illness and death may continue to
be harassed by hypochondriacal anxiety for the rest of his life, or at
least as long as the emotional matrix of his childhood brush with
illness and death remains untouched. It was for such reasons that
Poe was rarely able to free his art from preoccupation with the themes
of death, burial, and resurrection, and that Houdini was obsessively
committed to the art of escapology.

Like Poe—and like Doyle—Houdini employed his art as an instrument for the enactment of claustrophobic fantasies. Reminiscent of
both "The Pit and the Pendulum" and Doyle's "Adventure of the En-

gineer's Thumb" is a scene in Houdini's motion picture *The Master Mystery* which discovers the hero lying bound and helpless at the bottom of an elevator shaft and clearly destined to be ground to bits by the descending car. The same film, in which Houdini not only helped compose the scenario but also played the aptly named hero Quentin (San?) Locke, contained several "cannibalistic" episodes in which, like Jack of Beanstalk fame, he is faced by the prospect of being figuratively eaten alive. Like Houdini's real experience of being tied at the stake, surrounded by a ring of burning faggots and managing to get away just before the fire reached him, there is a scene in the film in which Locke performs a hair-raising escape from the straps of the electric chair *—where the condemned prisoner is said to "burn"—and another when he frees himself from coils of barbed wire (i.e., wire with "teeth"), just before his body is eaten away by acid.†

Like bailing out a badly leaking boat, these counterphobic measures were at best temporary expedients that may have postponed, but surely did not avert, an inevitable doom. For Poe that doom had been sealed in the pains and turmoil of a childhood which had been scarred by the birth of his sister Rosalie before he was two and wrecked less than a year later by the death of his mother. Clearly he was never able to erase those haunting memories, and he returned to them remorselessly, both in his literary art and in his personal life. When the narrator of "The Black Cat," awaiting execution for the murder of his wife, explains how the crime had been disclosed by the wailing of a cat he had inadvertently walled up with the corpse, he remarks that the cry had sounded "like the sobbing of a child."

Nor was Houdini able to free himself from his nightmarish preoccupation with bodily mutilation. Recalling the beheading of his brother in effigy in a family picture, and the decapitation of the portraits by the painter Frith, is a photograph in his scrapbook taken from an Australian newspaper in 1910 which shows six or eight human bodies spread upon the ground, their severed heads lying not far away. This ghoulish memento of his Australian tour carries the following inscription in longhand: "A real photo of how they treat pirates in Chinese [sic]. These men committed murder on the high seas and were executed publicly." (Figure 7)

It is not difficult to imagine the mixture of horror and fascination

---

* Compare Houdini's counterphobic gesture of installing a disused electric chair in his home.

† An enactment of being figuratively devoured and regurgitated can be discerned in Houdini's escape from a man-sized sausage skin.

that assailed Houdini as he gazed upon this chilling scene. It was a picture that was destined to haunt him throughout his life, and up until the very end he continued to explore methods by which he might exorcise that grim image from his troubled brain. Like Poe, he sought to master his fear by recreating it under his own authorship.

Christopher has in his possession an unfinished manuscript of a story, jointly attributed to Houdini and an unnamed collaborator, in which the great magician narrowly escapes decapitation at the hands of a mad scientist who has tied him to a surgical operating room table. Entitled "The Mania of Wangh Pagh" (or "Maugh Pagh"—it is hand-written and not too legible) or "Thoughts and Visions of a Head Cut Off," the inspiration for the story is freely assigned to an article on hypnotism in *The Encyclopaedia of Occultism*.

Appearing on page 222 is an account of an experiment in hypnosis allegedly performed on the celebrated painter Wiertz (1806–1865) which was designed to determine whether thought persists in a freshly severed head. Concealed beneath the platform of a guillotine, close to the place where the head of the condemned criminal would soon roll into the basket, the painter was supposedly put into a hypnotic trance and commanded to identify himself with the criminal and to report every thought and sensation that occurred to him during the execution. The effect was spine-chilling, for soon he began to utter pronouncements filled with torment: "The head!" he cried out, "it thinks and feels and does not understand what has happened. It seeks its body and feels that the body must join it." And after the lethal knife had fallen, and the head had dropped into the basket, the painter moaned, "I fly through space like a top spinning through fire. But am I dead? Is all over? . . . Have pity! Give it back to me that I can live again. . . . Oh! my wretched wife and children. I am abandoned. If only you would restore my body to me I should be with you once more. . . . Such suffering cannot endure forever; God is merciful. All that belongs to earth is fading away!" And then, when the hypnotist discovered that the head was quite lifeless, a change occurred in the painter's lamentations: "I feel a calm stealing over me," he sighed. "What a good sleep I shall have! What joy!"

The Encyclopaedia of Occultism, published in 1920, is in the Houdini Collection in the Library of Congress, and the section describing the foregoing hypnotic experiment is marked off with brackets in pencil. It is certain, therefore, that Houdini was familiar with the Wiertz story and undoubtedly participated in adapting it for "The Mania of Wangh Pagh." The mad scientist in the "Houdini" story, it should be noted, is identified as a reembodiment of the hypnotist of the Wiertz experiment.[7]

Here once again Houdini utilized the medium of creative fiction, like his escapes, as a vehicle for the depiction of claustrophobic anxiety and counterphobic defense. He would continue to battle against these fears until the very end of his life. With the indomitable spirit of his fictional namesake in the foregoing story, as the dying Houdini was being wheeled into the operating room in October 1926 he said to the two orderlies, "Go on, I can still lick the two of yez."

Rites of Passage

For each age is a dream that is dying,
Or one that is coming to birth.
　　　　　—Arthur O'Shaughnessy: ODE

Because of the crucial roles played by birth, death, and resurrection in claustrophobia, it is no surprise to discover traces of those themes in Houdini's escapes and in his fiction.

Several of his acts may indeed be interpreted as symbolic representations of stages of parturition. A depiction of the intrauterine state, for example, may be discerned in his "Water Can" stunt, in which he had himself locked into an air-tight galvanized iron container which was shaped like a milk can and filled with more than twenty buckets of water. It needs but a brief glance at a poster advertising this feat to perceive the resemblance between the sketch of the nearly naked Houdini crouched in this liquid-filled container and illustrations of the intrauterine fetus in obstetrical textbooks. (Figure 8a) The resemblance grew even stronger when, because it was being pirated by rival magicians, the "Water Can" was replaced by the more elaborate "Chinese Water Torture Cell," a device that enabled Houdini to be stationed upside down in a glass-enclosed tank. (Figure 8b) Now when the audience looked at him through the transparent wall they saw him, not in the upright position of a breech presentation, but suspended by his ankles from above and placed head downward in the conventional attitude of a proper fetus.

The very style in which he presented these stunts evoked something of the nervous excitement associated with confinement and childbirth. A master showman, endowed with an intuitive feel for what generates thrilling theater, he staged these acts like an obstetrician executing a

121

difficult delivery in a crowded surgical amphitheater. To insure the emotional participation of the audience, he began the act by inviting the spectators to start holding their breath at the very moment when he immersed himself in the water, so that they might gauge the strain of his imminent ordeal. Supporting his claim that man can live but a short while under water deprived of life-sustaining air, soon most of the audience was gasping for breath while he continued to remain submerged for what seemed like an unbelievable period. Following this endurance phase of the act, he emerged, had his wrists handcuffed, and re-entered the water-filled can. Now the top was fitted in place and fastened with padlocks. A curtain was drawn about the apparatus; after what seemed an eternity Houdini still failed to reappear, and the crowd began to grow restless. As the orchestra slowly and ominously played "Asleep in the Deep," people began to wonder whether something had gone wrong. Had he drowned? they asked. Why was his assistant, holding a fire axe in readiness, moving anxiously toward the can? Might he be compelled to cleave the can in two—as if he were performing a figurative Cesarean section—to release the imperiled creature within? The tension continued to mount until it became nearly unbearable. Then, suddenly, dripping with water, smiling and triumphant, out stepped Houdini, and the crowd went wild.

Although it is hardly likely that consciously Houdini grasped any such symbolic significance in these acts, at some level of awareness he seemed to recognize a kinship between his feats of escape and the phenomenon of birth. Writing to his friend and colleague, the celebrated Harry Kellar, to announce the arrival of a baby canary and the joy its birth had brought to Bess, he added the significant line: *"As it broke out of the shell, we called it Houdini."* Nor was this the only occasion when he linked the themes of birth and incarceration. In a telegram sent to Kellar on the occasion of his birthday, Houdini added the obscure statement: "Seventy-two years ago a great soul was imprisoned by the birth of a baby boy."

No symbolic depiction of the act of birth can surpass the description of Houdini's leap into the Detroit River in 1906, particularly in the revised version, according to which he had to swim around virtually blindly until he could find the elusive hole in the ice that led to the outside world. Nor was the atmosphere of an accouchement diminished by the claim that it was by listening to the voice of his mother that he was ultimately guided to the precious aperture.

It is also tempting to discern an obstetrical allusion in Houdini's "Suspended Upside-Down Escape"—his hanging by the feet is sugges-

tive of the position in which a newborn baby is held until spontaneous respiration is established. Performed outdoors, it was begun
in 1915 when Houdini, while playing in a theatre in Kansas City, conceived the idea of being strapped in a strait-jacket and suspended head
downward from the *Kansas City Post* Building. Trussed up in a
leather and canvas jacket, his heels fastened to a block and tackle
apparatus, Houdini's body was hoisted high above the heads of the
five thousand or so persons who had gathered to see this daring act.
Despite the assurance of the city police officials that escape was impossible, less than three minutes of wriggling and squirming by the
incredible Houdini was enough to set him free and to cause pande-
monium among the crowd.

Of his outdoor stunts, no less spectacular than the suspension act
and his daring plunges from high bridges were his bold underwater
escapes from submerged crates and boxes. Two months before the
Kansas City feat, a poster in New York announced, under the title
"Daring Dive," that "Securely handcuffed and leg-ironed, [Houdini]
will be placed in a heavy packing case, which will be nailed and
roped, then encircled by steel bands [and] firmly nailed. Two hundred
pounds of iron weights will then be lashed to this box containing
Houdini. The box will then be THROWN INTO THE RIVER.
Houdini will undertake to release himself whilst submerged under
water."

Proclaimed as "The Most Marvelous Feat Ever Attempted in This
or Any Other Age," this spectacle was destined to be presented in
many variations, each of which invariably created a sensation. One
source of the fascination it evoked lay in the fact that it was not a
stage performance, subject to the artifice and illusion of the theater,
but an open-air drama taking place on a river or canal. This natural
and unsophisticated setting conferred on it a stamp of innocence and
simplicity. The stunt began when a tug, hired by the magician, would
come alongside the pier and hoist the packing case containing Houdini
over the water by means of a crane swung out from the ship. Then,
amidst the growing excitement of the crowd, the crane would slowly
lower the box until it was submerged. After an anxious moment or so
the crane would begin to move again, now to lift its burden, and when
the box once more would come into view the incredulous spectators
would thrill to see Houdini sitting jauntily on top.

Like all of Houdini's amazing escapes, this one proved no less
baffling to the spectators. Quite logically the audience reasoned that
nailed within the packing case Houdini could hardly escape by push-

ing out its walls, which were further secured by ropes and encircling bands of steel. What the public failed to consider was that, anchored by a concealed hinge, one of the sides of the box could swing *inward*, thus permitting him to swim out between the ropes and bands, and then draw the wall closed behind him. This done, he would mount the top of the packing case and be lifted with it as the crane brought it out of the water.

What neither Houdini nor his cheering followers realized, in all likelihood, was that the drama just unfolded was a twentieth century version of a legend that is as old as recorded human history: the deliverance of the hero from a box or ark immersed in water. Characteristically this oft-repeated story concerns the unusual circumstances surrounding the birth of a hero, and as Rank demonstrated in his classic work, *The Myth of the Birth of the Hero,* it can be discovered in widely separated cultures.

In one version of the story of Oedipus, for example, the child was not exposed by his father on a mountain, but *"locked in a chest, which was lowered into the sea from a ship.* This chest drifted ashore at Sicyon where Periboea, King Polybus's queen, happened to be on the beach, supervising her royal laundrywomen. She picked up Oedipus, retired to a thicket and pretended to have been overcome by the pangs of labor. Since the laundrywomen were too busy to notice what she was about, she deceived them all into thinking that he had only just been born." [1]

Similar themes occur in the myths of Osiris, Dionysius, Perseus, and others. Like Oedipus, the infant Perseus, son of Zeus and Danae, was locked in a wooden ark with his mother and cast into the sea. Washed up on the shore near the island of Seriphos, the ark was broken open, revealing that both Danae and her baby were alive. The child was then taken to King Polydectes, who reared it in his own house.

The same theme appears in the story of Moses, who was placed as an infant by his mother in an ark of bulrushes and lowered into the water.

> And the daughter of Pharaoh came down to wash herself at the river; and her maidens walked along the river's side; and when she saw the ark among the flags, she sent her maid to fetch it. And when she had opened it she saw the child: and, behold, the babe wept. . . . And the child grew and [the woman who nursed it] brought him unto Pharaoh's daughter, and it became her son. And she called him Moses, and she said, Because I drew him out of the water.

It must be realized, however, that many of the escapes devised by Houdini—from the sea monster, the water can, the submerged boxes, and others—which have been regarded as symbolic of the act of birth were at the same time potentially dangerous, and even capable of bringing about his death. That Houdini himself was fully aware of such a risk is evident from a news item appearing in April 1909 in the London *Daily Mail*, which he pasted in his scrapbook:

> *Landshut, Bavaria.* A so-called Handcuff King, named Ricardo, who has been appearing at a music hall here, sprang this morning, heavily manacled, from the Luitpold Bridge, purposing to take off his handcuffs under water. He failed in the attempt and was drowned.[2] ("Failure meant a lingering death," added Houdini.)

The play of these opposing themes is especially evident in Houdini's fascination with Niagara Falls and his varied attempts to include that mighty spectacle in his professional repertoire. His projected but unrealized plan of going over the Falls in a nailed box represented not only a shocking dramatization of his death but a reassuring enactment of his rebirth or resurrection. A variation on this theme appeared in his Yar story, and again in his film *The Man From Beyond,* in which the hero rescues his beloved from certain death just as she is about to go over the Falls in a drifting canoe.*

Psychoanalytic explorations of fantasies and dreams of rescue, especially when they occur in relation to water, often concern the begetting of a child. Such an interpretation was suggested some years ago by Ernest Jones concerning the tragic fate of a young childless couple who met their deaths while on a visit to Niagara Falls. They had been standing on an ice bridge just at the foot of the Falls when suddenly it began to crack and drift downstream toward the terrible rapids that lead to the Niagara whirlpool. Although several opportunities to save themselves arose, some inexplicable inertia, particularly on the part of the woman, prevented their doing so. Even as they floated under the railroad bridge and the man successfully seized a rope that had been lowered from it some sixty yards above their heads, something again interfered with their salvation, for the woman unaccountably refused to trust the rope unless it was fastened about her, and her husband's fingers were too numbed with cold to do so. The last glimpse of them alive found them kneeling together and locked in each other's arms as they were sucked inexorably to their deaths.

* This attraction was evidently of long standing. As early as September 1897 his diary records that while playing an engagement there he visited the Falls "every day and night."

Whether Jones' conjecture was valid, namely that the irrational behavior of this couple was somehow a reflection of conflicts concerning the begetting of a child, is obviously incapable of proof. But although Niagara Falls is known as "The Baby City" because of the many conceptions originating in this favorite honeymoon resort, it is no less notorious for extending a beckoning finger toward a quick and a certain death.

In light of the affinity between Houdini and Sir Arthur Conan Doyle, it is interesting that a cataract also served as the locale for the interplay of the themes of birth, death, and resurrection in the career of Sherlock Holmes. Anticipating Houdini's fascination with Niagara, in the spring of 1893 Doyle chose to destroy Sherlock at the Reichenbach Falls in Switzerland, a "terrible place," he noted, "that would make a worthy tomb" for the Great Detective.[3]

This same "terrible place" had figured prominently in Doyle's personal history, for it was while gazing upon those Falls with his wife, Louise, during a holiday on the Continent early in 1893, that the idea of the destruction of Holmes first took root in Doyle's mind. The fact that but a few weeks earlier Louise had given birth to their son Kingsley suggests that that event had proved to be deeply disturbing to the new father, whose mind was now beset by thoughts of violence. Indeed, not long after the child's arrival Doyle had written a story entitled "The Curse of Eve," in one version of which a woman dies in childbirth and her distraught husband denounces the new baby as a murderer. In killing off Holmes, therefore, Doyle may have been displacing filicidal fantasies from his real to his fictional son.

Needless to say, death wishes aimed either at his wife or his new son were quite inadmissible to the conscious thought of Sir Arthur Conan Doyle, and thoroughly incompatible with his moral code. Once again fiction came to his rescue, for he revised the story and gave it a happy ending. And by diverting his black thoughts from Kingsley to Sherlock—the person who "took his mind off better things"—he spared himself the pain of overhearing his own whispered inner secrets or discovering the true identity of both the criminal and the victim. Best of all his undetected deed earned him no graver punishment than his mother's disapproval and a howl of indignation from his disappointed fans. Fortunately these lamentations did not go unheeded, for in time Sherlock was miraculously resurrected and, confronted by no further obstacles, continued in the pursuit of his brilliant deductions.

In tracing these seeming parallels between the fancied happenings at the Reichenbach and the Niagara Falls, it seems that for Houdini, no less than for his friend Doyle, the roar of the cascading waters succeeded in drowning out thoughts of malevolence. If the death of the fictional Sherlock served as a cloak hiding the wished-for death of a wife or a son, it is no less plausible that Houdini's projected plunge into the Niagara Falls also represented a destruction in effigy of some faceless foe, some unseen adversary that once had floated in his mother's "box." Through the device of displacement and the process of interchanging identifications, when Houdini imagined himself plunging over the Falls at Niagara, he may have unconsciously fused himself with an old rival and then consigned that rival to oblivion. Mercifully, this fratricidal deed became undone when, through the miracle of magic, Houdini—the impersonated victim—would appear unharmed and smiling on the shore.

Ironically, many years later in the winter of 1963, such a fatal plunge did occur—not at Niagara, but within view of the Hudson River in New York City. Alone, old, and like King Oedipus, virtually blind, the once distinguished Doctor Leopold Weiss, the last survivor of the children of Rabbi Weiss, groped his way to the roof of his apartment house, and as if yielding belatedly to the stern and Olympian command of his magician brother, leapt to his death on the pavement below.

XIII

The *Akedah,* or
the Binding of Isaac

Take now thy son, thine only son Isaac, whom thou lovest, and get thee into the land of Moriah; and offer him there for a burnt offering. . . .

—GENESIS 22:2

Viewed collectively, Houdini's several depictions of birth, death, and resurrection recall varieties of rites of initiation—those ceremonies of puberty that herald the transition from boyhood to manhood, from a mother's child to a full-fledged member of the adult community. Expressive of the fear and hostility which the older generation harbors toward the younger, these rites often expose the initiate to frightful ordeals and threaten him with castration or death before he is allowed to be "reborn" or "resurrected" and then reconciled with his elders. Sometimes, in fact, these tests unwittingly have proved to be fatal:

> A "pledge," or candidate to an American college fraternity, was blind-folded and tied to a railroad track in the course of his initiation, a few moments before the train was expected. Soon its approach was heralded by a growing roar which became deafening as it reached the helpless boy. Evidently he had been unaware that it was a double-track line, for after the train passed by and his celebrants came to release him from his bonds, they discovered to their horror that he was dead—of fright.

Throughout legend and history aggression toward the neophyte has assumed a wide variety of shapes and complexions. In some versions the attack upon the child-hero by the king or his surrogates has caused the boy to be permanently scarred or deformed. Such was the case with Oedipus, whose father, Laius, advised that the child would ultimately prove his undoing, snatched him from his nurse's arms, pierced his feet with a nail and, after binding them together, exposed him to perish

128

on a mountainside. (The maiming of the child's feet may be interpreted as a displaced expression of castration.)

In this legend, as in many others, the survival of the victim, often effected by the merciful intervention of a god or a father surrogate, is a reflection of the ambivalence of the father toward his son. Thus the future Zoroaster was torn from his mother's womb by a monster, but restored by the intercession of a god. Later when Duransarum, the prince of the realm, learned that the birth of this child would lead to his destruction, he sought to stab the boy, but miraculously his hands fell paralyzed at his side. The same theme appears in the legend of Christ, who was brought into Egypt in order to escape the wrath of Herod, who had sought to destroy him.

In the course of time these violent practices have undergone considerable modification. In the Abraham and Isaac story, another example of divine intervention in an infanticidal act, child sacrifice has given way to animal sacrifice. The story of the "sacrifice" of Isaac also reflects the shifting of the period of symbolic castration—i.e., circumcision—from puberty to the eighth day of life. (The enduring need among Jews for some form of puberty rites, despite these humane modifications of the old ones, is still reflected in the benign and bloodless ritual of Bar Mitzvah.)

In other societies, however, the practice of circumcision continues to exist as a principal feature of the ordeal of initiation. "When the little boy of the Murngin tribe is about to be circumcised, he is told by the father and the old men, 'The Great Father Snake smells your foreskin; he is calling for it.' The boys believe this to be literally true, and they become extremely frightened. . . . The women wail over the boys ceremonially; this is to keep the Great Snake from swallowing them." [1]

Frazer described an initiation ceremony among the natives of Ceram, an island in East Indonesia, in which the boys are led into the depth of the forest where a primitive shed has been built. "The high priest calls aloud upon the devil. As a testimony to the boy's death a dull chopping sound is heard inside, a terrible cry rings out, and a sword or spear, dripping with blood, appears on the roof of the shed," signifying that "the boy's head has been cut off and the devil has carried him away." [2] In the initiation ceremonies of the Yabim tribe of Papua the principal rite again consists of a circumcision. This is performed in a long hut which, reminiscent of Houdini's sea monster, represents the belly of the monster Balum, who is to swallow the novices. The old men of the tribe lead the procession of terrified boys to the monster, all the while raising a shrill song and sacrificing pigs in order to induce the monster to spare the lives of the candidates after they have been circumcised.

In *The Temptation,* Theodor Reik points out several elements of these ceremonies that occur in the story of Abraham and Isaac. Isaac is a lad at about the age of puberty at the time of his intended slaughter by a god for whom the father serves as executioner. Reik interprets the uncompleted sacrifice as a threat to castrate Isaac which is prevented by the last-minute substitution of a ram. It should be emphasized that Jewish theologians speak not of the averted sacrifice of Isaac but of the *Akedah,* or the *binding* of the boy.

> And they came to the place which God had told him of; and Abraham built an altar there; and laid the wood in order, and bound Isaac his son, and laid him on the altar upon the wood. And Abraham stretched forth his hand, and took the knife to slay his son.

This tale of Isaac's binding is solemnly recited in most Jewish communities on Rosh Hashanah (New Year).

As a rabbi's son, who possessed a Hebrew grammar and who surely received a religious education, young Ehrich Weiss, the future Houdini, must have been well-versed in stories of the Old Testament, and particularly in the story of Abraham and Isaac. He also must have been profoundly shocked by this fearsome tale of a father who was prepared to kill his trusting son and make of him a burnt offering to God—especially since Houdini doubtless had vivid memories of his own father circumcising his younger brothers!

It may be that as a child Houdini's reaction to this terrifying story, and especially to the image of Isaac's binding, was to transform the entire drama into a game in which either he or another boy played the role of the victim. Certainly during their adolescence Houdini and his brother Theodore engaged in rope-tying and escapes. While Theodore would "enthusiastically spend hours tying Harry . . . Harry would spend more strenuous hours wriggling out." Friends were also called upon to perform the same service. "Never in all the history of the Weiss family, which had produced a number of rabbis and Talmud scholars," wrote Gresham, "had anyone senselessly allowed himself to be tied with clothesline." [3]

From this playful activity it was but a small step to a repertoire of professional performances, marked by increasingly ingenious escapes from fetters, handcuffs, and strait-jackets.

Houdini's undisguised fascination with the theme of bondage is not the only hint of his identification with the story of Abraham and Isaac. When he allowed himself to be tied at the stake surrounded by burning faggots his inspiration may well have come from the frightening image of Isaac slated to serve as the burnt offering on the altar on Mount Moriah.[4] And in seeking a cemetery for his family, Houdini chose one bearing the name Machpelah. Machpelah, the oldest burial ground mentioned in the Bible, is the name of the cave where Abraham, his wife Sarah, and Isaac were buried.

Even the change in name adopted by Houdini during his adolescence is in keeping with Biblical tradition and with certain initiation ceremonies. Inasmuch as these rites commonly signify death and resurrection, the reborn initiate assumes a new name and a new identity. Hence, just as Abram became Abraham and Jacob became Israel, the reborn Ehrich Weiss assumed a new self under the name Harry Houdini.

The claim that Houdini saw himself as a latter-day Jewish patriarch and patterned his career as a master escapologist on the binding of Isaac might be considered somewhat at variance with his religious conduct as an adult. One lady who knew Houdini when she was a child recalls seeing a crucifix around his neck. Since she also reports that from time to time she still sees Houdini's old dog Charlie running in the street—although Houdini's diary clearly states that the dog died in 1909—her memory of the crucifix may be somewhat inexact. Be that as it may, throughout the years she has felt Houdini's presence in her life as a guardian angel, certain that his corporeal death has in no way diminished the living presence of his spirit. To her he has remained a saint.

Nor was she alone in ascribing the odor of sanctity to Houdini. While to his mother-in-law his magic was proof of his alliance with the devil, Houdini on the other hand clearly identified himself with Christ. Thanks to his Family Romance fantasies he could imagine himself, like Jesus, to be the Jewish child of a royal virgin, whose husband played a distinctly minor role in the child's life. Like Jesus, too, by the grace of magic he could cause the birds of the air to multiply and restore the seemingly dead to life. Moreover, in his vigorous opposition to the doctrine of spiritualism he undoubtedly saw himself as a savior —one whose apostolic zeal would save mankind from the scourge of madness, even as Christ had "cast out the spirit with his word [of the] many that were possessed with devils."

Whether or not he did wear a Catholic cross around his neck, much of the pageantry that bedecked his person and his art seems to have been inspired by scenes from the Christ legend. A BBC documentary film, entitled *The Truth About Houdini*, shows a stunt called "The Crucifix Trick" in which he ingeniously escapes from an apparatus that is identical to the Christian cross. (Figure 9) And his escape from a grave six feet below the earth discloses an unmistakable, if unconscious, allusion to the Resurrection.

Both in his marriage to a Catholic girl and in his erratic religious practices, Houdini showed himself to be a most inconstant Jew. Yet despite the fact that Houdini never became Bar Mitzvah, in paragraph eleven of his will he directed that his brother Hardeen was to receive his share of the estate only on condition that the latter's then "surviving children shall have been confirmed according to the Jewish law and tradition (Orthodox or Reformed) or shall be so within three months of my death." Ironically, the person assigned to determine whether this condition would be fulfillled was the executrix, Houdini's Catholic wife.[5]

His seeming confusion over his religious affiliation was again emphasized by an entry in his diary written in an English town in 1909, affirming his wish to say *Kaddish* on the anniversary of his father's death, but regretting the absence of any "Jewish churches" in that locality. The rabbi's son sent out Christmas cards regularly, and once, while commenting upon his escapes from manacles, likened his performance to an episode in the life of St. Peter, after he had been thrown into prison by King Herod in Jerusalem, and was bound with chains. "And behold, the angel of the Lord came upon him . . . and raised him up . . . and his chains fell from off his hands." [6]

It may be that deep within the uncertain heart of this gifted conjurer, who had repudiated so much of his onerous heritage, was a desire to employ his magic in order to transform himself into a Christian. And nothing more strongly suggested his identification with Christ and Christianity, nor better revealed the flexibility of his piety, than the funeral monument he designed for his parents—the exedra, whose crowning piece was his own sculptured head. In the foreground, kneeling before his chiseled form, is the stone figure of a grief-stricken young woman, an unmistakable portrayal of a sorrowing Pietà.[7]

Early in 1917, some two years after the amputation of her leg, the great Sarah Bernhardt was appearing in a theater in Boston at the same time that Houdini was in that city. One day, after watching his incredible stunts with amazement, she is supposed to have said to him, "Houdini, you must possess some extraordinary power to perform such marvels. Won't you use it to restore my limb for me? You can bring it back, can't you?" 8

Alas, in this request she had touched him in a most vulnerable spot, for it had been the threat and conquest of mutilation and death that had been the leitmotif of his career. Had he known how to grant the pathetic entreaty of the Divine Sarah, he would have attained his own most secret wish, for it was to reach that goal that he had become a conjurer just as it may be suspected that it was to evade the perils of the *Akedah* that he had become the King of Escapology.

XIV

The Magic Wand

With respect to the Queen's command to cut off the head of the Cheshire Cat,

The executioner's argument was that you couldn't cut off a head unless there was a body to cut it off from . . . [while] the King's argument was that anything that had a head could be beheaded.

—ALICE'S ADVENTURES IN WONDERLAND

Decapitation, like cannibalism, dismemberment, and castration, has been a recurring theme in mythology, legend, and art. And it is no surprise to discover that it has played a prominent role in the practice of magic.

The lore of widely disparate cultures is filled with the themes of sex and mutilation. In the myth of Cronos, for example, Cronos, urged on by his mother Gaia (Earth), castrated his father Uranos, whose phallus was thrown into the sea. A like fate befell Cronos who, having devoured his children, was himself castrated by his youngest son, Zeus. In an earlier myth Osiris, who was favored by his sister Isis, was slain by his jealous brother Set and torn into many pieces. Each of Set's accomplices was given a piece of the body, presumably to diminish their individual guilt, although none could bring himself to accept the prized phallus. By stealing the ogre's seven-league boots, Tom Thumb may also be seen as figuratively castrating the father. (In size Tom is surely a very small male, but as a symbol he may be viewed as an exceptionally large phallus.) Posed against these brutal deeds of mutilation are phases of restitution and rebirth: thus from the sea foam surging about the amputated phallus of Uranos sprang the goddess Aphrodite and body of Osiris was reassembled by his beloved sister Isis.

It is but natural that such miracles of resurrection are closely linked with the history of religion and magic. When the unlettered congregation, attending the sacrament of the Eucharist, heard the Latin *hoc est corpus* chanted during the awesome transformation of the bread and wine into the body and blood of Christ, the words came out as *hocus pocus,* the traditional watchword of conjuring.

Hence, although a head might appear to be beheaded, or a body decapitated or otherwise mutilated, a skillful magician could undo it all, and cause the body to become whole again. According to Christopher, such miracles were described as long ago as 3000 B.C., during the reign of Khufu (Cheops), the builder of the Great Pyramid at Gizeh, when a conjurer named Dedi achieved fame by his power of restoring severed heads, including those of birds. The continuing appeal of this theme is revealed by a similar tale of magic from fourteenth-century China:

Prefiguring Jack and the Beanstalk, a magician's assistant climbed into the clouds on a seemingly endless strip of leather. When he failed to return upon his master's command, the latter picked up a knife and climbed after him into the sky. Soon a hand, a foot, and then other parts of the boy's body came flying through the air and fell upon the ground. Then the magician slid down the leather strip from the sky, kissed the ground and carefully reassembled the pieces of the boy's anatomy. Finally he gave the entire body a kick, and lo and behold! the boy stood up, complete and erect.[1]

Five hundred years later the boy who was to become Houdini witnessed a similar miracle when his father took him to a magic show in Milwaukee.

While the principal leitmotif of demonstrations of mutilation has not changed for the past five thousand years, advanced techniques and innovations in publicity have greatly enriched the orchestration. To advertise the supposed riskiness of his theatrical act of sawing a woman in half, the magician Horace Goldin hired ambulances to weave through the city streets, carrying red-lettered signs which read: "We're going to Keith's in case the saw slips," while in the theater lobby a uniformed nurse stood in grim readiness by the side of a stretcher. Servais Le Roy, a British magician performing a similar stunt, invoked his classical learning in sounding the spirited clarion, "I came, I sawed, I conquered." [2] And an ingenious touch was supplied by the Hungarian Tihanyi, who placed two girls, dressed in costumes of contrasting colors, in adjacent boxes. After sawing them in two he rejoined the severed halves, but somehow they got wrongly connected, for although the girls were now intact again, each was wearing the bottom half of the other's costume.[3]

Shades of Edgar Allan Poe were recalled by the magician known as Fu Manchu, who suspended a sharp-edged pendulum that swung back and forth while it slowly descended to the position where it would presently slice through the prone body of the hapless victim. The same conjurer devised a sort of "Danse Macabre," a number performed in semidarkness in which luminous skeletons emerged from a coffin and danced about while their heads and extremities became detached and floated in the obscurity like disembodied ghosts, until at the end they were finally reassembled.[4]

Less poetic, but surely far more spine-chilling, was a gruesome exhibition of dismemberment presented by the South American magician Richiardi, Jr., who ran a circular saw through his assistant, causing a stream of blood to spurt out and soak the stage. Fascinated spectators filed down the aisle and across the stage "to view as ghastly a mess of entrails as can be found in any butcher shop." [5] This atmosphere of carnage is reminiscent of an initiation ritual in the highlands of Fiji. At one point the boys were taken to a sacred enclosure where they were exposed to the sight of "a row of men lying on the ground, covered with blood, and with their entrails protruding. The novices had to crawl over these bodies until they reached the High Priest, who sat at the far end. The High Priest suddenly uttered a yell, whereupon the corpses sprang to their feet and ran down to the river to wash off the pigs' blood with which they had been smeared." [6]

The substitution of animal for human "mutilation" was destined to become a prominent and popular feature in the practice of magic, and the enduring popularity of this colorful pageant of mutilation attests to its universal appeal. There is, to begin with, the thrill induced by a display of primitive brutality and the reciprocal satisfaction of the conjurer for having succeeded in shocking and horrifying his audience. He plays upon the credulity of the spectators, convincing them at one moment of the reality of his awesome deeds, and then, hocus pocus, transforming the nightmare of terror into the calm assurance that all was make-believe.

For the spectator there is the complementary pleasure of yielding passively to an omnipotent and mysterious force, of submitting helplessly to mounting swells of excitement where reason is overthrown and judgment scuttled. "The secret of showmanship," wrote Houdini, "consists not of what you really do, but what the mystery-loving public thinks you do." [7] But sometimes the mystery-loving public only pretends it is being fooled. This was characteristic of some members of Houdini's audience who appeared to maintain a devout belief in his magical powers long after books and pamphlets were available explaining how his tricks were done. Like people attending a performance of a Gilbert and Sullivan operetta who, although they know the score backwards and forwards, and the libretto by heart, strain not to miss a single line nor lose a single joke, many of Houdini's followers flocked to his shows, eagerly waiting to be fooled once again by stunts whose methods were known to them.

But clearly the fun goes deeper. For example, in bearing witness to the grim spectacle of a lady cut in two, the audience participates vicariously in an act of cruelty which, like the thrills of the circus and the drama of the bullfight, serves as a vehicle for a host of secret and forbidden impulses. Unlike the bloody wounds and killing deeds of the *corrida*, however, the transection of a pretty lady turns out to be mere illusion, and whatever guilt or other psychic pain may have been aroused is quickly erased when she leaps easily to her feet and stands smiling and unharmed upon the stage. Ultimately, the greatest appeal of such performances is their successful denial of the reality of mutilation.

Psychoanalytic as well as anthropological studies reveal that the widespread preoccupation with these themes arises from the conscious and unconscious fantasies and from the daydreams, nightmares, and anxieties of childhood, in most of which a central role is played by concern over genital mutilation, or castration. This is equally true whether the matter of mutilation concerns humans or birds, for as noted earlier the latter have always served as a symbol of the penis —the cock or pecker that in defiance of the law of gravity possesses the mysterious power of ascension. What indeed could be more magical than the phenomenon of penile erection? (It is claimed that an inspired *mohel*, or ritual circumciser, ordered a wallet to be made out of the foreskins he had collected over the years. When he protested at the price he was asked to pay, he was told that it was quite reasonable, for if properly stroked, the wallet might become an attaché case!)

Despite scattered and occasionally theatrical reports of men who have sought out surgical alteration of their genitals in order to create a facsimile of female antomy, and who are covertly envious of feminine sexual and biological functions, in the main, far from being an object of envy, the absence of the female phallus tends to be regarded as a warning of the fate that may befall the unwary and overly cocky male. Moreover, when the distress occasioned by the absent female penis is compounded by bleeding, the ensuing revulsion may attain such proportions as to cause the woman to become a tabooed object. In some societies this practice has become institutionalized, and menstruating women are forbidden under pain of death to touch anything that men use, or even to walk on a path that men frequent.

Except for such banishment or quarantine, the most common defense against this frightening evidence of the danger of castration is the psychological device of denial. And denial of the reality of amputation is the theme of the dramas of feigned mutilation performed by magicians on both humans and birds: if a severed head can be miraculously restored to its proper location, and the two halves of a body reunited, it follows that other apparent amputations—notably that of the female phallus—are equally illusory and reversible.

But man's ingenuity has devised still more persuasive measures to deny the distressing reality of the absent female phallus. In the Museo Nazionale in Rome, reclining among the Greco-Roman sculpture, is the chiseled figure of a hermaphrodite, a perfect specimen, endowed both with fulsome breasts and penis and scrotum, whose ancient date of execution attests to the ageless history of his human dilemma.

A delightful literary allusion to the fantasied phallic woman appears in Melville's *Typee*. In this story the narrator describes the remarkable effect produced upon the natives of a South Seas island when a missionary introduced among them his wife, the first white woman ever to visit their shores. Clearly supposing that she was endowed with the prized male genital, "the islanders at first gazed in mute admiration at so unusual a prodigy, and seemed inclined to regard it as some new divinity." But after a short while they began to explore her clothes and "pierce the sacred veil of calico in which [she] was enshrined. . . . Her sex once ascertained, their idolatry was changed into contempt; and there was no end to the contumely showered upon her by the savages, who were exasperated at the deception which they conceived had been practiced upon them." [8] Less artistic but no less desperate efforts to revise nature's objectionable handiwork are reflected by the practice of cosmetic surgery on the female genitals and the use of artificial penises or dildoes.*

The creation of the illusion of the female phallus plays the central role in the practice of fetishism in which the subject, averting his gaze from the intolerable reality of anatomy, fixes it compulsively upon some contiguous object—garter, girdle, stockings, boots, heels, hair and hair ornaments, or furs—and endows it with the significance

* The late Josephine Baker used to appear on the music-hall stage clad in nothing but a skirt composed of a bunch of bananas.

of the missing penis. It is also prominent in the related practice of transvestism, or the wearing of women's clothes by a man. As a female impersonator, the transvestite assures his male audience that they have nothing to fear, for beneath all the skirts and undergarments there is a real penis. So reassured, the audience is free to enjoy the charade, which accounts for the popularity of such public performances as well as for the fascination exerted by persons of uncertain gender.

Such a one was the Chevalier d'Eon, the notorious French transvestite, whose true sex allegedly remained a secret until his death in 1810 at the age of eighty-three, and whose name has been immortalized in the lexicon of perversions as *eonism*. (Figures 10a and b) Some notion of the excitement aroused by this enigmatic personage is conveyed by the report that his sex was a subject of wagering on the London Stock Exchange. (On November 11, 1775, for example, the odds on his being a female were quoted as seven to four.) Under the impression that he was a female, the chevalier received dozens of letters from young girls asking how they might make themselves into men in appearance so that they might follow "her" romantic example and serve with *éclat* in the king's army. Long a resident of London, permission to return to his native France was made contingent upon his acknowledging a female identity. By order of the king, the chevalier was commanded "to abandon the uniform of the dragoon that she is in the habit of wearing, and to resume the garments of her sex." [9] Despite its seeming severity, it is difficult to work up great sympathy for the plight of the Chevalier or Chevalière as far as his inability to persuade the French authorities to recognize his true gender was concerned. Since a post-mortem examination revealed the body of a perfectly formed male, it would appear that for reasons originating within his own psychological makeup, the Chevalier preferred to perpetuate the ambiguity that made him famous.

Despite certain similarities between the practices of fetishism and eonism, the fetishist is characteristically unconscious of the symbolic significance of the fetish, whereas the transvestite is often consciously aware of promoting the illusion of the female phallus. The very nature of the transvestite's performance often resembles a practical joke or a game. Indeed, certain types of play activity among adolescent boys can be seen as an attempt to ward off the castration anxiety induced by the frightening observation of the female genitalia. Both the absence of the penis and the evidence of bleeding have played a crucial role in the enactment of "damage games," the aim of which is to present a show of injury where in actuality none exists.

A common variant of the "game" involves a naked boy—before a mirror or in the presence of companions—pushing his penis and scrotum backward between his compressed thighs to create the illusion of their absence. A number of such devices employed to ward off castration anxiety, as well as other dreaded eventualities, bear a resemblance to many of the classical feats that have been performed throughout the long history of magic. More than a hint of fetishism, for example, can be discerned in Christopher's account of a charming Egyptian legend of magical recovery. A prized turquoise hair ornament had been dropped accidentally out of a boat by a lady of the court. Pronouncing a magic spell, a conjurer placed one half of the lake on top of the other, so that he could walk across the dry bottom, find the missing jewel and return it to the lady. Then he restored the superimposed half of the lake to its original location. Viewed symbolically, the disappearance of her valued adornment from its accustomed place nestled in her hair represents the calamitous loss of her phallus, that prized possession that only a skilled magician can retrieve.[10]

The pretense of sawing a body in two is similarly related to the "cripple game," just as the substitution of a person of one sex for the other represents a magical version of transvestism. By the same token the miraculous transformation of a caged girl into a snarling caged feline evokes the theme of fur fetishism. An even more compelling allusion to fetishism is the classical conjuring device of "misdirection." Just as the fetishist avoids a confrontation with the repellent reality of the female genitalia by fixing his gaze upon some contiguous object, so does the magician accomplish his feat by misdirecting the attention of the audience from the reality of his action toward a distracting maneuver.

Equally striking are the parallels between some of the "damage games" and a number of the celebrated acts in Houdini's repertoire. Games of playing dead, for example, in which the player remains immobile for extended periods of time or tries to see how long he can hold his breath, recall Houdini's stunt of live burial and his prolonged immersion in a galvanized iron box. Likewise there is an undisguised resemblance between Houdini's strait-jacekt and wet-sheet escapes and games of playing crazy—hardly surprising since Houdini conceived these escapes after visiting a mental asylum.

The similarities between certain feats of magic and the so-called damage games suggest that psychologically both serve a common purpose. Like Houdini's strait-jacket routine, they convert a passively endured or anticipated traumatic experience into an adventure under the active control and direction of the "player."

Like damage games, terrifying feats of magic not only enable the performer to cope with his own anxieties but permit the spectator to undergo a similar experience. In the end both the magician and the audience may take satisfaction in the realization that, despite all appearances, nothing really dreadful has occurred.

> "What fun!" said the Gryphon, half to himself, half to Alice.
> "What *is* the fun?" said Alice.
> "Why, *she*," said the Gryphon [meaning the Queen]. "It's all her fancy, that; they never execute nobody, you know."

Despite the Gryphon's reassuring words, it is doubtful that Houdini would have drawn much comfort from them, for throughout his life, both on the stage and off, he was ruled by irrational fears that caused him to engage in a never-ending warfare against the threat of castration. And it may be these fears which led to his unfeigned interest in twins.

Like Poe, he was fascinated by that subject, which he regarded as "one of Nature's special miracles." Indeed, it was this fascination, wrote his friend Melville Cane, that formed a particular bond between himself and Houdini, for Cane was the father of twin girls, and Houdini never tired of sending him a steady supply of news items and pictures on the subject. When he met Cane's three-year-old identical daughters, Houdini confessed he had been toying with the idea of using identical twins to perform a modified version of the "Sawing-a-Woman-in-Half" trick, namely "Sawing-a-Woman-into-Twins."

To what extent he pursued this plan is unclear, but the importance of it lies in its relevance to the easing of his castration anxiety. For even more persuasive than the demonstration that a man cut to pieces can be put together again is the unimpeachable evidence supplied by nature that human beings exist in duplicate. Doubling, wrote Anna Freud, "is of course very closely related to the mechanism of denial, namely *turning the dreaded absence into the duplicated presence*" (italics added). That miracle of duplication, and even multiplication, is standard fare in the repertoire of all magic is well known to anyone who has ever sat enthralled while witnessing the marvelous transformation of a single bird into two, or even more.

Twinning also played a role in the creative imagination of Robert-Houdin, and it is probable that Houdini's idea of sawing a woman into twins was inspired by a passage, mentioned earlier, in the celebrated *Memoirs*. In this passage Torrini describes "The Trick of the Two Pages," a seeming doubling of a single person, which depended upon the extraordinary physical resemblance between the twins Antonio and Antonia. Although such a conception is biologically unsound—fraternal twins bear no greater resemblance to each other than do random siblings—it provided the illusion of a total similarity between brother and sister, a similarity which included to be sure their sexual anatomy. It is apparent that such a notion is intimately associated with the themes of homosexuality and transvestism. Torrini's Antonio, it will be recalled, was "a charming lad . . . with a tenor voice, feminine face, small waist and timid demeanor . . . [who] looked like a boarding school miss in men's clothes."

It may be that Houdini's fascination with the phenomenon of twinning was also aimed at erasing the difference between the sexes. There is evidence that he may have entertained some confusion about gender identity. In changing the name Balsamo to Balsoma, for example, wittingly or not he was affixing a feminine ending to the given name of Count Cagliostro. Similarly, in referring to the latter's wife as Lorenzo instead of Lorenza he was providing her with the name of a man. Although there is no known evidence that Houdini engaged in true transvestism, it is true that he sometimes appeared in seances and in public wearing a wig and other disguises. And for some undisclosed reason, after Houdini's death, Conan Doyle hinted that, in his mind at least, the magician evoked an allusion to that perverse practice, for Doyle likened him to the Chevalier d'Eon.[11]

Be that as it may, just as Houdini employed the art of magic in warding off the peril of castration, so did he turn to the doctrine of Spiritualism, espoused by Sir Arthur, in pursuing his quest for life beyond the grave.

XV

A Magician Among the Spirits

Glendower: I can call spirits from the vasty deep.
Hotspur: Why, so can I, or so can any man;
But will they come, when you do call for them?
—HENRY IV, PART I

Like the psychoanalyst who said he didn't believe in superstition because it had always brought him bad luck, Houdini, despite his vigorous and often belligerent opposition to Spiritualism, was highly susceptible to its appeal. A superstitious man, especially about Friday the thirteenth, he made a number of solemn pacts with friends to communicate after one or the other should have died, and he never ceased watching for "signs" from the dead. His wife related how he once worked himself into a state of wild excitement when he heard an odd telegraphlike tapping at the window, which he insisted was produced by the efforts of his dead secretary to reach him. Less suggestible than her husband (though hardly free of superstition herself), Bess soon discovered that the "spirit telegraphy" was caused by a loose shutter swaying in the wind.

Following the death of his mother, Houdini became increasingly involved with Spiritualism. He sought consultations with countless mediums, ostensibly to receive from her the celebrated "blocked message" she was supposed to have tried to send him just before she died. During the six months of a tour in England and Scotland in 1920 he is said to have attended more than a hundred seances, sometimes as many as two in a single day. It was this inexorable search for the shade of his dead mother that led him to Sir Arthur Conan Doyle and Lady Doyle and to the establishment of a friendship with them that was ultimately destined to come to grief.

Early in 1920, when the friendship began, however, an atmosphere of cordiality prevailed. On April 9 Houdini wrote:

Dear Sir Conan Doyle, I am very anxious to have a seance with any Medium with whom you could gain me an audience. I promise to go there with my mind absolutely clear and willing to believe. I will put no obstruction of any nature whatsoever in the Medium's way, and will assist in all ways in my power to obtain results.

Less than a week later, on April 14, his diary mentioned a visit to the Doyles. "Had lunch with them. They believe implicitly in Spiritualism. Sir Arthur told me he has spoken six times to his son. No (?) chance for trickery. Lady Doyle believes and had tests that are beyond belief." He was unmistakably charmed by Sir Arthur, whose voice and mannerisms, he declared, were "just as nice and sweet as any mortal I have ever been near." Despite sudden disclosures of doubt concerning Sir Arthur's testimony—"All this is ridiculous stuff," he wrote in his diary on April 25—he continued to make the rounds of seances and "trumpet meetings."

He was evidently still torn by ambivalence when, on June 17, 1922, during their visit to America, the Doyles invited him to their hotel room in Atlantic City to attend a seance of automatic writing in which Lady Doyle would try to receive a letter dictated by Houdini's mother.

When the three were alone—Bess, for some reason, was excluded—Lady Doyle was suddenly seized by a spirit. "Her hands shook and beat the table, her voice trembled, and she called the Spirits to give her a message. Sir Arthur tried to quiet her, asked her to restrain herself, but her hand thumped on the table, her whole body shook, and at last, making a cross at the head of the page, started writing . . . " what was purportedly a letter dictated by the late Mrs. Weiss:

Oh, my darling, thank God, thank God, at last I'm through. I've tried, oh so often—now I am happy. Why, of course I want to talk to my boy—my own beloved boy—friends, thank you with all my heart for this. You have answered the cry of my heart—and of his—God bless him a thousand-fold for all his life for me—never had a mother such a son—tell him not to grieve—soon he'll get all the evidence he's so anxious for—yes, we know—tell him I want him to try to write in his own home. It will be far better so.[1]

And so it went. What happened next became a matter of some controversy.

According to one account, Houdini objected vigorously to the entire proceedings on several grounds: first because Lady Doyle had placed a Christian cross at the top of the page on which she was presumably taking down a spirit message dictated by his Jewish mother. Sir Arthur, discounting any religious significance, explained that the cross was simply a measure to guard against "lower influences," adding, "We find it protective." [2] Next, Houdini pointed out that, despite his mother's proficiency in five other languages, she was unable to speak English, which was the language employed in the writing seance. Doyle met this objection easily by stating that, when a medium is not in trance, "it is the flood of thought and of emotion which strikes her and has to be translated by her in her own vocabulary as best she can." In short, Lady Doyle had practiced a sort of simultaneous translation.[3] On another occasion Houdini asserted that privately Sir Arthur had explained to him that a spirit becomes more educated the longer it is departed and that his blessed mother had been able to learn the English tongue in heaven.[4]

Yet another objection raised by Houdini arose from the curious coincidence that the seance had been held on the anniversary of his mother's birthday. "If it had been my Dear Mother's spirit communicating with a message," he declared, "she, knowing her birthday was my most holy holiday, surely would have commented on it." [5] * Nonsense, replied Doyle, "What are birthdays *on the other side?* It is the death day which is the real birthday." [6]

It should be pointed out, however, that Houdini's skeptical reactions to the Atlantic City seance did not arise at once. Not until December 15, six months afterward, did he complain to Sir Arthur about the matter of the language. He had refrained from mentioning this at the time of the seance, he explained, "because of my emotion in trying to sense the presence of my Mother, if there was such a thing possible, to keep me quiet until time passed, and I could give it the proper deduction." [7] What Houdini meant by the phrase "the proper deduction" was apparently an effort to escape from his tormenting conflict. There can be no question that he approached the seance in a state of excited anticipation. "I was *willing* to believe, even *wanted* to believe," he wrote. "It was weird to me and with a beating heart I waited, hoping that I might once more feel the presence of my beloved Mother. . . . I was determined to embrace Spiritualism if there was

* Something is wrong here, for on a number of occasions Houdini gave the date of his mother's birthday as the sixteenth, not the seventeenth, of June. Maybe her Spirit knew what it was about.

any evidence strong enough to down the doubts that have crowded my brain for the past thirty years." [8]

For a time his desire to believe won out. Directly after the seance, Doyle declared, Houdini was in a state of elation, asserting two days later that he had been "walking on air ever since." [9] Others confirmed Doyle's impression. "There is no doubt," wrote a friend, "that Houdini wavered from time to time in the firmness of his convictions. . . . The Doyle message is a case in point, for he seems to have been deeply and emotionally influenced at the time, and only afterward did he come out with the statement that 'There was nothing to it.' " [10] Indeed, so urgent was his ultimate need to disavow his recent credulity that six months after the Atlantic City seance he filed an official and legal disclaimer, signed and witnessed before a notary, setting forth "The Truth Regarding a Spiritualistic Seance Given to Houdini by Lady Doyle." [11]

Evidently his position on the issue of Spiritualism was insufficiently affirmed by his notarized statement, for during the ensuing months he launched a campaign against it of such intensity that it assumed the character of a divine mission. Appareled in the shining armor of reason, Houdini rode forth under the banner of truth to do battle with the evil forces of Spiritualism. Now reminiscent of his earlier repudiation of others he had once cherished, he leveled his lance and charged at Sir Arthur, reviling him as "a menace to mankind"—a shocking epithet for the knight whose noble head was crowned, said Robert Louis Stevenson, with a white plume.

A menace to mankind! Even the usually tolerant Doyle was unable to ignore such slander. "I am very sorry this breach has come," he wrote to Houdini in May 1923, "as we have felt very friendly toward Mrs. Houdini and yourself, but 'friendly is as friendly does,' and this is not friendly, but on the contrary, it is outrageous to make such statements with no atom of truth in them. . . . How long a private friendship can survive such an ordeal I do not know, but at least I did not create the situation." [12]

Whatever else may have prompted Houdini to condemn his old friend as a menace and to denounce the doctrine of Spiritualism, the principal issue, he insisted, was the prevention of insanity. In support of his contention that Spiritualism caused madness he marshaled what he considered to be expert opinions. He asserted that "a famous mental specialist," whom he neglected to identify, had estimated that "thousands of persons" had been driven to the asylum through Spiritualism, to which Houdini added, "A truly pitiful record." [13] Elsewhere he cited another authority, an English doctor, also unnamed, who put the number of such cases at a million. "The list is not limited to European countries," he went on, "we have a goodly share of baneful results right at home." It is a well-established fact, he added gratuitously, "that the human reason gives way under the exciting strain of Spiritualism." [14]

As an example he cited the case of a young college girl who, having been an ardent student of Spiritualism, fell in love with a spirit and finally "was driven to suicide in order to join him." [15] He also mentioned a man who shot his sons because his dead wife sent him a message saying she wanted the children with her. In his book *A Magician Among the Spirits,* Houdini aimed his warning message to all Americans, citing the case of Charles J. Guiteau, the assassin of President Garfield and "a pronounced Spiritualist," who had been driven to commit his quasi-parricidal deed by the dictates of the "Spirits."

No less fierce than his denunciation of Spiritualism was Houdini's attack on the *Ouija* board, the magical parlor game named for the French and German words for "yes" that became the rage during the 1920s. He cited a Doctor Williams of the Cleveland State Hospital who said that the Ouija board craze was a direct cause of sending folks to the madhouse, an opinion that was shared by a Doctor Bennett of the Eloise State Hospital and Insane Asylum. In the course of giving a show at the Lakeview Insane Asylum, Houdini learned of seven people who had been admitted in one month because of the Ouija board. Although the director remarked that some claimed that these people would have become crazy anyway, it was not necessarily true, and they might have remained sane all the rest of their lives had not the stress of the Ouija board been put on their minds. Another authority cited by Houdini was a Doctor Curry, "Medical Director of the State Insane Asylum of New Jersey," [sic] who had issued a warning about the noxious influence of the Ouija board, which was especially serious, he pointed out, "because it is mainly adopted by persons of high-strung neurotic tendency, who become victims of actual illusions of sight, hearing, and touch at Spiritualist seances." [16]

In the single month of March, 1920, Houdini pointed out, according to the newspapers no less than five persons living in the little town of Carrito (probably El Cerrito), near San Francisco Bay, had been driven mad by the diabolical board. One shudders to think of Houdini's reaction had he lived to learn the tragic story of fifteen-year-old Mattie Turley who, acting on the instruction of her Ouija board, killed her elderly father with a shotgun so that her mother, a former beauty queen, could marry a handsome young cowboy. "Mother asked the Ouija board to decide between father and her cowboy friends," Mattie reported. "Suddenly it spelled out that I was to kill father. It was terrible. I shook all over. . . . We asked about the law, and it said not to fear the law, that everything would turn out all right. We asked how much the insurance would be, and it said five thousand dollars. I tried to kill father the next day, but I couldn't. I lost my nerve. A few days later, though, I followed him to the corral. I raised the gun and took careful aim . . . and fired." [17]

That Houdini's connection of Spiritualism and kindred matters to insanity suffered from serious methodological flaws goes without saying. Bereft of the most elementary understanding of psychiatry [18] and basing his conclusions on undocumented hunches, he arrived at a formulation that is quite the reverse of the truth. For far from being a cause of madness, when it is not a manifestation of it, Spiritualism is often the refuge of those caught in the grip of unendurable anguish. "The history of Spiritualism," wrote Houdini's friend Dunninger, "is as old as human hope." The dedication to Spiritualism of two of its most devout adherents, Sir Oliver Lodge and Sir Arthur Conan Doyle, owed much of its force to the deaths of their sons. Like them and the late Bishop James Pike, those who have turned to the beliefs and practices of Spiritualism are essentially no different from the untold millions of troubled souls who, since the beginning of time, have turned to religion, to mysticism, superstition, and other irrational beliefs in their hour of despair.

Clearly such beliefs are not restricted to the uneducated masses. A Gallup survey undertaken during the economically and politically troubled period of November 1973 disclosed that fifty-one percent of persons interviewed believed that Unidentified Flying Objects, or Flying Saucers, are real and not just a figment of the imagination. College-educated persons are as likely to say that they had seen them as those with less formal education. The thirteenth floor of the New York Hospital is labeled 12A.

Even Freud succumbed periodically to the seductive appeal of telepathy, and like Houdini vacillated between skepticism and credulity. Hoping that he had not given the impression that he was "secretly inclined to support the reality of telepathy in the occult sense," in a paper entitled "Dreams and Telepathy" (1922) he went on to state that he was "anxious to be strictly impartial. I have every reason to be so," he continued, "for I have no opinion. I know nothing about it." Yet he made no secret of his fascination with the subject and once wrote that if he had his life to live over again he would devote himself to psychical research rather than to psychoanalysis.[19]

However sincere Houdini may have been in insisting that his opposition to Spiritualism arose from a desire "to stop people from going to the madhouse," his recurring tendency to project upon external forces and agencies his inner fears and impulses, together with the intense zeal with which he pursued his uninformed attacks against the supposed enemy without, lead to the suspicion that foremost among those whom he sought to protect from that ominous fate was himself.

No less insistent than his haunting obsession with death and graveyards and his morbid fascination with crime and prisons was the spell cast upon him by madness and mental institutions. He seemed never to tire of visiting "insane asylums"; his diary records three such visits in a single week in March 1925 when, as in his tour of prisons, he performed for the inmates. He was clearly moved by what he saw, for he wrote, "There ought to be a law to put them out of their misery. I would not do it myself, but some of the cases are terrible." And then, hinting at a potential kinship with them, he added, "We humans who are normal ought to thank God for so being, and not at times bemoan our fate." Perhaps here he was whistling in the dark, for to judge from Bess's report there were times when she had misgivings about Houdini's mental balance.

She told her husband's biographer Kellock of an experience with Houdini and his brother Theodore, not long after her marriage, that gave her a "bad scare." One night in Coney Island, after the show, Houdini asked her and his brother to take a walk with him. He led them into the country where he bade them stop on a "dark lonely bridge spanning some swiftly running black water. . . . In the middle of the bridge he halted us . . . and clasped his brother's hand and mine together, raised them aloft and cried: 'Beatrice, Dash [Theodore], raise your hands to heaven and swear you will both be true to me. Never betray me in any way, so help you God.'

"His brother and I repeated the vow after him. Then Houdini kissed me and shook Theodore's hand. 'I know you will keep that sacred oath,' he said.

"By this time I was in a state of panicky terror. The eerie sky, the lonely bridge in a waste of marshland, the black water—and then this dramatic and terrible vow—these things seemed wholly abnormal and strange. It was apparent that this Houdini whom I had known less than two weeks was an inexplicable person, probably a madman, and his brother was no better. . . . As soon as I got to a firm road, to a lighted street, I would make a break for it and find my way home to my mother.

"But there were no more dramatics that night. Houdini sensed my fears and immediately began to lead me away and reassure me. By the time we reached the lighted streets his gentleness and tenderness had restored my tranquility." [20]

Despite Bess Houdini's reputation for having seasoned Kellock's biography with the spice of her own fancy, there is a sufficient supply of familiar themes in this somber gothic vignette to lend to it at least some credibility: the sudden fit of distrust, the swift and dramatic readiness to discern a foe where just now a friend had been, the imperious command, the theatrical oaths, and the appeal for divine protection—all unfurled in an unnatural setting exuding paranoia and nightmarish unreality.

Just as he enacted his obsession with death by encasing himself in boxes and caskets, and just as he advertised his affinity with crime by getting himself locked into cells and shackles, so did he acknowledge his kinship with madmen by surrendering his body to strait-jackets and wet packs, which were promptly incorporated into his professional routine. Under the guise of entertainment he enacted a medley of games in pantomime in which he toyed with frightful peril, while assuming a posture of limitless and foolhardy audacity. Yet the very magnitude of that audacity, as well as the supremely staged theatricality in which it was displayed, implies that these feats were quasi-magical gestures designed to ward off a deep and abiding terror. That he feared madness as much as he dreaded death is supported not merely by these "crazy games," but by the recurring allusions to insanity that permeated his utterances and his writings.* From what has already been noted about his psychological makeup, it seems that his fears were not altogether groundless.

The unspoken logic involved here was impeccable: Charles J. Guiteau was a Spiritualist. The Spirits commanded him to kill President Garfield, i.e., to commit symbolic parricide. Houdini had impersonated Guiteau by getting himself locked into the assassin's death cell. Hence, if Houdini should yield to Spiritualism, his identification with Guiteau might become complete, and in obedience to the Spirits he might go crazy and kill his father or a father surrogate. The only

---

* "Treat me as you would the most dangerous of the criminal insane," Houdini advised the attendants who were strapping him into a strait-jacket for an escape act in Pittsburgh in November 1916.[21]

way to combat this dreaded eventuality was to attack the external forces that drove men to commit such madness.

As in his conflict with Robert-Houdin, Houdini's fight with Conan Doyle over Spiritualism would appear to have been in the last analysis a battle within himself, a struggle to expel an unwanted and feared facet of his own psychological makeup. In *The Unmasking of Robert-Houdin* he had aimed to cleanse himself of moral stain, ascribing to his deposed idol those unbecoming traits he sought to disown within himself; in *A Magician Among the Spirits,* his diatribe against Spiritualism, he hoped to rid himself of his own irrationality. Like the animosity he ultimately came to direct at his French mentor, the hostility he finally aimed at his British friend arose from a matrix of affection and admiration. Indeed, in turning against Sir Arthur he behaved like a skittish virgin, mistrustful of his own ability to resist temptation and constrained, therefore, to view his erstwhile friend as if he were a devilish seducer plotting to coax him down the primrose path of lunacy.

XVI

The Edge of the Unknown

"I see nobody on the road," said Alice.

"I only wish I had such eyes," the King remarked in a fretful tone. "To be able to see Nobody! And at that distance too! Why, it's as much as I can do to see real people, by this light!"

—THROUGH THE LOOKING GLASS

The preceding chapter should serve as a caution to those who like to assign people to neat little categories, and to slip their personalities and beliefs into nice little compartments, for, although it is undeniably tempting to nominate Doyle as the Apostle of Spiritualism and Houdini as his Uncompromising Foe, this is clearly a gross oversimplification. It would be more correct to say that Doyle, the Believer, set up an *alter ego* in Sherlock Holmes to register opposition to his own irrationality, and that Houdini, the alleged Arch Enemy of that same dogma, sought to enlist its services in furthering his frantic efforts to communicate with his dead mother.

Although from an early period in his life Doyle was successively attracted to telepathy, theosophy, hypnotism, and later occultism, Buddhism, and finally, Spiritualism, there was another Doyle who, according to one biographer, "went out of his way to make Holmes deny all belief in the supernatural, because Holmes—whom he had set up as a calculating machine—must click with absolute consistency, like a machine from beginning to end." [1]

"I take it in the first place," Holmes tells Doctor Watson in "The Adventure of the Devil's Foot," "that neither of us is prepared to admit diabolical instrusions into the affairs of men. Let us begin by ruling that entirely out of our minds." And in "The Adventure of the Mazarin Stone," Holmes remarks, "I am a brain, Watson. The rest of me is mere appendix."

Nor did Doctor Doyle confine his scientific rationality to the fictional Holmes. When Lady Doyle first developed her interest in automatic writing, Doyle himself displayed signs of skepticism. Noting how "some power seemed to take possession of [her] arm and write things which purported to come from the dead," he had wondered, "How can you tell that she is not unconsciously dramatizing strands of her own personality?" It was a question he might have posed with equal cogency six years later when she was frantically taking down the message that supposedly was being dictated by the spirit of Houdini's mother; but by that time such vestiges of his scientific training had disappeared from his personal life, and he had become a dedicated advocate not only of his wife's spirit writing but of her ability to ward off "diabolical intrusions" and "lower influences" with the sign of the crucifix. Thus is Mephistopheles undone in *Faust*.

Like Doyle, Houdini used the medium of art to reveal his supposedly rejected beliefs. Echoing Doyle's ringing message, THEY ARE NOT DEAD! is the theme of reincarnation that resounds in several of Houdini's movie scenarios. One, bearing the strange title *Il Mistero di Osiris, A Mystery Tale of Old Egypt,* attributed to one Giovanni Deadota (whose name is enclosed within quotation marks), is a story of metempsychosis, or the transmigration of souls. "Thus it represents the harmony of the universe," reads the introduction, "and for it nothing in the world becomes lost. Out of this faith was born the legend of Carma. . . ." [2]

This is hardly the kind of stuff one might expect to be promoted by a zealous scoffer of the doctrine of life after death. The same might be said of Houdini's movie *The Man From Beyond,* in which the central leitmotif is the miracle of resurrection. A further indication that this dedicated opponent of Spiritualism was not altogether disposed to shut the door against that belief with uncompromising finality was a press release issued at the time of the showing of that film: at the present time, it stated, Houdini was "writing the effort of his life, a Spiritualist book which he will call *The Safe and Sane Side of Spiritualism.*" [3] As might be expected, Doyle wrote most enthusiastically about Houdini's resurrection film, pronouncing it "the very best sensational picture I have ever seen . . . one of the really great contributions to the screen." [4]

It appears, then, that at least from Houdini's standpoint, what created his rift with Sir Arthur was basically not a matter of ideology, for at certain levels of thought they seemed to be in complete accord. On the contrary, the fundamental difficulty lay in Houdini's inability to tolerate any close relationship that carried the seeds of rivalry. In the thick of his crusade against Spiritualism he seemed to lose sight of the real issues in the smog of his competitiveness. Exulting over the popular success he was meeting in posing as the savior of mankind from the evils of Doyle's dogma, he was unable to divorce his own noble image from earthy considerations of box-office appeal. "Wait till Sir A.C. Doyle hears of my lectures! Whew!!!" he crowed in his diary on April 16, 1923. And three weeks later he wrote: "Bess goes to Doyle lecture; says my lecture is more interesting and convincing. But I told her Doyle is an historical character, and his word goes far—in fact further than mine," to which, in another hand, hers presumably, was added, "I don't think. B.H."

Far from a metaphysical controversy, the atmosphere surrounding his conflict with Doyle more closely resembles Houdini's noisy verbal bout with the heavyweight champion Jess Willard. Indeed, Houdini's debunking of Spiritualism turned into another theatrical performance which, like his spectacular escapes, became a sure-fire number in his professional repertoire. That Doyle himself recognized that his opponent was somewhat wanting in pure idealism, and perhaps personal integrity as well, was conveyed by a comment made after Houdini's death: "One could not wish a better companion," he wrote, "so long as one was with him, though he might do and say the most unexpected things when one was absent." [5]

No less remarkable than the dissolution of this friendship is the enigma of how it came into being in the first place, for it is not easy to imagine what bonds might have linked two such dissimilar persons as the Edinburgh-born Sir Arthur Conan Doyle, the most highly paid short story writer of his time, and Harry Houdini, the son of an obscure Hungarian rabbi, who became the King of Handcuffs. Seen through Houdini's eyes, the friendship with a British knight, some fifteen years his senior, must have been most flattering. And by enabling him to bask in the warm paternal glow of Sir Arthur's fame and station, it must have brought rich nourishment to his unappeasable hunger for the fulfillment of his fantasies of the Family Romance. Assigned to such a role, it was inevitable that like Robert-Houdin, his father-surrogate predecessor, Doyle, would ultimately fall victim to figurative parricide.

As for Doyle, like millions of others he was fascinated by Houdini, whose feats, he insisted, despite the latter's emphatic denials, were done with the aid of spirits and by means of Houdini's "great mediumistic powers." He refused to listen to Houdini's protests, when he asked, "What can cover all [the] facts, save that there was some element in [Houdini's] power which was peculiar to himself and that could only point to a psychic element—in a word, that he was a medium?" [6] Houdini's remarkable ability to free himself from shackles, he went on, was due to the phenomenon of "the passage of matter through matter—of the wrists through metal handcuffs," which he found no more amazing, he added, than the invention of the wireless or flying.[7]

Citing the remarks of the rabbi at Houdini's funeral that the magician "possessed a wondrous power that he never understood, and which he never revealed to anyone in life," Doyle argued that "such an expression coming at so solemn a moment from one who may have been in a special position to know, must show that my speculations are not extravagant or fantastic when I deal with the real source of those powers." [8] If, Doyle continued, Houdini had maintained that his magic was accomplished strictly by material means . . . "no matter how baffling it is to the layman," [9] it was simply because an admission that "half his tricks were done by what his brother magicians would regard as illicit (that is, Spiritualistic) powers" would have ruined him professionally.[10] When Doyle was told that Houdini was practically out of the submerged packing cast before it reached the water, he replied, "Considering that the screwed and corded box was in full sight of hundreds of spectators as it sank beneath the waves, it is difficult to accept such a solution as this. I admit that I am at a disadvantage when opposed to the technical and expert knowledge of such men as Goldston and Thurston, but on the other hand I have my own technical and expert knowledge of psychic possibilities. . . . Are we children that we should be expected to believe that such things can be done by a mere knack?" [11] (Evidently Doyle had forgotten a remark of Sherlock Holmes: "If I told you how I did it, Watson, I would no longer seem so remarkable.")

Doyle's argument was enlarged by J. Hewat McKenzie, in a book bearing the arresting title *Spirit Intercourse: Its Theory and Practice*:

Without disturbing any of the locks, Houdini was transferred from the tank direct to the back of the stage in a dematerialized state. He was there materialized and returned to the stage front dripping with water. . . . Not only was Houdini's body dematerialized but it was carried through the locked iron tank, thus demonstrating the passage of matter through matter. This startling manifestation of one of nature's profoundest miracles was probably regarded by most of the audience as a *very clever trick* [italics added].[12]

There were times, it seems, when Houdini himself appeared tempted to join Doyle and the other Spiritualists in acknowledging that he possessed supernatural gifts. Doyle claimed that Houdini had admitted that he responded to "a voice which was independent of his own reason or judgment [and] told him what to do and how to do it. So long as he obeyed the voice," Houdini supposedly confessed to him, "he was assured of safety." [13]

Doyle also described a scene, involving a friend of his named Captain Bartlett and Houdini, which offered further evidence of the latter's acknowledgement of his special powers. When Houdini was asked by Captain Bartlett about his box trick, "instantly his expression changed. The sparkle left his eyes, and his face looked drawn and haggard. 'I can't tell you,' Houdini said, in a low tense voice. 'I don't know myself, and what is more I always have a dread I should fail.' " Evidently the entire household shared the Captain's perceptions of the witchery emanating from the person of Houdini, for when the latter "stooped to stroke our cats . . . to our amazement they fled from the room with their tails in the air, and for some minutes they dashed wildly up and down stairs." [14]

Just what significance Houdini himself attached to this spooky display of feline enchantment was not recorded, but it would be a mistake to assume that he ignored it, for despite his apparent commitment to scientific rationality and his insistence that Spiritualism, like hypnosis, was pure fakery, his actual behavior suggested that he nourished a lingering suspicion that perhaps telepathy and communication with the dead were possible after all. At any rate he wasn't taking any chances, for in a bank vault he left copies of messages addressed to his wife, to Doyle, and others, which he would endeavor to send after his death. But, although for many years on the anniversary of that event his wife would sit by an "eternal light" waiting for a message to come through, none ever reached her or anyone else. In the opinion of Bernard Ernst, his close friend and biographer, Houdini remained "a sort of half-believer" in communication with the dead to the end of his days. Among the thousands of books he bequeathed to the Library of Congress there are no less than seven copies of a book entitled *Future Life in The Light Of Ancient Wisdom and Modern Science,* by Louis Elbe, as well as innumerable books on Spiritualism, fortune-telling, ghosts, theosophy, and kindred subjects.

Both Houdini and Doyle were preoccupied with cemeteries. Like Houdini, Doyle had a penchant for visiting the graves of famous men, and during his stay in America he went to see where Lowell, Longfellow, and other great persons were buried.

There were similarities, too, in their attitudes toward women. Both were inordinately attached to their mothers and apparently equally dependent upon them for their approval and opinions. While Houdini always spelled "mother" with a capital M, Doyle invariably referred to his mother as "The Ma'am."

A major issue that drew the two men together was the suffering each had experienced over the years from deaths. When, referring to the seance of 1922, Houdini spoke of the doubts about communicating with the dead "that had crowded [his] brain for the past thirty years," he was clearly alluding to something that long antedated the death of his mother in 1913—presumably the loss of his father in 1892. By the same token, although Doyle's interest in Spiritualism extended back many years, it was markedly increased following the death of his first wife, Louise, in 1906. This long-expected event—she had been stricken by tuberculosis in 1892, less than a year after the birth of his son Kingsley—ushered in a number of symptoms suggestive of depression: lassitude, insomnia, and what was called "nerves." Inasmuch as Louise's death now left him free to marry Jean Leckie, with whom he had been in love for some nine years, it is a reasonable assumption that both his psychological symptoms and his deeper involvement with Spiritualism were as much expressions of guilt as grief.

The most powerful impetus to Doyle's commitment to Spiritualism, however, followed the death of the twenty-seven-year-old Kingsley at the conclusion of World War I. The War, wrote one of Doyle's biographers, "produced a new Doyle, who was determined to spread the evangel, writing books and lecturing all over the country." Even when he learned that his son was dying, he refused to cancel a speaking engagement, declaring, "Kingsley would wish it so." [15]

Like Houdini's yearning to speak to his "Sainted Mother," after the death of Doyle's mother in 1921, he sought to communicate with "The Ma'am." In his memoir he described a seance during which "in the darkness the face of [his] mother shone up peaceful, happy, slightly inclined to one side, the eyes closed." A woman sitting next to him, who had not known his mother in life, remarked on seeing her during the seance, "how wonderfully like she is to her son," which caused Doyle to comment that this would show "how clear was the detail of the features." [16] His one aim in life, he asserted, "is that this great truth, the return and communion with the dead, shall be brought home to a material world which needs it so badly." [17]

Although both men longed passionately to break down the barrier of death, the manner in which they went about it was quite different. Richly endowed with literary genius and creative imagination, Doyle was able to discharge much of the conflict between his heart and his head through the medium of fiction.[18] The same pen that etched the sharply chiseled adventures of Sherlock Holmes was equally capable of weaving fancies about imps and tiny green men with their merry little faces as if he were reporting unimpeachable truth. In a chapter entitled "Dwellers on the Border" in his book *The Edge of the Unknown,* Doyle, the scientist and creator of Holmes, the thinking machine, proceeded seriously to discuss the nature of the so-called Fairy Rings that can be seen in meadows and marshland. It is quite true, he admitted, that they come "not from the beat of fairy feet," but from fungi. So far so good. Yet once formed, continued Doyle the spiritualist, these Fairy Rings would "offer a very charming course for a circular ring-a-ring dance for the little people." [19]

Such a faculty for splitting his mental processes was less easy for Houdini, who maintained his mental equilibrium by clinging to the safety of simple certainties and pious platitudes, while ascribing to his adversaries those beliefs and those traits that he spurned, or had at least relinquished. Indeed, in Houdini's inflexible personality there is a hint of Doctor Watson himself, a man, said Doyle, who never had shown a gleam of humor nor made a single joke.

Temperamentally Houdini was no more suited to the contradictions in Doyle's personality than was Doyle to Houdini's mawkish pabulums, such as "God couldn't be everywhere, so he made mothers." Cheered on by such slogans, Houdini marched forward like a reformed sinner, and much as he yearned to believe in the possibility of communicating with the dead, and especially with his mother, he came to look upon the whole idea as a snare, viewing his ultimate rejection of Lady Doyle's spirit-writing seance as a narrow escape from a diabolical plot.

While in Doyle's eyes Houdini's hostility to Spiritualism "bordered upon a mania," [20] his own dedication to the cause on which he spent over a quarter of a million pounds suggests that, in measuring the comparative irrationality of the two combatants, there was little to choose from. In light of Doyle's intellectual endowments, moreover, and particularly his medical background, one might have expected a greater degree of sophistication in his approach to the subject of mental illness than is conveyed, for example, in a statement in his journal for 1912 that "one should put one's shoulder to the door to keep out insanity all one can," or another declaring that Nietzsche's philosophy is "openly founded on lunacy, for the poor fellow died raving." [21]

There were instances in which this man, who complained that Houdini was "not a clear thinker" and "had no logical process in his mind," [22] was himself skating rather precariously on the thin ice of rational thought. In *The Edge of the Unknown* he wrote about the "well-known case of a famous French actress" who had been hounded for a period of two years *after his death* by a suitor whom she had rejected. In Doyle's opinion the "unmanly persecution to which he subjected her . . . proved the wisdom of her rejection of him." [23] And it is a fine commentary on Doyle's capacity for self-deception to discover that a few years before making these judgments he had written: "I do not wish to blow my own trumpet, but after all, I am a doctor of medicine, a trained man of science, an authority upon deductive reasoning and a man of the world who has proved his judgment to be correct upon public questions many times." *

Each impelled to defend his own mental stability by mutually conflicting measures, it was inevitable that in time the frail bonds that linked Houdini and Doyle in so unlikely and tenuous a friendship would ultimately break. And it was fitting that the final rupture of their relationship took place during that celebrated crisis in the history of American Spiritualism—the investigation of the famous Boston medium Mina Crandon, the Queen of Psychical Research and darling of Sir Arthur Conan Doyle, who was known to the public as Margery.

Margery was the wife of Doctor Le Roi Crandon, a distinguished professor of surgery at the Harvard Medical School, who was himself a strong proponent of her mediumistic powers. In 1924 she had attained such confidence in her gifts that she had decided to contend for the prizes offered by the *Scientific American* magazine for authentic spiritualist demonstrations. The validity of her claims was to be judged by a committee composed of eminent members of the scientific community, as well as the famed escape king and declared foe of Spiritualism, Harry Houdini.

Conceivably some members of this distinguished gathering may have been distracted by certain aspects of Margery's conduct, for The Witch of Beacon Hill, as some called her, was an attractive and flirtatious medium, who laced her spirit stuff with a generous dash of sex.

---

* Apparently some deterioration in Doyle's scientific thinking had occurred in his later life, especially in psychological matters. Recent investigations indicate that in 1891 Sherlock Holmes was in Vienna, where he was treated for cocaine addiction by Sigmund Freud.[24]

She attended Spiritualist seances wearing nothing beneath her kimono but silk stockings and slippers, and it was rumored that on occasion she sprinkled her bosom with phosphorescent powder, so that when she exposed herself in the dark by throwing open her robe, the assembled company might be treated to some luminous titillation.

But Margery possessed other attributes that were even more interesting. Emerging through a slit in her dressing gown—as she snored peacefully during the seance—a limp and flaccid mass appeared which seemed to originate in her genitals and was claimed to be the materialization of a psychic substance called ectoplasm. (Figure 11) On other occasions the thing assumed the shape of a long tonguelike structure. In the opinion of her brother Walter, the protrusion of these pseudopods from between his sister's thighs proved that they were a form of supernatural birth. Walter's opinions are of more than passing interest, for although he attended all the 1924 seances and was an active participant in them, some thirteen years earlier, in 1911, he had been killed in a railway accident!

Lest there be any doubts concerning the authenticity of these manifestations, the reader has but to consult the reports on the Margery Mediumship, recorded in Volumes 20 and 21 of the *Proceedings of the American Society for Psychical Research* for the years 1926–1927. Plates five and six are reproductions of photographs of the "crude teleplasmic mass" that issued from Margery's accomplished genitals.

When one observer suggested that the medium should wear tights to make certain that the ectoplasm "was not some material substance that was smuggled out of her body by legerdemain," [25] both Margery and her husband objected vigorously, for reasons which will in time appear. Moreover, Margery seemed to relish holding sittings in the nude—for which she can hardly be blamed—for it is not every day that a girl from Boston has a chance to display her ectoplasmic phallus and to have it photographed, too. The paths that led to this height of good fortune and the role that Houdini was to play in it will be traced in the pages to follow.

XVII

The Witch of Beacon Hill

"There's no use trying" [said Alice]. *"One* can't *believe impossible things."*

"I daresay you haven't had much practice," said the Queen. *"When I was your age I always did it for half-an-hour a day. Why sometimes I've believed as many as six impossible things before breakfast."*

—THROUGH THE LOOKING GLASS

Doctor Crandon's fascination with Spiritualism, which ultimately gained vicarious expression through his wife's mediumship, was aroused not only by the American lecture tours of Sir Arthur Conan Doyle but by a book he happened on early in 1923, *The Psychic Structures at the Goligher Circle.* This is an account of some seances conducted by the author, an Irish engineer named William Jackson Crawford, with members of a Belfast family named Goligher. Emanating from the bodies of several persons in the group who were said to be mediums, a strange substance was discovered by Crawford which he described as "viscous, damp, and clammy," and which gave off a sickly or unpleasant smell. Extruded in small portions from various body orifices, this substance, which came to be called *ectoplasm,* often assumed the shapes of hands and faces. Photographs taken of the medium while in a state of trance showed a white flowing material oozing from the lower part of the body and endowed with a remarkable power. Indeed, the ability of the ectoplasm to cause the tilting of the seance table prompted Crawford, drawing no doubt on his background in engineering, to label the stuff a "psychic cantilever."

Unfortunately, it was discovered that photographic studies, like those later performed on Margery, were hampered by the fact that when white light happens to strike the ectoplasm, the material quickly withdraws into the body of the medium, often inflicting harmful effects upon the physical health of the "psychic." This limitation, necessitating that most of the work be performed in the dark or at least under a dull red light, was not the only obstacle, however, to a complete acceptance of Crawford's researches. Some critics proposed that less supernatural explanations might be responsible for the phenomena he had been attributing to ectoplasm. Might not the table-tilting and the other remarkable occurrences that he had been ascribing to the "psychic cantilever" be produced, say, by the sly meanderings of someone's naughty foot?

Crawford dismissed such suggestions outright, countering them with the argument that he knew all the participants, that he liked them and trusted them, and that they had no possible reason to cheat. The Goligher Circle, he insisted, was a private matter, a sort of religious ceremony, a family affair. Under the circumstances, why should they cooperate to produce a fraudulent result? The phenomena were genuine; this, Crawford believed, could not be doubted. (When Mark Twain was shown the tomb of Adam in the Holy Land, he wrote: "There is no question that he is actually buried in the grave which is pointed out as his—there can be none—because it has never yet been proven that that grave is not the grave in which he is buried.") The noted French spiritualist E. E. Fournier d'Albe, however, came to the conclusion that the Goligher phenomena had been produced by fraudulent methods. Whether Crawford ultimately began to share some of the misgivings of his critics is not known, but in time he suffered what was called a nervous breakdown, and one day in 1920, presumably in a fit of melancholy, he killed himself by taking poison. Four days earlier he had written: "I have been struck down mentally. It is not the psychic work. I enjoyed it too well." [1]

No hint of any skepticism concerning the findings in the Goligher Circle was breathed by Doyle, however, who not only acclaimed Crawford's work in Belfast as "splendid" but went on to assert that the results of these studies were, in his opinion, "among the most notable of any investigation which had ever been recorded." Indeed, Doctor Doyle quite outdid Engineer Crawford in recognizing the extraordinary importance of ectoplasm, which he hailed as a "new form of matter, with unheard of properties, lying latent in all probability within each of us." [2] Although the views of the early investigators often had been ridiculed by scientific men, he noted, later studies have "shown that in this as in other matters the early spiritualists were the pioneers of truth, and that they had come upon the most singular manifestation of matter with which we have any acquaintance —a form which might almost be called a *half-way house to Spirit* [italics added]." [3]

Doyle was no less impressed by the photographs of the ectoplasm taken under red lamps—"red being, as in photography, the one bearable color." It was testified by witnesses, he wrote, "that there oozed from the medium's mucous membranes, and occasionally from her skin, this extraordinary gelatinous material. The pictures are strange and repulsive," he admitted, "but many of nature's processes seem so in our eyes. You can see this streaky viscous stuff hanging like icicles from the chin, dripping down to the body, and forming a white apron." Like Crawford, Doyle was familiar with the sensitivity of ectoplasm to white light, for when "undue light came upon it, it writhed back into the body as swiftly and stealthily as the tentacles of a hidden octopus. If seized and pinched, the medium cried aloud. It would protrude through clothes and vanish again, leaving hardly any trace upon them." [4]

The phallic and seminal allusions implicit in the foregoing remarks were even more emphasized in Sir Arthur's enthusiastic account of one of Crawford's Belfast experiments (in this report, as in all other cases referred to, the medium is a female):

> Her ectoplasm "was used for the making of rods or columns of power, which protruded from the body of the unconscious girl, and produced results such as raps, or the movement of objects at a distance from her." Then calling on his rich imagination, Doyle engaged in speculations concerning the vast possibilities inherent in such an extraordinary endowment. "Such a rod of power," he reasoned, "might be applied, with a sucker attachment, under a table and lift it up, causing the weight of the table to be added to that of the medium, exactly as if she had produced the effect by a steel bar working as a cantilever, and attached to her body." [5] *

Needless to say, the transfer of this powerful stuff must necessarily occur at the expense of the medium's internal energy, for now, with a third or more of her own substance outside herself, the medium would become a mere residuum, the difference showing itself rather in a "refining of the whole body" than in a visible loss of substance. It was hardly to be wondered at, Doyle added, "that under such abnormal circumstances, any rough disturbance of the conditions which caused the external third to fly back with unnatural speed to the body would cause physical suffering." Indeed, Doyle reported having known of a medium who suffered a "broad weal from breast to armpit through the

---

* Doyle's generous imagery of phallic power is reminiscent of the story of the visit of a British lady to a hospitalized soldier whose genital had been damaged by shrapnel. "Dear me," said her Ladyship when she learned the details, "Did it go through the bone?" In reply, the wounded man gave a brisk salute, remarking, "The bone? My compliments to his Lordship."

sudden elastic recoil of the ectoplasm. Is it any wonder," asked Doctor Doyle, "that spiritualists object to the type of researcher who suddenly flashes a powerful electric torch in the middle of a seance?" [6] A cynic might suspect that Sir Arthur objected to shedding light of any description upon all Spiritualist phenomena.

Surely he was far from directing any powerful beams of scientific skepticism toward Margery, who quite clearly made a most favorable impression on him. During her triumphal tour of France and England in 1922 she was invited to give a private seance in London for Sir Arthur, who found her "marvelous"—which tribute may have been not unrelated to the fact that during the seance Margery had placed her feet in his lap. Later he would write that he had seen numerous photographs of the ectoplasmic flow from Margery and that he had no hesitation in stating "that it is unquestionably genuine, and that the future will justify the medium against her unreasonable critics." [7] How he felt about her decision to apply for the prizes offered by the *Scientific American* magazine for "spirit photographs" and for a medium who could produce "all genuine physical phenomena" like raps and levitations, can be inferred from his stated disapproval of giving the prizes in the first place. "Why offer prizes at all," he asked, "when there is already in existence a quantity of indubitable evidence?"

By the summer of 1924 when she decided to hold seances to demonstrate her qualifications for the award, Margery's husband invited the magazine's committeemen attending her seances to stay on at their Lime Street home in Beacon Hill, Boston, as his guests. Despite such an obvious conflict of interest, neither the invitation to become guests of the Crandons nor the decision to hold the testing sessions in Margery's own seance room appears to have greatly troubled the members of the committee—that is, until Houdini appeared on the scene in late July. By this time Margery had held over fifty sessions with the committee, and armed by the combination of their gullibility and her own artfulness, she seemed well on the road to victory. On one occasion a member of the committee became suspicious when he discovered a piece of string attached to the leg of a stool that had miraculously "walked" across the floor in the direction of a grating that communicated with a room on the floor below. But when he suggested that someone in that downstairs room might have caused the stool to move by pulling on the string which had been passed through the grating, Margery responded "with indignation and uncontrollable laughter," and the suspected string was identified as merely a frayed part of the carpet. The *Scientific American* prize was virtually within her grasp: "Margery the Boston medium passes all tests," reported *The New York Times*. "Scientists find no trickery in a score of seances."

When Houdini learned that the magazine was on the point of awarding her the prize he flew into a rage, enlisted the support of the magazine's publisher and succeeded in being included in subsequent seances. From this moment on, there was a radical change in the format of the investigation.

Armed with an encyclopedic familiarity with tricks and trickery, he introduced an array of safeguards and precautions that seriously jeopardized Margery's miracles. It was due to his aggressive and challenging policies that the committee, originally disposed in her favor, became increasingly critical.

To begin with, Houdini rejected the invitation to stay at the Lime Street house, arguing that it was not possible to perform an objective test in an atmosphere of social intimacy. More important was his insistence upon strict surveillance of the medium's actions and behavior and upon guarding against fraud and collusion. He pointed out that it does no good to isolate or "control" a medium by holding the hands or restraining the feet in the dark if someone who is sympathetic to the medium—a husband, for example—is free to transmit clues and signals. This came as a severe blow to the Boston medium, for on many occasions prior to Houdini's arrival at the Margery investigation, the person chosen to act as her "control" was none other than Doctor Crandon himself! Houdini finally succeeded in having the sessions take place in the more neutral location of a hotel, where the medium would be obliged to sit in a contrivance designed by him that presented many fewer opportunities for trickery. Despite this precaution, on at least one occasion it was found that the cabinet had been tampered with, for which Margery blamed her brother Walter.

For his aggressive methods, which one participant labeled unnecessarily "cruel," "brutal," and "caddish," [8] Houdini soon found himself persona non grata both on Beacon Hill and in the entire Spiritualist community. Margery's brother Walter was especially hostile to the brash magician from New York, and unlike his gentle sister, was loud, sarcastic, and profane. At one point during some acrimonious mutual accusations Walter screamed, "Houdini, you goddam son of a bitch, get the hell out of here and never come back!" [9] * To be sure, it was such uninhibited language that persuaded many persons that the

---

* To this name calling Houdini responded with a show of mocking distress. He buried his face in his hands, groaned, and almost wept, and cried out, "Oh, this is terrible. My dear sainted mother *was* married to my father!" [10]

words originated in a spirit, for the refined Mina Crandon was judged incapable of knowing such words, let alone uttering them.

As the investigation progressed, Doctor Crandon became no less hostile to other members of the committee, accusing some of them of inflicting physical injury on his wife, or as he called her, "Psyche." For ignoring the "extreme sensitivity" of the ectoplasmic rods and their "intimate connection with the vitality of the medium," he accused one member of the committee of causing severe damage by squeezing them. As a result of this vigorous handling, the Doctor insisted, "Psyche" began to vomit on the floor after the seance. "This had never happened before," he continued, and worse yet her "catamenia . . . came on at once, and out of time, and persisted for seventeen days." (In short, the rascals had snapped off Margery's ectoplasmic phallus.) During the same period she had "persistent crossing of the eyes, violent headaches, and other alarming symptoms," which one physician, who never examined her, suggested might be due to "sleeping sickness." "In our total of over four hundred sittings," lamented the Doctor, "with over five hundred different sitters, no such assault has been made before." [11]

There were others, however, who gave a rather different version of the seance in question, asserting that neither Walter nor Margery had been aware of the squeezing of the rod while it was taking place, or for that matter until some forty-five minutes later when, after the lights had been turned on, an account of the session was being dictated to the stenographer. It had been only at this point that Margery began to gag and cough and act as if she were ill. Despite her husband's account of her violent symptoms and his claim that she had been confined to bed for four days, when one of the committee members visited the Crandon home on the day after the critical squeezing session, he failed to find Mrs. Crandon "any the worse for the experience. She ran up and down the stairs easily and seemed in excellent spirits." [12]

As for some unseemly implications concerning the ectoplasmic rod protruding from his wife's genitals, Doctor Crandon was no less piqued. He objected vigorously to one participant who *"with obvious intent* described it as 'like a stick covered with leather,' " and when another member of the committee quipped that "the watchamacallit feels to me like an—[censored]" Doctor Crandon drew himself up to his full Beacon Hill height and declared, "Whether you agree with me or not, it is my decision that such a comparison constitutes behavior impossible for a gentleman." [13]

Less impressionistic was the evidence adduced by psychologist William McDougall of Harvard that enlargements of the photographs of the ectoplasm displayed "certain ring markings which strongly resembled the cartilaginous rings found in the mammalian trachea." This discovery led to the suspicion that the ectoplasmic stuff had been faked from some animal lung material, an opinion that was shared by the eminent physiologist Professor Walter B. Cannon and Doctor H. W. Rand, Associate Professor of Zoology, both of Harvard. (As a surgeon, it should be noted, Doctor Crandon had easy access to animal laboratories in several Boston hospitals.)

Soon the Walter charade began to crumble, for during photographed sequences it was noticed that when he laughed the corner of his sister's mouth drooped; both of "them," moreover, pronounced the word larynx as *larnyx*. As for Walter's mysterious thumb prints, which had caused a good deal of perplexity, they were ultimately traced to the thumbs of the dentist who not only took care of Margery's teeth but showed her how to prepare dental wax to receive impressions. He had given her two slabs into which his thumb prints had been deeply pressed.

At the conclusion of this dramatic inquiry, despite some thinly veiled bribes offered by Doctor Crandon, Houdini delivered a most unequivocal opinion of Margery's mediumship: "My decision," he declared, "is that everything which took place at the seances which I attended was a deliberate and conscious fraud, and that if the lady possesses any psychic powers, at no time was the same proven in any of the above dated seances." [14] While other members of the committee rendered a more qualified judgment, in February 1925 the *Scientific American* announced that by a vote of four to one it had decided that Margery did not merit the award upholding her supernatural powers. The verdict came as a severe blow both to her and to her eager promoter/husband.

Undoubtedly the decision proved to be no less disappointing to those hopeful souls who had looked to her and to her spectral brother as a bulwark against man's most abiding fears—death and castration —for the seeming vitality of Walter had given promise of the truth of life after death, while the ectoplasmic rods issuing from her genitalia offered proof of the reality of that most elusive prize—the female phallus.

In short, Margery, the "light around which countless visionaries danced and paid homage," wrote committeeman Doctor Walter Franklin Prince, turned out instead to be the central figure "in the most ingenious, persistent, and fantastic complex of fraud in the history of psychic research." [15]

It was only fitting that this personage, who was endowed both with such spectacular mediumistic powers and flashy genital paraphernalia, should have established her initial contact with her future husband and Spiritualist mentor in a gynecological operating room. Early in 1917, in the seventh year of her faltering marriage to a grocer named Rand, the twenty-nine-year-old Mina was admitted to a private hospital in Dorchester, Massachusetts, where Doctor Crandon was called in to operate on her. Although the surgery was some sort of gynecological procedure, its precise nature was not stated, for the doctor did not wish to reveal the alterations he had made in what was termed Mrs. Rand's "most convenient storage warehouse." [16] Whatever it was, Mina later claimed it had resulted in profuse menstrual flow.

It was not many months later that her relationship with Rand came to an end; by the close of the year she left him and, taking her little son with her, returned to her mother. Soon thereafter she obtained a divorce. Doctor Crandon, meanwhile, divorced his wife (his second one), whom he charged with cruelty and abuse, and some time in the fall of 1918 he and Mina were married. Gossip had it that she was quite pleased by the improvement in her social status resulting from her replacing her "small-time grocer" spouse with a Harvard professor.

There is reason to suspect, however, that her new-found gratification was short-lived, for within four years of her marriage, and independent of her husband's influence, she began to become interested in Spiritualism—a step which may be regarded as an unfailing indication of emotional unrest. Some time in 1922, according to a news item in the *Boston Herald* of December 20, 1924, she had visited a medium in the South End of Boston, where she was told that she possessed unusual powers. Interested in the suggestion, she began to experiment with automatic writing with which she soon established a reputation. Precisely what specific circumstances in her life prompted her venturing into the realm of the occult is unknown, but to judge from such examples as Conan Doyle, Sir Oliver Lodge, Bishop James Pike, and others, whose dedication to Spiritualism was closely associated with the loss of a child, it is likely that her turning to the "faith" was similarly determined by a desire to seek release from the mental torment occasioned by the death of a close family member.

No one can read the accounts of her seances without remarking upon the central role played in her mediumship by her dead brother

Walter. In his own distorted way, Doyle understood this when he wrote, "What Houdini failed to take into account was that the presiding spirit, Walter, the dead brother of Mrs. Crandon, was a very real and live entity, who was by no means inclined to allow his innocent sister to be made the laughing stock of the Continent. It was the unseen Walter who checkmated the carefully laid plans of the magician." [17]

Intentionally or not, Doctor Crandon was also a party to her utilizing her spiritualist seances as a means of denying her brother's death. On one occasion when she was apparently resisting Doctor Crandon's orders, he sternly rebuked her, asserting, "Little sister will do exactly as big brother says." [18]

The fiction of Walter's presence was joined with the conception of her assuming his identity, of his living on through her. Whether she is viewed as a malingerer or a hysteric, there is something poignantly pathetic—like Houdini's pitiful efforts to reach his dead mother—in her attempts to impersonate the dead Walter, as if she might annul his death and effect his resurrection through her own person. Mina sought to recreate her brother Walter by incorporating him within herself, adopting the quality of his voice, the timbre of his laugh, the range of his language, the character of his manners and, above all, the very physical makeup of his person. Her embrace of Spiritualism was clearly prompted by a passionate need to deny two intolerable realities: the death of Walter and the absence of her own phallus. [19]

In her later years Mina Crandon, the woman who had been hailed as "the most brilliant star in the firmament of alleged psychical mediumship that America has seen in fifty years" [20] and the "white hope of the believers" in their battle with the skeptics, went into eclipse, her melancholy somewhat assuaged by the soothing effects of spirits of another sort. During her final bedridden days when she was asked by the "psychic researcher" Nandor Fodor to confess the truth about her past, she shot out, "All you 'psychic researchers' can go to hell. Why don't you guess? You'll be guessing for the rest of your lives." [21]

"Ah, Mina, there was a heartbreaker for you," an acquaintaince once remarked. "A natural blond with the most devilish eyes I ever saw in my life. And there was pure enchantment in her voice, no other way to describe it. I understand that she went to pieces rather badly before she died and all the loveliness and the laughter were no more." [22]

Possessed of such devilish eyes, imbued with the ghost of a departed brother, and equipped with the spectral genital of the male, it is no wonder that Mina Crandon seemed bewitching, especially to those men who, like her thrice-married husband, were caught in a constant search for a woman who gave subtle promise of hidden phallic power. Whether Houdini was beguiled by those charms is not recorded, nor is it known how he responded when she flung her unclothed legs about under the seance table, ostensibly searching for clues.

Such erotic antics could hardly have failed to complicate his ambivalence toward Spiritualism, for despite his bombastic efforts to denounce it, even in the face of so patent a fraud as Margery he was still assailed by gnawing doubts and a relentless longing to believe. On January 5, 1925, in a letter to Harry Price, a well-known investigator of psychic phenomena, he wrote: "Another strange thing happened: with the aid of spirit slates, I produced a photograph of Mrs. Crandon's brother Walter, who was killed, and of all the miracles in the world, I ran across the photograph of the boy as he was crushed between the engine and the tender of the train, and which was taken one minute before he died . . . I doubt very much if there are any duplicates about." 23

It is easy to see why Margery was called a witch, for even if she carried no broomstick to fly her through the sky, in her ectoplasmic rod she held its counterpart. Just as in *The Wizard of Oz* Dorothy destroys the Wicked Witch of the West by dousing her with a bucket of water, so, by tinkering with her ectoplasmic phallus, did the committeemen of the *Scientific American* cause Margery to become "violently ill" and make her injured genitals bleed for seventeen days. For his part in thus castrating the Witch of Beacon Hill, Houdini was destined to pay a heavy price.

Sincerely, no doubt, Doyle claimed that, like the Crandons, he had become seriously alarmed for Houdini's safety, but if the Crandons were as alarmed as he implied, they had a strange way of showing it, for Margery threatened to have her friends give Houdini a thrashing if he were to denounce her from the stage where he was appearing. When she added that she didn't want her son to read in the papers that his mother had been called a fraud, Houdini snapped back, "Then don't be a fraud." 24

But an uglier threat was uttered in the fall of 1924 when Margery, speaking through her spectral brother, put the hex on Houdini, announcing that he would die within a year. To this Houdini retorted that if it turned out to be true it would be by God's will, not Walter's.25 Be that as it may, God or Walter, the latter's ominous prediction was not far wrong, for within two years of the fateful prophecy Houdini was dead.

XVIII

Halloween

Fair is foul, and foul is fair:
Hover through the fog and filthy air.
—MACBETH

Like King Acrisius, whose death at the hands of Perseus had been foretold by an oracle, Houdini advanced into the twilight of his life as if his fate, too, had been similarly preordained. Although he had emerged the victor in his combat with Margery and her spectral brother, and although he continued to wage his attacks on seers and mediums with undiminished vigor,* as he moved into the final months of 1926 there was a change in the temper of his belligerence. The bold blasts of defiance that had once roared out his disdain for death became shriller and increasingly mingled with the chill breath of superstition.

"My experience with him for the last three months of his life," noted the writer Fulton Oursler, "was most peculiar. He would call me on the telephone at seven o'clock in the morning and he would be in a quarrelsome mood. He would talk for an hour, telling me how important he was and what a great career he was making. In his voice was an hysterical, almost feminine note of rebellion, as if his hands were beating against an immutable destiny. . . . In all these cases Houdini portrayed to me a clear sense of impending doom. . . . I believe that Houdini sensed the coming of his death, but did not know that it meant death. He didn't know what it meant, but he hated it and his soul screamed out in indignation." [1]

He made a similar impression on the celebrated magician Dun-

* The leader of the Mission of Love on Dearborn Street, Chicago, filed a libel suit against Houdini, charging him with harassing his spirits, which he claimed were no longer as communicative as they had once been.[2]

ninger, who reported that in the early hours of one morning he had been awakened by Houdini on the phone, who insisted that he come over at once to see a pair of live hands he had obtained. "They're a pair of human hands," Houdini shouted. "And they're *alive,* Joe, they're *alive!*" Perplexed and understandably curious, Dunninger got dressed and rushed over to Houdini's house on 113th Street. There on the library table was a plaster cast of Houdini's hands. "There they are, Joe," exclaimed Houdini excitedly. "Don't they look as though they're really alive? Just think of it—my hands, *my poor hands* immortalized, preserved forever! Isn't it wonderful?" [3]

On another occasion during that same period, when Dunninger was helping him move some belongings from his house, Houdini expressed an even more explicit presentiment of his death. After they had loaded the car and had driven as far south as Seventy-second Street, Houdini suddenly ordered Dunninger to turn back to the house. Had they forgotten something? Dunninger wondered, but he received no explanation. It was raining, but when they reached 113th Street, Houdini got out of the car and stood bareheaded on the sidewalk, looking up at the house. When he got back into the car he was crying, and as they drove off again he said, "I've seen my house for the last time, Joe. I'll never see my house again." And a little later he began to speak of the bronze coffn he had had made for his submersion stunt and said to Dunninger, "Joe, I made it to be buried in." [4]

His preoccupation with his own death continued unabated. On the day he left New York for what would prove to be his final tour, he called Oursler on the phone and declared he was doomed. "I am marked for death," he told him. All over the land, Doyle would later write, "loud warnings of danger arose. . . . In my own home circle, I had the message a year or so ago: HOUDINI IS DOOMED, DOOMED, DOOMED!" [5]

The events that followed seemed to bear out these gloomy forebodings, for from the very start the tour was beset by an inexorable parade of misadventures.

On Thursday, October 7, while he was fulfilling an engagement in Providence, Rhode Island, Houdini awoke to find to his dismay that Bess was sick and feverish, presumably from so-called ptomaine poisoning. Although hospitalization was not advised, Houdini worried about her greatly, and despite the availability of good nursing care, when her fever continued on Friday he insisted on staying up with her throughout the night.[6] On Saturday she was still running a fever, but was well enough to travel. Following the evening performance and in the company of a nurse she took the train for Albany, where Houdini was scheduled to begin a run on Monday, the eleventh. After seeing them off at the Providence station, Houdini boarded a late train for New York, dozing fitfully on the long and uncomfortable journey.

There was no slackening of his restless pace after he reached New York. He dashed about taking care of various matters until the late afternoon when he appeared at the apartment of his attorney, Mr. Bernard Ernst, with whom he had an appointment. When he found that the family had not yet returned from the country, he lay down on the living room sofa for about twenty minutes to snatch what was virtually his first sleep in three days. During his conference with Ernst after dinner, Houdini seemed less alert than usual, and on two occasions he phoned Albany to find out about Bess's condition. After concluding his affairs, he took an early morning train for Albany and arrived there at 7:00 A.M. on Monday. Once again he had gone through the night with virtually no sleep. On his arrival he found Bess much improved, and he managed to rest for an hour before hurrying out again to see that everything was in readiness for the night's opening.

It was on this night, October 11, that the peal of doom sounded again as preparations were being made for the "Water Torture Cell" stunt to be performed during the second act of the show. Houdini seemed to be extremely fatigued as the mahogany stocks were applied to his ankles. Then, as his assistants pulled on the hoist to lift him into the air by the feet in order to lower him head first into the cell, the apparatus gave a sudden jerk, and Houdini gasped as he felt something snap in his left ankle. He was quickly lowered to the stage, and as he sat there rubbing his ankle he called out to the audience to ask if there was a doctor in the house.

There was, and when the physician examined the ankle he told Houdini he believed it was broken and advised him to end the show and go at once to the hospital for an X-ray. Predictably, Houdini declined, and although he was in severe pain and unable to bear any weight on the foot, he insisted on limping through the rest of the performance. Later that night an X-ray examination confirmed the doctor's diagnosis.

> Though Acrisius sought to flee the presence of Perseus, the latter happened to be nearby while he was competing in some funeral games. When it came to the discus-throw, his discus, carried out of its path by the wind and the will of the gods, struck Acrisius's foot and killed him.

Word of Houdini's injury traveled quickly. The next day Oursler reported an unknown woman claiming to be a medium came to him bearing a letter from "a departed spirit" which read: "The waters are dark for Houdini. He thinks he has broken his ankle, but his days are almost over." [7]

Despite these forebodings and despite a newspaper report that the fracture might keep him off the stage "for some time to come," Houdini refused to submit to his mishap; aided by bandages, splints, and a brace, he managed to continue his two more scheduled days in Albany, followed by three more in Schenectady. The next stop was the Princess Theater in Montreal, where he was due to open an engagement on Monday, the eighteenth, and continue through Saturday, the twenty-third. His ankle continued to be painful, but Houdini proceeded with his schedule of performances, and in addition gave a lecture at McGill University on Spiritualism. On the afternoon of the nineteenth, before an enthusiastic audience of faculty and students, he talked about frauds and phony seances and recounted many of his experiences in unmasking seers and mediums, including the famous Margery of Boston, whom he dubbed the "slickest medium that ever lived." [8] For this display of hubris he seemed to feel destined to pay dearly, for once again he alluded to his own death. "If I should die tonight," he remarked, "the Spiritualist mediums would hold a national holiday." [9] *

On Friday morning, the twenty-second, while he was relaxing on a couch and going over his mail in his dressing room, he received a visit from several of the students who had heard his lecture. One of them, a man named J. Gordon Whitehead, reputed to be a college boxing star, tried to engage Houdini in a discussion about miracles mentioned in the Bible, but aside from wondering what people of those ancient times might have thought of his own miraculous stunts, Houdini failed to show any particular interest in the subject.

Next Whitehead asked if it was true that, despite his fifty-two years, Houdini's physical condition was so good that he could withstand blows to his body without injury. When he was invited to put it to the test and believed he had received permission to do so, Whitehead let loose with a barrage of punches—apparently before Houdini had time to prepare himself. It was said that he gasped and clutched his abdomen, signaling the young man to stop. Then he braced himself and invited Whitehead to hit him again. This time Houdini was ready and the blow didn't hurt.

* Houdini is said to have made virtually the same prediction as he was being wheeled into the operating room in Detroit one week later.

Something else did, however, for during the matinee Houdini began to feel pain in his abdomen and it had become tender to the touch. By nightfall the discomfort was worse and kept him awake. On Saturday he began to have chills and sweats and spells of fatigue. Characteristically, he insisted on going through with the final Montreal performance that night, but at the end of it he had to be helped in changing his clothes. He then took the train to Detroit. When a doctor finally succeeded in getting to him after the long night's journey, he found him setting up props at the theater for the Sunday night show. Despite a fever of 102° and the doctor's advice for immediate hospitalization, Houdini refused to give in. Later, when he heard that the house was sold out, he said, "They're here to see me. I won't disappoint them." [10]

And he didn't. True to form, now with a fever of 104°, he played through to the end and then collapsed. Only after he had talked on the phone to his New York physician did his resistance weaken sufficiently to allow him to consent to be admitted to the hospital in the early hours of Monday morning. There was no question that surgery was imperative.*

At the operation he was discovered to have a ruptured gangrenous appendix, which was removed. He did not get well, however, for he was afflicted by a fulminating streptococcal peritonitis, against which in those days there were, alas, no magic medicines. Despite a display of what his physician found to be an extraordinary will to live, in time he, too, realized that the end was near. On Halloween morning, Sunday, October 31, he whispered to his brother Theodore: "I'm tired of fighting. . . . I guess this thing is going to get me." And at one twenty-six in the afternoon he died.[11]

He was laid to rest in the same bronze coffin he had purchased as a prop for his submersion stunt and which he had recently told Dunninger he had acquired to contain his dead body. In accordance with his own instructions, he was interred in the family plot in the Machpelah Cemetery:

"My body is to be embalmed and buried," he directed in chapter nineteen of his will, "in the same manner in which my beloved mother was buried upon her death, and my grave [is to] be constructed in the same manner as my beloved mother's last resting place was con-

* It has been asserted that he asked the surgeon to see to it that "some unpleasant relatives" be prevented from seeing him after the surgery. Presumably this meant the ostracized Leopold. Houdini's other brothers, Nathan and Hardeen (William had died the year before), and his sister Gladys came to Detroit on the following day.[12]

structed for her burial, and I also direct that I shall be buried in the grave immediately alongside that of my dear departed mother."

At long last her cherished words would now be close to him forever, for a black bag containing her letters to him was placed beneath his lifeless head. Nor would this prove to be the sole reward conferred upon him by the angel of death, for now, lying motionless in an escape-proof box and buried deep within the bosom of the earth, he could abandon his grim counterphobic games and, secure in death's embrace, yield to those mad fantasies that in his living hours he had sought in vain to banish.

Despite the temptation to attribute his destiny to the gods and to view his madness as a prelude to his destruction by them, an inquiring mind may justly seek an answer to the question: Why did Houdini die?

In the spirit of scientific reality it will be said that he died of a streptococcal peritonitis caused by the rupture of a diseased appendix. Others will cite the blows aimed at his abdomen some nine days before his death when, aside from a broken ankle, he was apparently in perfect health. Yet a computerized search of the medical literature as well as random inquiries among experienced surgeons reveals not a single instance of acute appendicitis resulting from physical injury. Although the English literature contains reports of three instances of disease of the appendix following blunt trauma to the abdomen, in none of them was there a bona fide appendicitis. Whatever inflammatory process existed was apparently secondary to physical damage to the appendix, namely its being torn from its base.[13] During the 1930s a Works Progress Administration Commission in Washington concluded that "there is no such entity as traumatic appendicitis," an opinion that evidently still holds.[14] On the other hand, trauma has been known to cause rupture of the large intestine, and indeed the preoperative diagnosis by Houdini's surgeon, Doctor Charles S. Kennedy, had been a traumatic rupture of the sigmoid colon. At operation, however, the colon showed no signs of perforation, while the appendix was not only ruptured but lying on the left side.

Abdominal trauma has also been cited as a cause of peritonitis when it has resulted in the rupture of an already diseased organ or abscess. This raises the possibility that Houdini had been afflicted with an inflamed appendix *before* he had been punched in the abdomen by Mr. Whitehead. Although there is no record of his having suffered symptoms referrable to such a condition prior to the blow, one observer, Doctor William D. Tait, professor of psychology at McGill, who escorted Houdini to the lecture platform on the afternoon of the nineteenth, noted that at the conclusion of his talk he sat down immediately, "as he was suffering great pain from his fractured ankle." Conceivably it was his abdomen that was causing his distress and not the ankle, which had been fractured eight days earlier. This account appeared in the November first issue of the *Montreal Daily Star* under a headline which read: "Houdini . . . looked ill at lecture." A newspaper reporter claimed to have seen "the stamp of death on his countenance."

Needless to say, no clinician would be tempted to place great reliance on such impressionistic evidence, set down nearly two weeks after the event. Indeed, all that can be said with any degree of confidence is that Houdini's unrelieved anxieties concerning damage and death caused him to ignore dangerous signs of ill health and surely contributed to his dark destiny. If this employment of the psychological device of denial be viewed as courage, it is difficult to distinguish it from folly, for it paved the way to his own destruction.

Perhaps this was Houdini's unconscious intention—an intention that he sought to conceal by ascribing his destiny not to himself but to his stars, from whence he learned the ghostly premonitions of his unhappy fate. Perhaps it was also a manifestation of the same psychological device that enabled him to displace his own fierce aggression upon another person, upon one who could unleash a blow to the abdomen, such as an angry child might aim at the swollen belly of a faithless mother. Thoughts of his mother were indeed with him to the very end. Two days before he died, when Bess was at his side, he whispered to her, "Mother never reached me. If . . . anything happens . . . you must be prepared. Remember the message. . . . When you hear those words . . . know it is Houdini speaking." [15]

Even in death he displayed extraordinary vitality. In January 1929 the newspapers reported that through the spiritualist medium, the notorious Arthur Ford, Bess had finally received a message from Houdini, deciphered by code words known only to herself and to her late husband. From Boston, Margery, his old nemesis, exulted, "Harry Houdini in death has furnished the world with evidence which conclusively refutes the theories which he so vigorously defended in his life." [16] But soon the miraculous seance proved to be a hoax and the secret code turned out to be no secret at all, for it had been revealed to Kellock by Bess when he was gathering material for the biography of Houdini he had published the preceding year.

To the lady who knew him when she was a child and recalled seeing a crucifix about his neck, he was immortal. Indeed, one morning some twenty years ago when an ex-soldier rang her door bell, she recognized at once that it was Houdini, and she invited him in and cooked him the sort of breakfast she remembered from her childhood that Houdini liked. And when a year or so ago this writer called her on the telephone to request an interview, she registered no surprise; she had expected him, she explained, for only a few nights before Houdini had appeared to her in a dream and had predicted the call.

Although it is now a half century since his death, his legendary name lives on, enveloped in an atmosphere of mystery and magic. Reports of buried codes and hidden clues concealed among the stones and inscriptions of the gravesite, purporting to contain the keys to his professional secrets, continue to haunt the news from time to time.

As recently as April 10, 1975, his name burst into the newspapers again, when it was reported that his stone bust, dominating the exedra in the family burial plot in the Machpelah Cemetery, had been smashed to pieces, evidently by a sledge hammer. (Figure 12) Although neither the perpetrator of this act of vandalism nor its motive was identified, it offers renewed affirmation of the enduring vitality of his spirit and of his unfailing ability to rouse the public passion.

Who might have committed such a brutal deed? The vengeful victims of his fickle faith, like Robert-Houdin or Conan Doyle? The angry shade of his brother Leopold, once exiled from that very cemetery? Walter, the infamous brother of Margery, the Boston medium, the butt of Houdini's mockery and scorn?

No, none of these. Before his death Houdini had made his peace with Robert-Houdin, his boyhood hero and mentor, and Doyle was too forgiving a man to hold a grudge. As for the doctor, Houdini's brother, soon after his death some dozen years ago, permission was granted that his body be admitted for burial in the Machpelah plot, and now, appeased, he reposes with his family. Finally, Walter's spectral thirst for revenge was surely satisfied when, obedient to his grim prediction, Houdini had died within a year or two of his sister's humiliation and defeat.

There is one ghostly hand, however, that might have smashed that granite bust—the hand of Ehrich Weiss, the rabbi's son, who from an early age had heard the injunction against the fashioning of graven images. Perhaps like a wrathful Moses destroying the calf of gold, reconciled at last to the faith of the patriarchs, the shade of Houdini's most secret self made one last escape, stole from the grave and performed his most amazing trick—his own decapitation.

Notes

Introduction

1. Herbert Muller, *The Uses of the Past* (New York: Oxford University Press, 1952), pp. 34–35.

2. Milbourne Christopher, *Houdini, The Untold Story* (New York: Pocket Books, 1970), p. 101. Originally published by Thomas Crowell, New York, 1969.

3. Maurice Zolotow, *New York Times* Book Review of *Houdini, The Untold Story*, by Milbourne Christopher, March 23, 1969.

4. Joseph Campbell, *The Hero with a Thousand Faces* (New York: Pantheon, 1949), p. 4.

I. The Family Romance

1. The picture of Houdini's mother in the photo insert was taken by a professional photographer in Essen, Germany, shortly after her "coronation" in Budapest. Although the dress has an undeniably regal appearance, and is without doubt the gown he had bought for her in London, there is some question whether it was actually designed for Queen Victoria.

On seeing the photograph, Mrs. D. Langley Moore, the Founder and Adviser of the Museum of Costume in Bath, England, and an authority on the Queen's wardrobe, gave the opinion that the dress could "*not possibly* have belonged to Queen Victoria." She noted that in later life Her Majesty was "incredibly fat," and and that neither her generous waist—it measured fifty-one inches!—nor her fat arms could have fitted into the slim gown and narrow sleeves shown in the picture. She cited several other details in support of her opinion. Her concluding sentence, however, appears to diminish the force of her initial impression, for she wrote, "Houdini was a loyal son and an ingenious man . . . but his mother must have been an odd shape—unless the Queen's dress was much altered for her." Inasmuch as Christopher reported that the gown had been altered to fit Mrs. Weiss, it is not impossible that it had been designed for the Queen. If on the other hand the dress was not what it was said to be, two possibilities remain: either Houdini had been duped by the London shopkeeper who sold it to him, or what would be more likely in light of Houdini's notoriously inventive imagination, he himself had concocted the entire story.

2. Harold Kellock, *Houdini, His Life-Story* (New York: Blue Ribbon Books, 1928), pp. 148–149.

3. The argument that the discrepancy was caused by a different system of dating is invalid: the Gregorian calendar was in use in nineteenth century Hungary.

4. *Proceedings of the Houdini Birth Research Committee*, Lawrence Arcuri, Chairman, Exhibit F.

5. In one version the age difference between Houdini's parents was given as thirteen years; in another, twenty-five. The former is more reliable. The latter source also claimed that the rabbi's first wife was Rose Czillag, a popular opera singer, while Christopher maintains that it was her sister.

6. *Proceedings, op. cit.*, Exhibit I.

7. Christopher, *op. cit.*, p. 9.

8. *Ibid.*, p. 11.

9. *Ibid.*, p. 13.

10. Milbourne Christopher, *The Illustrated History of Magic* (New York: Thomas Crowell, 1973), p. 340.

11. Melville Cane, *The First Firefly* (New York: Harcourt Brace Jovanovich, 1974), p. 85.

II. Robert-Houdin, Hero and Guide

1. Christopher, *Houdini, op. cit.*, p. 11.

2. Houdini was not the only magician to identify himself with the celebrated Frenchman. Inspired by Robert-Houdin, William Henry Palmer (1826–1878), a magician from Canterbury, England, changed his name to Robert Heller. As noted earlier, a heel from one of his shoes was among Houdini's prized possessions. It is not known whether Houdini knew the origin of Heller's nom de guerre.

3. Robert-Houdin, *Memoirs of Robert-Houdin, King of Conjurers*, with a new introduction and notes by Milbourne Christopher (New York: Dover, 1964), pp. 21–22.

4. *Ibid.*, p. 27.

5. *Ibid.*, p. 32.

6. *Ibid.*, p. 71.

7. Ernst Kris, "The Image of the Artist" in *Psychoanalytic Explorations in Art* (New York: International Universities Press, 1952).

8. William L. Gresham, *Houdini, The Man Who Walked Through Walls* (New York: Henry Holt and Co., 1959), p. 24.

9. Robert-Houdin, *op. cit.*, p. 91.

10. Kellock, *op. cit.*, p. 149.

III. The Sin of Ham

1. Gresham, *op. cit.*, p. 90.

2. Harry Houdini, *The Unmasking of Robert-Houdin,* with *A Treatise on Handcuff Secrets* (London: George Routledge and Sons, Ltd., 1909), p. 141.

3. *Ibid.,* p. 115.

4. *Ibid.,* p. 318.

5. W. B. Gibson and M. N. Young, *Houdini's Fabulous Magic* (Philadelphia and New York: Chilton Book Co., 1961), pp. 205–206.

6. Houdini, *op. cit.*, p. 299.

7. Christopher, *Houdini, op. cit.*, p. 6.

8. *Ibid.,* p. 193.

9. Maurice Sardina, *Where Houdini Was Wrong,* trans. Victor Farelli (London: George Armstrong, 1950), p. 90.

10. Robert-Houdin, *op. cit.*, p. 326.

11. In the original French version, with which young Weiss was surely not familiar, the figure given is twenty-five.

12. Robert-Houdin, *op. cit.*, p. 48.

13. 1803, according to the French version.

14. Robert-Houdin, *op. cit.*, p. 56.

15. *Ibid.,* p. 326.

16. Sir Arthur Conan Doyle, *The Edge of the Unknown* (New York: G. Putnam's Sons, 1930), p. 43.

17. John N. Hilliard, *Greater Magic: A Practical Treatise on Modern Magic,* eds. Carl W. Jones and Jean Hugard (Minneapolis: Privately Printed, 1938).

18. It seems possible that Houdini's susceptibility to the prestige of academic status originated in his childhood. Christopher owns what is said to be the earliest known signature of Ehrich Weiss, in a Hebrew grammar, written by one I. Mayer, "Dr. Ph, Professor of the Oriental Languages." The fact that another Hebrew scholar, his father, also bore the name Mayer, may have encouraged the son to indulge in reveries in which he endowed his father—and himself, too, perhaps—with similarly impressive titles and degrees.

19. Henry R. Evans, *The Old and the New Magic* (London: Open Court Pub. Co., and Kegan Paul, Trench, Trübner, Ltd., 1906), p. 32.

IV. The Mark of Cain

1. Harry Houdini, *Houdini: A Magician Among the Spirits* (New York: Harper and Bros., 1924), Dedication.

2. Fulton Oursler, *Behold This Dreamer* (New York and Toronto: Little, Brown, 1964), p. 188.

3. Houdini, *A Magician Among the Spirits, op. cit.*, p. 151.

4. Kellock, *op. cit.*, p. 241.

5. *National Magazine,* Vol. 44, May 1916, pp. 340–341.

6. *Ibid.,* p. 307.

7. W. B. Gibson, *The Original Houdini Scrapbook* (New York: Corwin Sterling Co., 1976), p. 176.

8. *Ibid.*, pp. 175–176.

9. Kellock, *op. cit.*, p. 231.

10. The only exception was to be his wife, for whose burial by his side his will provided. Ironically, before her death in 1943, she had again embraced her native faith and she received a Catholic burial in the Gate of Heaven Cemetery in Westchester County, far from her husband's side.

11. Kellock, *op. cit.*, p. 236.

12. *Ibid.*, p. 286.

13. *Ibid.*, p. 264.

14. *Ibid.*, p. 265.

15. *Ibid.*

16. Leopold's fate was destined to undergo a dramatic reversal. Excluded from the family burial plot by Houdini's edict, Leopold and Sadie arranged for their ultimate interment in a mausoleum in the Mount Neboh Cemetery, located across the highway from the Machpelah Cemetery. But the marriage fared badly, and in the late 1920s Leopold went to Reno, Nevada, where he obtained a divorce. When Sadie died in 1935 he did not attend the funeral. Now he found himself lacking a burial place for himself in both cemeteries. Meanwhile he had lost much of his fortune in the financial crash of 1929, and worse yet, in time his eyesight began to fail him—a calamitous fate for a roentgenologist. Except for his estrangement from Houdini, he had remained a loyal and supportive brother to his siblings. Ultimately he outlived them all, but when death finally overtook him, it came in the form of violence.

V. A Doll's House

1. Kellock, *op. cit.*, p. 300.

2. *Ibid.*, p. 384.

3. *Ibid.*, p. 49.

4. Gresham, *op. cit.*, p. 27.

5. Kellock, *op. cit.*, p. 299.

6. Zolotow, *op. cit.*

7. *Ibid.*

VI. Of Human Bondage

1. Only in the case of one of his stories—"Imprisoned with the Pharaohs," which was published in the July 1924 issue of *Weird Tales*—was his collaboration with Lovecraft acknowledged.

2. © 1921 by Harry Houdini.

3. *Ibid.*

4. R. E. Littman and C. Swearingen, "Bondage and Suicide," *Arch. Gen. Psychiatry* #27, July, 1972, pp. 80–85.

5. E. Kronengold and R. Sterba, "Two Cases of Fetishism," *Psychonal. Quart.* #5, January 1936, pp. 63–70.

6. J. Mulholland, *Quicker Than the Eye* (Indianapolis: Bobbs Merrill, 1932), p. 153.

7. While presiding over the Magicians' Club of London Houdini contrived to sit on a special chair raised high off the floor, so that his head was well above the heads of the other members. "My soul would have been quite different if I had not stammered, or if I had been four or five inches taller," wrote W. Somerset Maugham. In his novel *Of Human Bondage,* Philip the protagonist is afflicted by a club foot.

8. Littman et al., *op. cit.*

VII. A Virtuoso of Imposture

1. Kellock, *op. cit.,* p. 19.

2. Houdini, *Handcuff Secrets, op. cit.,* p. 70.

3. W. Gibson, *Scrapbook,* p. 172.

4. Although the charlatanism of Cagliostro (1743–1795) and his oneness with Balsamo generally have been taken for granted, from time to time there have been attempts to rehabilitate him. Trowbridge, for example, who denied any connection between the two individuals, insisted that "there is not a single authenticated instance in which Cagliostro derived personal profit from imposture." He ascribed the well-known hostility of the medical profession toward Cagliostro to jealousy over his remarkable skill and miraculous cures. Such a view corresponds to the encomiums pronounced in Cagliostro's own day, like one inscribed under a portrait engraving by Guérin: *Il prolonge la vie, il secourt l'indigence. Le plaisir d'être utile est seule sa récompense.* (He prolongs life, he rescues the indigent. The pleasure of being useful is his only reward.)

When he was in Paris, Benjamin Franklin was urged to avail himself of the remarkable medical skills of the great Cagliostro. W. R. H. Trowbridge, *The Splendour and Misery of a Master of Magic* (London: Chapman Hall, 1910), p. 124.

5. Evans, *op. cit.,* p. 68.

6. In his story, "The Marvelous Adventures of Houdini," the yacht carrying him and his lady friend arrives at a place called Felice Island, which is said to be near Honolulu. Since no such island is listed in the standard Atlas, the name was presumably invented by Houdini.

7. While Houdini belittled the importance of the Cagliostro touch in the performance at St. Cloud, asserting that his seals were by no means rare and really formed no part of the trick anyway, artistically it was clearly of a high order, of far greater importance, one might say, than the question beggared by Houdini whether Robert-Houdin was indeed the indisputable originator of the trick.

8. Evans had stated her name to be Lorenza Feliciani, although he acknowledged that she had called herself Countess Serafina Feliciani. The section on Pinetti, the Italian conjurer, does contain a few inaccuracies. Houdini could hardly have objected to Evans's account of the Pinetti-de Grisy feud which Evans, too, accepted as authentic, although for some inexplicable reason he never mentioned the name Torrini, always referring to Pinetti's apocryphal nemesis as de Grisy.

9. William Frazee, "When Houdini was President," *M-U-M,* November 1953, p. 218.

10. Gresham, *op. cit.,* p. 54.

11. In his fictional life of Houdini, Zolotow depicted a similar identification

of his hero with Cagliostro: "More and more resembling his archetype, Cagliostro (Balsamo), became a charlatan, pandering to the fears and aspirations of the populace and coining money from its superstitions."

12. Oakland (California) *Tribune,* February 17, 1967.

13. Edmund Wilson, *Classics and Commercials* (New York: Farrar, Straus, 1950), p. 150.

VIII. The Dance of Death

1. Kellock, *op. cit.,* p. 185.

2. How far he had strayed from his pious father and the family fold can be gauged not only by his geographic removal and the altered spelling of his surname but by the nature of his adopted profession.

3. Melville Cane, *The First Firefly* (New York: Harcourt Brace Jovanovich, 1974), p. 80.

4. Gresham, *op. cit.,* p. 175.

5. Kellock, *op. cit.,* p. 371.

6. *Ibid.,* pp. 2–3.

IX. The Premature Burial

1. Kellock, *op. cit.,* p. 257.

2. Christopher, *Houdini, op. cit.,* p. 146.

3. Kellock, *op. cit.,* p. 257.

4. Christopher, *Houdini, op. cit.,* p. 146.

5. Kellock, *op. cit.,* p. 257.

6. Houdini, "Confessions of a Jail-Breaker," in W. B. Gibson *Houdini Scrapbook,* p. 172.

7. Christopher, *Houdini, op. cit.,* p. 7.

8. Kellock, *op. cit.,* p. 88.

9. *Ibid.,* p. 139.

10. Robert-Houdin, *op. cit.,* p. 28.

11. J. Meerloo, "Sea and Airsickness and Man's Hidden Fears," in *Child Family Digest:* 17: 3, 1958.

X. A Modern Icarus

1. Kellock, *op. cit.,* p. 214.

2. Christopher, *Houdini, op. cit.,* p. 123.

3. The others are "The Balloon-Hoax," "The Angel of God," and "Mellonta Tauta." The pun shallowly buried in the hero's name—Pfaall—is not merely an example of Poe's humor, but an unsubtle allusion to the underlying fear he was seeking to banish by the magical effect of flight. That he was aware that concealed behind this fear lay a self-destructive wish is plainly disclosed in "The Narrative of A. Gordon Pym" when, seeking to descend to the bottom of a steep cliff, the

narrator finds himself "consumed with the irrespressible desire of looking below
. . . my whole soul was pervaded with a *longing to fall;* a desire, a yearning, a
passion utterly uncontrollable."

4. Marie Bonaparte, *Life and Works of Edgar Allen Poe: A Psychoanalytic
Interpretation* (London: Imago, 1949), pp. 71 and 410.

5. Antoine de Saint-Exupéry, *Lettres à Sa Mère* (Paris: Gallimard, 1955), p. 64.

6. Antoine de Saint-Exupéry, *Flight to Arras,* trans. Lewis Galantière (New York:
Reynal and Hitchcock, 1942), p. 46.

7. Douglas D. Bond, *The Love and Fear of Flying* (New York: International
Universities Press, 1952), pp. 21–26.

8. Houdini was not the only magician to become enamored of aviation. His
work on Robert-Houdin states that the celebrated Italian conjurer Pinetti, the
adversary of the fictional Torrini, was similarly fascinated by flying and devoted
his later years as well as his fortune to ballooning.

XI. Claustrophobia

1. Zolotow's fictional recreation of Houdini's life contains recurring allusions
to his hero's claustrophobia, which is attributed to a frightening childhood experience of being accidentally locked in a hope chest (!) while fleeing from his
enraged father.

2. Was this a sly allusion to the claustrophobic myth of Daedalus? The suspicion that Doyle may have been responding to echoes of ancient Greece gains
support from the first name of the villain of this story—Lysander. This was the
name of the Spartan naval commander in the Peloponnesian War.

3. Those familiar with *Struwwelpeter,* that awesome primer on the evils of
thumbsucking (and other pleasurable practices), may wonder whether the fate of
the engineer alluded to a similar conflict in Doyle's childhood.

4. B. Lewin, "Claustrophobia," *Psychoanal. Quart.* #4, 1935, pp. 227–233.

5. S. Asch, "Claustrophobia and Depression," *Jour. Amer. Psychoanal. Ass.* #14,
Oct. 1966, pp. 711–729.

6. One great advantage of being a writer, wrote W. Somerset Maugham in
Cakes and Ale, is "that you can rid yourself of a painful experience by projecting
it on paper."

7. What is surprising about Houdini's purported collaboration in this story
is the fact of his well-known prejudice against hypnosis. The magician Dunninger
asserted that Houdini claimed it was a fraud and a delusion shared by both hypnotist and subject.

XII. Rites of Passage

1. Robert Graves, *The Greek Myths* (Baltimore: Penguin, 1955), vol. 2, p. 9.

2. Kellock, *op. cit.,* p. 162.

3. Samuel Rosenberg, *Naked is the Best Disguise* (New York: Bobbs Merrill,
1974), p. 32.

XIII. The *Akedah,* or the Binding of Isaac

1. Theodor Reik, *The Temptation* (New York: George Braziller, 1961), p. 130. The similarity of this ritual to the story of "Jack and the Beanstalk" hardly needs to be pointed out. In both instances castration is equated to devouring and the victim is identified or discovered by his smell.

2. *Ibid.,* pp. 103–104.

3. Gresham, *op. cit.,* p. 19.

4. On page 208 in *The Unmasking of Robert-Houdin* is a photograph of Houdini standing at the "long-neglected grave" of the celebrated magician Robert Heller in the Mount Moriah Cemetery in Philadelphia.

5. As in other sections of Houdini's will, this proviso bears the arbitrary character of someone wanting to throw his weight around, for the boys' mother was not Jewish, and conceivably may have taken not too kindly to the pressure that was being exerted by her brother-in-law.

Although Houdini's stipulation was carried out—in a distinctly perfunctory manner, it would appear—Hardeen's two sons grew to manhood without any seeming sense of a Jewish affiliation.

6. One of his Christmas cards displayed these several themes as well as allusions to birth and flying. It is a folded card which, when closed, showed Bess "caught" behind a much bolted and locked door, labeled Newgate Prison. When opened it revealed an empty prison cell with sunlight streaming through the small barred window, discarded shackles on the floor, and the word: "flown."

7. Far from serving as an argument against the thesis that Houdini's professional life was determined in some measure by an identification with Isaac, the foregoing evidence of his seeming personification with Christ supports it. "The Christ story," wrote Reik, "is a complete myth that reached its logical aim. It renewed the old idea and superstitions, resulting from the belief that the adolescent boys in primitive societies are killed during their initiation and then reborn." Reik, *op. cit.,* p. 212.

8. Kellock, *op. cit.,* p. 16.

XIV. The Magic Wand

1. Christopher, *Illustrated, op. cit.,* p. 1.

2. *Ibid.,* p. 289.

3. *Ibid.,* p. 418.

4. *Ibid.,* p. 420.

5. *Ibid.,* p. 422.

6. Lord Raglan, *The Hero* (New York: Vintage Books, 1956), p. 41.

7. Houdini, *The Unmasking, op. cit.,* p. 303.

8. Herman Melville, *Typee* (New York: New American Library, 1964), p. 19.

9. M. Coryn, *The Chevalier d'Eon, 1738–1810* (New York: Fred Stokes Co., 1932), p. 174.

10. The theme of this legend anticipated certain details in *The Arrow of Gold,* one of the last novels of Joseph Conrad. Both the title, which refers to the precious hair ornament worn by the androgynous heroine, and the fetish-laden content of the book reflect the author's interest in the theme of the phallic woman.

11. According to Rosenberg, Doyle was preoccupied by the subject of uncertain gender and made frequent allusions to the matter in his writings. A fictional example appears in the Gerard story, "How the Brigadier Lost His Ear," a tale set during Napoleon's occupation of Venice, in which the themes of both castration and transvestism are readily recognized: because she has taken a French officer for a lover, a Venetian lady has been sentenced to undergo the amputation of the lobe of one ear. Seeking to spare her this calamity, her French lover dresses himself in her clothes and hides in her prison cell, where gallantly he submits to the mutilation in her place.

XV. A Magician Among the Spirits

1. Houdini, *A Magician Among the Spirits, op. cit.*, pp. 152–153.
2. Sir Arthur Conan Doyle, *Strand Magazine*, London #74, Sept., 1927, p. 266.
3. Doyle, *Edge, op. cit.*, p. 39.
4. Houdini, *A Magician Among the Spirits, op. cit.*, p. 154.
5. *Ibid.*, p. 152.
6. Doyle, *Edge, op. cit.*, p. 44.
7. Houdini, *A Magician Among the Spirits, op. cit.*, pp. 157–158.
8. *Ibid.*, p. 152.
9. Doyle, *Edge, op. cit.*, p. 39.
10. B. M. L. Ernst and H. Carrington, *Houdini and Conan Doyle: The Story of a Strange Friendship* (New York: Albert and Charles Boni, 1932), p. 173.
11. *Ibid.*, p. 170.

It was characteristic of Houdini to buttress his own wobbly convictions as well as his faith in other persons with documents, oaths, and legalisms. Paranoid and suspicious, just as he kept carbon copies of the letters he wrote to various ladies, so he seemed to believe he could iron-clad the truth with papers and seals. Persons employed by him professionally, for example, were often required to sign an oath that began: "I . . . do hereby solemnly and sincerely swear on my Sacred Word of Honour as a man, and before The Great God Almighty, that I will ever hold sacred the secrets of Harry Handcuff Houdini . . ." and ended, "I solemnly swear to the above oath verbally, by taking the oath in the usual manner so HELP ME GOD ALMIGHTY AND MAY HE KEEP ME STEADFAST."

12. *Ibid.*, p. 200.
13. Houdini, *A Magician Among the Spirits, op. cit.*, p. 143.
14. *Ibid.*, p. 181.
15. *Ibid.*
16. *Ibid.*, pp. 187–188, 190.

A Dcotor Marcus Curry was Medical Director of Greystone Park Psychiatric Hospital in New Jersey for many years prior to his death in 1950. Doctor Frank D. Fenimore, the present director, stated that he had no recollection of any discussion by Doctor Curry of "metaphysical matters" nor is there any indication that Doctor Curry issued such material for publication.

17. Paul Sann, *Fads, Follies and Delusions of the American People* (New York: Crown, 1967), p. 143.
18. The Houdini Collection in the Library of Congress contains the book *What*

is Psychoanalysis? by Isadore Coriat, M.D. Whether Houdini ever read it is not known.

19. Ernst Jones, *The Life and Work of Sigmund Freud* (New York: Basic Books, 1957), vol. 3, p. 392.

20. Kellock, *op. cit.*, p. 53.

21. Gibson, *Houdini Scrapbook*, p. 47.

XVI. The Edge of the Unknown

1. John D. Carr, *The Life of Sir Arthur Conan Doyle* (New York: Harper and Bros., 1949), p. 276.

2. Like *Yar, The Primeval Man*, and several other film scenarios, *Il Mistero di Osiris* was printed by Houdini for the apparent purpose of establishing copyright. Despite his evident endorsement of the work, its exact authorship is obscure. On page 308 of the June 1908 issue of his *Conjurers' Monthly* magazine, Houdini recommended to American audiences an Italian conjurer and sword swallower, named Joseph Deodato, who was born on December 18, 1867 in Mesuraca, Province of Catanyaro (probably Catanzaro in Calabria). Whether this was the same person to whom the movie scenario was somewhat cryptically attributed is not known, but in light of Houdini's erratic writing and spelling habits, not too much should be made of the discrepancies in the names: Deodato and Deadota, Joseph and Giovanni. The text reads as if it had been translated by someone with the same proficiency in English that is sometimes found on the directions accompanying imported espresso coffee machines, e.g., "I persecute you in the life and into death"; "Here everything smells death," etc. The spelling is often Italian: *metempsicosi, Tebe* (Thebes), *Faraone* (Pharaoh), *Carma*, etc.

3. Library of Congress Collection.

4. *Ibid.*

5. Doyle, *Edge, op. cit.*, p. 34.

6. The magician John Mulholland pointed out that although the notorious Fox Sisters confessed to the fraudulence of their "rapping" and other manifestations, and although one of them actually went on tour *exposing her own tricks,* they continued to be venerated as authentic by Spiritualists.

7. Doyle, *Edge, op. cit.* p. 53.

8. *Ibid.*, p. 20.

9. Houdini, *A Magician Among the Spirits, op. cit.*, p. 165.

10. Doyle, *Edge, op. cit.*, p. 34.

11. *Ibid.*, p. 60.

12. J. H. McKenzie, *Spirit Intercourse: Its Theory and Practice* (London: 1916; New York: 1917).

13. *Strand Magazine, op. cit.*, p. 134.

14. *Ibid.*

15. Hesketh Pearson, *Conan Doyle* (New York: Walker and Co., 1961), p. 232.

16. Sir Arthur Conan Doyle, *Memories and Adventures* (Boston: Little, Brown and Co., 1924), pp. 393–394.

17. Sir Arthur Conan Doyle, *Private Papers*, July 2, 1926.

18. An example of how Doyle used his art as a means of resolving mental conflict is afforded by the matter of the knighthood which was offered him in 1902. Although initially tempted to refuse it, he finally gave in after "The Ma'am" insisted that such an action would be an insult to the king. In the end, however, Doyle got his own way, for in the story "The Three Garridebs" he had Holmes turn down an offer of knighthood which was to have been conferred, incidentally, on the very date when Doyle himself was scheduled to be so honored.

19. Doyle, *Edge, op. cit.*, p. 173.

20. *Ibid.*, p. 14.

21. Pierre Nordon, *Conan Doyle, A Biography* (New York: Holt, Rinehart and Winston, 1964), trans. by Frances Partridge, pp. 32, 238.

22. Doyle, *Edge, op. cit.*, p. 48.

23. *Ibid.*, p. 130.

24. Nicholas Meyer, *The Seven-Per-Cent Solution* (New York: E. P. Dutton & Co., Inc., 1974).

25. E. J. Dingwall in "The Margery Mediumship" in *Proceedings of the American Society for Psychical Research,* vols. XX and XXI, 1928.

XVII. The Witch of Beacon Hill

1. N. Fodor, *An Encyclopedia of Psychic Science* (Secaucus, New Jersey: Citadel Press, 1966), p. 69.

2. Doyle, *Edge, op. cit.*, p. 217.

3. *Ibid.*, p. 218.

4. *Ibid.*, p. 221.

5. *Ibid.*, p. 231.

6. *Ibid.*

7. Thomas Tietze, *Margery* (New York: Harper and Row, 1973), introduction.

8. Dr. Edmund Overstreet. Personal communication.

9. Christopher, *Houdini, op. cit.*, p. 209.

10. J. M. Bird, *Margery the Medium* (Boston: Small, Maynard and Co., 1925), p. 433.

11. *Proceedings of the American Society for Psychical Research,* p. 383.

12. *Ibid.*, p. 742.

13. *Ibid.*, Letter dated May 26, 1926.

14. Tietze, *op. cit.*, p. 60.

15. *Ibid.*, p. 164.

16. *Ibid.*, p. 117.

17. Doyle, "Houdini the Enigma," in *Strand Magazine,* vol. 74, July, 1927, pp. 134–143.

18. Tietze, *op. cit.*, p. 21.

19. The fact that after Walter's death more than ten years elapsed before his attempted resurrection by his sister suggests that her emotional reaction to his death was rekindled by a subsequent loss, namely the guilt-ridden destruction of an unborn child. An abortion indeed may have been the unspecified gynecological procedure performed by Doctor Crandon in the Dorchester hospital, and may have

been responsible, too, for recurring allusions to babies in subsequent seances at Lime Street. In the unconscious mind, a baby is often symbolically equated with a phallus.

20. Gresham, *op. cit.*, p. 243.

21. Tietze, *op. cit.*, p. 184.

22. Gresham, *op. cit.*, p. 255.

23. Fodor, *op. cit.*, p. 213.

24. Christopher, *Houdini, op. cit.*, p. 209.

25. *Ibid.*, p. 213.

XVIII. Halloween

1. Doyle, *Edge, op. cit.*, p. 16.

2. Christopher, *Houdini, op. cit.*, p. 239.

3. Gresham, *op. cit.*, pp. 276–277.

4. *Ibid.*, p. 278.

5. Doyle, *Edge, op. cit.*, p. 15.

6. It is possible that Houdini's anxiety was heightened by the perhaps un-conscious realization that Bess's illness had erupted close to the anniversary of his father's death—October 5. In the past he had been very attentive to this date.

7. Oursler, *op. cit.*, p. 187.

8. *Montreal Gazette*, October 20, 1926, p. 7.

9. *Ibid.*

10. Christopher, *Houdini, op. cit.*, pp. 256–257.

11. *Ibid.*, p. 261.

12. Dr. Dale Boesky. Personal communication.

13. J. W. Gatewood and W. J. Russum, "Injuries to the Appendix Secondary to Blunt Trauma," *American Journal of Surgery*, vol. 91, April, 1956, pp. 558–560. Also D. A. Geer, G. Armanini and J. M. Guernsey, "Trauma to the Appendix, A Report of Two Cases," *Arch. Surgery*, vol. 110, April, 1975, pp. 446–447.

14. F. Boyce, *Acute Appendix and Its Complications* (New York: Oxford University Press, 1949), pp. 384–391.

15. Gresham, *op. cit.*, p. 286.

16. Christopher, *Houdini, op. cit.*, p. 270.

Bibliography

Bond, Douglas, D. *The Love and Fear of Flying*. New York: International Universities Press, 1952.

Campbell, Joseph. *The Hero With a Thousand Faces*. New York: Pantheon Books, 1949.

Cane, Melville. *The First Firefly*. New York: Harcourt Brace Jovanovich, 1974.

Christopher, Milbourne. *Houdini, The Untold Story*. New York: Thomas Y. Crowell Co., 1969.

———. *The Illustrated History of Magic*. New York: Thomas Y. Crowell Co., 1973.

———. *Mediums, Mystics and The Occult*. New York: Thomas Y. Crowell Co., 1975.

———. *Panorama of Magic*. New York: Dover Publications, 1962.

Coryn, M. *The Chevalier d'Eon*. New York: Fred A. Stokes Co., 1932.

De Camp, L. Sprague. *Lovecraft, A Biography*. Garden City: Doubleday, 1975.

Doyle, Arthur Conan. *The Edge of The Unknown*. New York: G. P. Putnam's Sons, 1930.

Ernst, Bernard M. L., and Carrington, Hereward. *Houdini and Conan Doyle: The Story of a Strange Friendship*. New York: Albert and Charles Boni, Inc., 1932.

Evans, Henry Ridgely. *A Master of Modern Magic: The Life and Adventures of Robert-Houdin*. New York: Macoy, 1932.

———. *The Old and The New Magic*. Chicago: The Open Court Publishing Co.; also London: Kegan, Paul, Trench, Trübner Ltd., 1906.

Gibson, Walter B. *Dunninger's Secrets*. By Joseph Dunninger. Secaucus, N.J.: Lyle Stuart, 1974.

Gibson, Walter B., and Young, Morris N. *Houdini on Magic*. New York: Dover Publications, 1953.

———. *Houdini's Fabulous Magic*. Philadelphia and New York: Chilton Co., 1961.

———. *The Original Houdini Scrapbook*. New York: Crown Sterling Co., 1976.

Gresham, William L. *Houdini, The Man Who Walked Through Walls*. New York: Henry Holt and Co., 1959.

Houdini, Harry. *A Treatise on Handcuff Secrets*. London: Geo. Routledge and Sons, Ltd., 1909.

————. *A Magician Among The Spirits*. New York and London: Harper and Bros., 1924.

————. *The Unmasking of Robert-Houdin*. London: Geo. Routledge, 1909.

Kellock, Harold. *Houdini: The Life Story (From the Recollections and Documents of Beatrice Houdini)*. New York: Blue Ribbon Books, 1928.

Mulholland, John. *Quicker Than the Eye*. Indianapolis: The Bobbs Merrill Co., 1932.

Reik, Theodor. *The Temptation*. New York: Geo. Braziller, 1961.

Rinn, Joseph F. *Sixty Years of Psychical Research*. New York: The Truth Seeker Co., 1950.

Robert-Houdin, Jean Eugène. *Memoirs of Robert-Houdin, King of Conjurers*. Translated from the French by Lascelles Wraxall, with a New Introduction and Notes by Milbourne Christopher. New York: Dover Publications, Inc., 1964.

Sardina, Maurice. *Where Houdini Was Wrong*. Translated and edited with notes by Victor Farelli. London: Geo. Armstrong, 1950.

Tietze, Thomas R. *Margery*. New York: Harper and Row, 1973.

Wilson, Ermund. *Classics and Commercials*. New York: Farrar, Strauss and Co., 1950.

Zolotow, Maurice. *The Great Balsamo, World Renowned Magician And King of Escape Artists*. New York: Random House, 1946.

Index

Biscuits O'Bryan
Texas Storyteller

Biscuits O'Bryan
Texas Storyteller

Monte Jones

State House Press

McMurry University
Abilene, Texas

Library of Congress Cataloging-in-Publication Data

Jones, Monte.
    Biscuits O'Bryan : Texas storyteller / Monte Jones.
        p. cm.--(Texas heritage series ; no. 5)
    ISBN 1-880510-91-X (cloth)
    1. Jones, Monte--Childhood and youth--Anecdotes. 2. Country
life--Texas, West--Anecdotes. 3. Ranch life--Texas, West--Anecdotes.
4. Storytellers--Texas, West--Biography--Anecdotes. 5. Texas, West--
Social life and customs--Anecdotes. 6. Sonora Region (Tex.)--Social
life and customs--Anecdotes. 7. Sonora Region (Tex.)--Biography--
Anecdotes. I. Title. II. Series.

    F386.6.J66 2005
    976.4'879063'092--dc22

                                                    2004029810

State House Press
McMurry Station, Box 637
Abilene, TX 79697-0637
(325) 793-4682
www.mcwhiney.org

Printed in the United States of America

1-880510-91-X
10 9 8 7 6 5 4 3 2 1

Book Designed by Rosenbohm Graphic Design

Contents

Foreword

I used to wonder how the Rev. Monte Jones could have lived so many lives. He's been a teacher, a preacher, a Green Beret, a cowboy poet, and his list of careers will only grow as he moves further into what he calls "retirement."

Now I know Monte's secret: early career training.

Monte lived a thousand lives during the 1940s. He explored jungles, climbed skyscrapers, swam oceans, flew fighter planes (sometimes parachuting from doomed aircraft) and staged daring raids on enemy troops.

He did it all before age twelve and without leaving West Texas.

How? Imagination. In those days—before television, video games, instant messaging, and the Internet—kids learned early how to entertain themselves from the material at hand.

Monte and his computer-deprived buddies turned cane poles, scavenged cloth, and baling wire into a "spectacular human kite." They invented near-lethal games from innocent props like stilts and croquet sets, then dared each other not to play. (All these years later Monte still remembers the classic dare of his day, delivered to him from a friend on the high board at San Angelo's Municipal Pool: "Scaredy cat, scaredy cat. Stay down there and be a rat." Naturally, he had to take the dare—and the plunge.)

Monte grew up in a world without OSHA, MTV, or Amber Alerts. He and his boyhood pals didn't need virtual reality because they enjoyed the real thing. They knew the joy of bare feet and mud squishing through toes. They enjoyed "tomatoes that tasted like tomatoes." They swam in stock tanks, treasured dead snakes for their practical joke value, and walked themselves home from the movies. They didn't surf the World Wide Web. They explored the world, walking along creeks "looking for whatever boys that age looked for."

"And," Monte writes, "miracle of miracles, we survived."

Monte's collection of stories about his childhood captures the magic—and mild wildness—of a boyhood when children had the run of the world just beyond their back yard.

There were no televisions, no cell phones, no video games, or "other electronic marvels," he writes. "We could go outside and play. What a wonderful difference."

In this collection of stories, Monte goes back to that magical time to play, and he takes us along. Through Monte's words we get to feel what it's like to slide down the shiny brass pole in San Angelo's old Central Fire Station. We taste the "chicken-fried steak swimming in cream gravy" at Steve's Ranch House restaurant. We hear the Torpedo firecrackers exploding in ant beds. We run, breathless, with him, dashing home (under a full moon) from a wolf man movie at the Angelus Theater.

"Life was good," he writes. "We were happy. What more could anyone ask for?"

With his book, Monte answers that question. He revisits boyhood memories. We share the adventures.

Rick Smith
San Angelo, Texas

Introduction

These are stories told by Biscuits O'Bryan, cook for the I.O. Everbody Ranch. My career as Biscuits began in 1986 on the stage of the Covered Wagon Dinner Theater at the Caverns of Sonora. I was serving as Rector of St. John's Episcopal Church in Sonora at the time, and a group of several Sonorans met and decided we needed something to pull more tourists off Interstate 20 to enrich their culture and Sonora's economy. We came up with the idea of an outdoor dinner theater with music and storytelling. Our hope was to record and preserve some of the oral history and culture of the area.

Having earned two degrees in drama prior to going to seminary, this seemed like a perfect outlet for some of my creative urges, so I decided to create a storytelling character of an old chuckwagon cook. After much research, I formed a persona and named him Biscuits, and O'Bryan just seemed to fall into place.

Biscuits came alive on the Covered Wagon stage for what I assumed would be a one-time performance. Little did I realize at the time, but things happened, such as the first National Cowboy Symposium and Celebration in Lubbock, where Biscuits was one of the featured performers on the big Saturday night show. A conversation with Stella Hughes, the authority on chuckwagon cooking, led me into, as we say in West Texas, "a whole 'nother career."

Biscuits was selected as the first cowboy storyteller on the touring roster of the Texas Commission on the Arts. He began to be invited to schools and chamber of commerce banquets. Biscuits was taking up so much of my time that I had to retire from full-time parish ministry in 1998 to be able to fulfill all of Biscuits' commitments. In the summer of 2003, Biscuits received the Will Rogers Award as Outstanding Cowboy Storyteller/Humorist by the Academy of Western Artists.

One of the most pleasant aspects of living Biscuits' life was remembering things that happened to me in my childhood and translating them into Biscuits O'Bryan happenings. My cousin, Don Odam, a real, live person, lived next door to me in San Angelo during our childhood, and we had many adventures while playing, which, in the summertime, was an all day and as far into the evening as permitted affair.

We both managed to survive, which, in retrospect, sometimes seems miraculous. So here are the "Don" stories, along with a few other adventures. All of these stories are, to varying degrees, based on actual childhood experiences. I'm sure you know that no self-respecting chuckwagon cook would ever exaggerate. Right?

I am especially grateful to my brother, Hank Nasworthy, for his input, editing, and inspiration, and my cousin Don Odam for his contributions to my wonderful growing-up years. I appreciate my friend Rick Smith, one of my favorite writers, for taking the time to read and comment on this book. It would never have come to pass had it not been for Janie Vaughan and the Friends of the Menard Public Library.

(The Rev.) Monte Jones
a.k.a. Biscuits O'Bryan

The Big Bang

Firecrackers were perfectly legal and an acceptable form of amusement for kids when I was young, carefree and totally invincible. And man alive, did we have *firecrackers*: M-80's, Cherry Bombs, Baby Giants, and a whole host of other explodables.

We terrorized red ant beds and empty tin cans and probably scared any critters in our vicinity, although we never intentionally hurt any animals. One of our most fun things was to shoot cherry bombs out over Lake Nasworthy with slingshots made from forked tree limbs and old inner tubes. It's truly a wonder that we never had injuries beyond minor burns.

One time, I really did get hurt, but it wasn't due to an explosion. It was my very small little brother. Back then he was Johnny Gus, but he's now matured, somewhat, into just plain Gus, which was our Papaw's name. Gus, Joe Lee and

Carolyn (Sissy) are my half-siblings on my Dad's side of the family, and one Christmas I was there in their little house on Holmsley Street in Midland.

Gus must have been around three or four years old, and I was a very grown-up early teen-ager. My most special present, to my way of thinking—not being thrilled with socks and shirts—was a box of Torpedos. Torpedos were not-quite-round rough skinned balls about half the size of a ping pong ball, and they exploded when thrown on the sidewalk. There were probably a couple of dozen of them packed in sawdust in a thin cardboard box. I was ecstatic at the thought of all the bangs I could cause. Then tragedy struck. That pesky littlest brother reached both of his grimy little paws into my box of treasured Torpedos, removing at least six or seven, stepped out the front door and let them drop to the sidewalk, all while I had turned away for only a couple of seconds.

I hollered at him, telling Gus that those were mine and he wasn't supposed to be messing with them. He took off down the sidewalk and I went charging out to assess my losses, hoping there might be one or two which didn't discharge.

As I knelt down searching fruitlessly for an unexploded Torpedo, all the while telling Gus of my immense displeasure, all of a sudden, the lights went out.

I learned right then that Gus didn't take criticism well. He picked up a substantial cast iron water sprinkler, walked up behind me and laid me out cold. Joe Lee told me I shouldn't pick on Johnny Gus, because he didn't like to be fussed at. Quite an understatement, but a point well made and taken.

I almost hate to tell my next explosive incident, but do so as a serious warning to anyone reading this. When we were around fourteen or so, cousin Don and I found a blank 30.06 cartridge. We carried it around for a few days until a brilliant idea came to me. I mused aloud, "Don, I'll bet if we held that cartridge with a pair of pliers and used a hammer and nail, we could shoot it."

That's all it took to send Don off to the tool shed. He quickly returned with the necessary equipment. By this time, I was experiencing a growing degree of trepidation, so I began my retreat as Don knelt down at the edge of the carport slab. Securing the bulletless shell casing with the pliers, which he held down with his knee, he placed the end of the nail on the primer, raised his hammer, and, for a minute, it sounded like the end of the world.

If you're a hunter, you know how loud a deer rifle is when fired, but what you probably don't know is that an unrestrained cartridge fired al fresco is at least twice as loud and a thousand times more dangerous.

How Don is still among the living today seems totally miraculous. The shell literally exploded into brass shrapnel, creating a serious gash in one of Don's fingers, but otherwise doing no harm. The fireball from the blast eliminated a serious quantity of his eyebrows, yet his eyes were not damaged. I think Don must have at least two or three guardian angels.

That incident prepared me for the biggest blast of all. My brother Hank and I had been moved to Lake Buchanan by our mother and great-aunt when I was a sophomore in high school and Hank was in grade school. Our neighbors were the MacDonalds. Mr. Mac was a rancher, his wife ran a small grocery store down from the motel my grandfather bought for my mother, and the two MacDonald children, Henry and Jeanette, were our closest playmates.

One day Henry and I went with his dad to the ranch, which was between Buchanan Dam and Llano, and while he was busy, we went exploring. During our scouting tour, looking for arrowheads and critters, I spotted something incongruous to the natural setting and we went to see what it was. It was a rusted out antique small barrel that had once held TNT. It had to have been well over fifty years old, and there were big chunks of dark gray material lying scattered near the still-visible stenciled cask.

Naturally, ol' big mouth me sounded off and asked the question, "Henry, I wonder if that stuff still burns?"

I have no idea why Henry MacDonald had a book of paper matches in his pocket, because neither of us had any inclination to smoke tobacco. But he did. He set a piece of the well-aged blasting material on a rock about a foot above the barrel and broke off a match. I broke into one of my speedier hundred yard dashes.

Fortunately for him, Henry chose to stand back and toss the match at the same time he began his sprint. What happened next was a sight to behold. With an unnervingly loud WHOOSH, a two-foot wide column of flames leapt thirty or forty feet straight up, followed by a truly fascinating smoke ring about fifteen feet across. This was followed by an eerie silence as the circle of smoke slowly drifted south toward Llano.

Henry and I remained anchored to the spot—both of us, I'm sure, thanking the Creator for not choosing that moment to open the gates to eternity.

The next time I experienced something like that was in demolition training for becoming a Green Beret.

A Shocking Story

Young people are totally clueless nowadays when I tell them about having lived without electricity, indoor plumbing, central heat and air conditioning, television, and other things they take for granted. It comes very close to making me feel old, but I quickly shake off that silly notion. I think about the kind of world my grandparents grew up in, and I realize I haven't really been around since the Stone Age.

When I was a little kid, the REA hadn't quite made it all the way to the ranch, and one of the things my Dad really liked to do was listen to ball games on the radio. This was way before transistors, and battery radios were expensive and batteries didn't last very long. So Daddy decided that we needed a wind charger to electrify our abode.

I was about five when this wonder of modern science arrived by truck. I helped dig the footing holes for the tower.

Daddy used a pick and a crowbar to dig through the caliche and rock, and I used a tuna fish can to scoop out the rubble.

Before long, there it stood: twenty-five feet of angle iron firmly anchored to the ground, just outside our box and strip garage. With some able assistance from the local windmill man, they mounted the wind-turned generator connected to a two-blade, three-foot propeller on the front, and a swiveling tail at the rear. Unlike our windmills, which had long wooden handles to turn the tails ninety degrees and make them stop turning, the wind charger had a little hand-cranked windlass which tightened or loosened the wire running up to the tail mechanism.

None of that, nor even the purpose of this marvelous contraption, concerned me very much. What I saw instead was a great make-believe airplane. Daddy built me a wooden platform on the tower about five feet off the ground. That was as high as he would let me climb on the wind charger. But that was more than sufficient for imaginary flights of fancy. In my mind, I soared high above the ranch and traveled all over the world.

When Don came for the summer, I had to show him my "airplane." Don, being more adventurous and, occasionally, inclined to ignore the rules, had to be called down a couple of times for exceeding the height of our airplane seat platform. If I'm not mistaken, the second time was reinforced with a bit of manual instruction applied to his hip pockets. That time, he got the point.

All was going well in our world of imaginary aviation until one day I noticed for the first time that there was a big black wire running from the wind charger to the garage. In a moment of curiosity, I said, "Don, I wonder what that wire does?"

Well, it became imperative that we find out, so we landed our airplane. This meant we cranked the windlass, causing the wind charger to quit spinning. Then we climbed down and headed for the garage. There on a low wooden platform sat a series of batteries to which the wire from the charger was attached by a couple of brass fittings. We fiddled around with them but with no response.

My quick-thinking, scientific mind arrived at the conclusion that perhaps the wind charger had to be running before anything happened with the wire.

"Don," said I, "why don't you stay here and watch where the wire's hooked up to these whatchamacallits, and I'll go start the airplane."

As an afterthought, I suggested that he might hang on to those metal fittings to see what would happen.

Cousin Don Odam is on the left. He was younger—and shorter.

I scurried back to the crank and unleashed what was to become the fury of direct current. It was a typical West Texas day with a twenty-knot breeze, so the charger immediately sprang into action when the wire was loosened. The response from the garage was instantaneous. I would never have guessed that Don could make a noise like that. The closest I can come to describe it would be a severely wounded hyena hooked up to one of those vibrating fat burners.

In a flash of good judgment, I cranked the propeller to a quick stop and ran to see what Don had experienced on the other end of the wire. There he stood with tear tracks down his cheeks. His hair stood up, making him look like a wind-blown porcupine, and his hands were emitting the distinct aroma of barbecue. That kept him from making fists and beating me to a bloody pulp.

Mama had some kind of soothing salve to ease his pain. She wrapped his poor paws in gauze, then made him wear mittens to bed so he wouldn't get that greasy balm all over the sheets. He finally talked to me again in a couple of days and tried to describe his experience. It cured me of ever wanting to be an electrician.

Several years later, Don had a similar encounter with a table-top radio he was trying to repair. His mother, my Aunt

Louise, heard him hollering "Maaaaamaaaa" and found him standing there, unable to release the radio and doing quite an innovative dance step. He finally managed to back up far enough to pull the plug from the wall socket. It was salve, gauze and gloves all over again.

First Scary Movie

Do you remember your first horror movie? The modern fright films leave little to the imagination as blood gushes and splatters and dismembered limbs and internal organs realistically litter the screen. Back when Don and I were kids, even monster movies were kinder and gentler, but still scary enough at the time.

The summer that I turned six—Don had to wait until November to reach that kind of maturity—we tagged along with our grandmother when she went down to Hemphill-Wells to do some shopping. Our movie experiences had been virtually non-existent at that point in our lives. I had been with my family to one of those singing, dancing, romancing films that didn't do much for me. When we were about to go into the store, I glanced across the street and there it was on the marquee of the Angelus Theater, "Frankenstein Meets

The Wolf Man!" Being the precocious child that I was, I was able to read already. Don and I began the litany, "Mom, can we go to the picture show, please, please, please?"

Back then, it was perfectly safe for kids to run around in downtown San Angelo, and this was her chance to get rid of us for a couple of hours and do some serious shopping. Besides, her house was only three blocks from the movie, so she said it would be all right.

"Come right straight home as soon as the picture's over," she instructed us.

"Yes, ma'am, we will," we assured her, and away we went.

I had a whole dollar. I bellied up (or "chinned" up) to the ticket window, paid our seven cents apiece, and in we went. I also splurged two nickels so we could each have one of those big wax paper cones of popcorn. This was in the days before movie moguls learned about the outrageous prices they could get for refreshments. Kids nowadays find this 1940s high finance hard to fathom.

When we got into the theater, the place was completely packed with kids. We couldn't even get a seat on the front row, so we had to step over and on a whole bunch of feet to get to the middle seats on the fourth row. Just as we sat down, the lights dimmed and on came the previews of com-

Remembering my first scary movie, I still like to dress up as the wolf man on Halloween and pass out candy to any kids brave enough to come to the door.

ing attractions. Then we were treated to two cartoons, one of which was Bugs Bunny, and I can't remember what the other one was. Next came a Buck Rogers serial, and they left ol' Buck in such a fix that I didn't see how he could possibly get out alive.

Then it began: the main feature. That little black and white Universal world spinning around led us into the titles, "Frankenstein Meets The Wolf Man, starring Lon Chaney, Jr., Bela Lugosi, and Maria Ouspenskaya." Even the titles were scary because they were in weird script that just came on and melted away while very spooky music played.

The tension in the theater was high. Don and I were getting nervous.

The movie opened on a dark night in a graveyard where a couple of less-than-stellar looking fellers were discussing the fact that someone had been put in a crypt wearing some gold jewelry that they planned to take off the body. The one who knew about it said the corpse would be in bad shape because he'd been in there two years. One guy carried a lantern with a candle in it. The other had a pry bar. This was really spooky.

There it was: the crypt with the name "Talbot" inscribed in the stone above the door. One man pulled on the big, iron ring while the other pried. With a terrible shriek, the door slowly swung open. Inside were several wooden coffins sitting on saw horses. Our two would-be felons began dusting off nameplates until they located the one that read "Lawrence Talbot."

Just then, the heavy stone door slammed shut and we all jumped about three feet straight up. Both men pushed, but they couldn't budge the door. One said not to worry, they could climb out the narrow open window, so they went on with their skullduggery. The coffin creaked even louder than the door as it opened with a breathtaking bang. There lay ol' Lawrence, looking fresh as a daisy.

He was surrounded with a bunch of dried weeds. Number two guy asked what those were. The chilling words echoed in the concrete tomb, *"wolfbane!"* We all knew what that meant and so did numero dos, who said, "I'm getting out of here right now." The head honcho told him he would be right behind him as soon as he got that gold ring off the body's finger.

Through the window on the opposite side of the crypt, a big full moon shone its light on Lawrence Talbot. He began twitching. Hair started popping out on his face and hands. His fingernails grew into claws. His teeth and nose got longer, all in a blurry, spooky cinematic sequence.

The wolf man's eyes popped open. He grabbed that grave robber by the wrist. Almost all the kids in the theater—including Don and me—were squatting down behind the back of the seats in front of us. Don was screaming bloody murder. I was reassuring him in a quavering voice, "Don't worry, Don. It's just a picture show. He can't really get us!" Those words were as much for my own benefit as for Don's.

The scene switched to a calmer setting, much to my relief, until I realized what I had done. A ten-year-old girl, who was sitting next to me, was hunkered down with the rest of us. In my panic, I had a hammerlock on her right leg with my left arm. I blushed so hard I'm sure I created a red glow throughout the theater. She thought it was funny.

We made it all the way to the end of the picture, when the wolf man and Frankenstein's monster were blown up when the dam was dynamited. We hoped they were dead and gone forever but couldn't be real sure about that prospect. In order to calm down a bit, we stayed and watched the previews and the two cartoons and sat through the serial one more time, hoping that maybe old Buck would get out of his dire situation, but he didn't. Then we decided we'd better head home.

There was a major complication. When we went into the movie, it was daylight, but when we came out, it was *dark*, and we had to walk home.

The first two and a half blocks weren't a problem. There were streetlights and people around. But when we got to the corner of Twohig and Oakes, by the Cactus Hotel, we had to make a critical decision. If we went straight home, we had to walk by the Masonic Lodge, which had a narrow, dark alley at the rear, shielded by a big cedar tree, the perfect spot for a wolf man to be lurking. We could go across the street, but then we would have to go by the two-story haunted house where the crazy woman with the butcher knife lived, and she hated little boys. We chose to take our chances on the alley.

Just as we neared the black-as-pitch alley, a full moon emerged from behind a cloud. We had no doubt whatsoever that the wolf man was waiting for us. We ran by that perilous spot as fast as we could. Don had a bit of a speed advantage over me, so I hung back a bit and gave him a little head start. I was sure that the wolf man would grab him and I could scoot on by.

In those days, people often sat on their front porches in the evening to visit, and they must have wondered what was going on as two little boys ran down the sidewalk, screaming at the top of their lungs.

We hit the terrace in front of the house, scooted up it and down the walk to the front door, barreled in, and locked the door behind us. We continued at full speed down the hall to my granddaddy's gun closet, jumped inside, pulled the string to turn on the light and made double sure the door was locked. When the folks came to see what was going on, we told them not to open that door until the sun came up, and we spent that whole night huddled in that closet with the light on.

I now own a videotape of that movie, and it's really not very scary at all. Yet sometimes when I'm out at night and a big full moon appears, the hairs on the back of my neck kind of rise as I remember that time when Frankenstein met the wolf man.

First Haircut

Some of my childhood memories are clear as a bell. Others are a bit hazy. Then there are those which are fortunately totally forgotten, but which others fondly recall. That's the story of my first haircut.

My grandmother—Mom—decided, when I reached the ripe old age of two, that I needed a real live store-bought haircut. She yanked me up and headed for the Cactus Barber Shop, presided over by Roy Matheson.

Roy put a leather-covered board across the arms of his big, swiveling barber chair, which stood in front of the mirror that ran all the way down the wall of the white-tile room. The shelf in front of the mirror was lined with bottles of hair tonic, hair oil, after-shave and talcum powder. Under that were drawers holding the implements of the barber trade.

Mom plopped me down on that board and Roy snuck up behind me and started to strangle me with a tissue-paper collar followed by a big white cloth which he tied around my neck. That must have been when I figured out that they were out to get me. I panicked and let out a resounding whoop followed by wailing that would have made an Irish keener proud. I then began my quest to evacuate the premises.

Mom and Roy were both grabbing for me. Roy had to be careful, because he had scissors in one hand and a comb in the other. I was little, but I was quick and determined. I've been told it caused quite a stir in the shop that day. It was a struggle, but Mom was determined I would lose those golden locks. She grabbed my ankles and turned me upside down. She yelled for Roy to move the board. Then she sat in the barber chair, holding my feet around her neck with my shoulders resting on her knees.

Out of breath, she hollered, "Roy, cut it!" And he did.

My first haircut was done while I was inverted. I don't remember it, but I certainly heard it told often enough, because every time I went to Roy's Appointment Barber Shop on South Oakes Street, he found someone in the shop who would listen to the story. Then he would laugh that great laugh of his.

Thankfully, I've never had another haircut like that first one.

P.G.–My First Hero

My first childhood hero was my great-grandfather, Frank Grubbs, whom we all called P.G. That, I suppose, stood for Papa Grubbs. He and Mama Grubbs may or may not have been divorced. I never really knew. I just know that she lived in San Angelo and P.G. lived in Brownsville, which, I suppose, was as far away as he could get from her and still be in Texas.

P.G. passed on to greater glory when I was about four years old, so my memories of him were from my earliest days of recollection. He always sported a great suntan and a large white moustache. He drove a Model A Ford which he had converted into a pickup by cutting off the back half of the roof and building a wooden truck bed. I was too little to remember specific details, but I thought his vehicle was pretty special. It must have been quite an adventure driving that car/truck from the Valley to San Angelo.

Although Mom, my grandmother, really loved her dad, I think his visits always created a certain amount of fear and worry. Considering the fact that P.G. was a kid during the War Between the States, he was definitely from a different era, but his manners were anything but Deep South graciousness.

Mom's most embarrassing moment with P.G. came one evening at the dinner table. She and Pop had invited company for supper and P.G. showed up unexpectedly. Of course, he was invited to join them at the table. Hot rolls were served, and P.G. juicily licked his table knife before cutting off a slab of butter – to keep the butter from sticking to the knife. Eyebrows rose around the table. Mom quickly whisked the butter dish off and replaced that particular stick. P.G. was totally oblivious to his grievous breach of etiquette.

P.G. had mastered the unbridled use of "salty" language. Profane epithets flowed freely and naturally in his conversation. Since he was my hero, it seemed natural that I would emulate him in as many ways as possible, so it was from P.G. that I made my first attempt at cussin'.

We were all around the table eating lunch when, in my innocent three-year-old voice, I said, "Please pass the damn butter." This created a brief moment of laughter, but my request was ignored. A bit more forcefully I repeated, "Pass

My great-grandfather, P.G., was my first hero. He taught me how to cuss.

the damn butter!" This time, my mother was not amused. She let me know that such language was not acceptable. Again, there was laughter around the table.

But no one passed the butter! So I upped the ante a bit by shouting, "God da...." That was as far as I got before being rudely snatched up by my suspenders and hauled off to the back bedroom, where a bit of manual education was applied to my nether parts and I got my first taste of Life Buoy Soap.

After I recovered my composure, I slunk back to the table, still snuffling a bit. After I was seated, Mom kindly asked me if I would like some butter. In a still-shaky voice, I replied, "Hell no. I won't ever eat anymore damned butter!" That not only brought down the house, but the wrath of Khan had nothing on that of my mother.

When P.G. came to visit, he got to share my bed upstairs. Back then, we didn't have central heat, and the gas space heaters were all turned off at night. That necessitated quite a bit of cover on the bed. If you've never slept under a pile of quilts, you have no idea how cold a bed can get. It would take a good fifteen to twenty minutes to get the covers up to a bearable temperature. I had to decide what position I wanted to sleep in, because once the quilts were pulled up, they were too heavy to allow much tossing and turning.

P.G. and I were settled in for the night. The sheets were nearly warm enough for me to relax from being in a tight knot when PG quietly slipped out of his side of the bed. In the moonlit room, I saw him kneeling beside the bed. Although I had already said my prayers under the covers, I wasn't about to be outdone by my hero. I slipped out and knelt on my side of the bed.

My devotions were interrupted when P.G.'s gravelly voice loudly whispered, "What are you doin', youngun?"

"Well, P.G.," I proudly replied, "I'm doin' the same thing you are!"

"You'd better not be," he said. "There ain't a chamber pot on that side of the bed."

A Costly Escapade

The summer that I turned eight (Don was still seven) we were taught a very expensive lesson.

It was at the height of World War II. Every evening at six o'clock, the whole family would gather around the big console radio in the living room and listen to news about how the war was going. It was awfully exciting hearing about daring raids by commandos, especially the paratroopers and rangers. Radio let us use our imagination, conjuring up fantastic mind pictures of the way things were. We didn't have graphic images like those presented in modern movies such as *Saving Private Ryan*, and our thoughts were not nearly as bloody or violent.

I was the idea man and Don was the man of action and, once again, that unfortunate combination of talents was about to get us into a serious predicament.

One of my mother's most prized possessions was a set of sea-foam green satin sheets and pillowcases she had received as a wedding gift from her bridesmaid and best friend, a lady of means. She cherished these linens and only our most privileged guests ever had the pleasure of sleeping on them. One fine summer evening, after a particularly inspiring news broadcast, I got to wondering out loud to Don if that satin was what parachutes were made of.

That's all it took as far as Don was concerned. Those sacred sheets were kept on the top shelf of Mama's linen closet. Everyone else was still in the living room listening to "One Man's Family." Don quietly took one of the kitchen chairs and, stretching to his full four-foot height, snagged those pillow cases, tossed them down to me, and we put everything else back in place and headed for the barn.

It was a typical barn with a hayloft upstairs and a large door up there opening out to a pen below. Daddy had moved the calves from that pen earlier in the day, so our would-be drop zone was clear of obstructions. Up the stairs we went to the nearly empty hay loft, and that barn became our transport to greater glory.

Our imaginary pilot cranked up the engines, roared down the runway, and headed for France. No SST has ever made it

Don and I are ready for action. We were nearly always ready for action.

across the Atlantic that speedily, because we were ready for action. As we approached the area behind enemy lines where the Free French forces awaited our much-needed assistance, we got ready. We checked our make-believe equipment and rifles, firmly grasped each side of the open end of our pillowcase parachutes, and waited for the green light.

It was our earnest intention to shout "Geronimo" as we began our descent to fame, glory, and a chest full of medals for valor. What ensued was more like "GerAAAAHHH-EEEEE!" followed by a loud *SPLAT*! Don was the lead man, and I bailed out right behind him. He lost his grip on the left side of his chute, but I managed to hang on firmly to my pillowcase. I don't think it made one whit of difference about how fast we descended. At the time, it seemed considerably faster than twenty-eight feet per second per second.

Don landed almost horizontally in a puddle of bovine-enhanced mud. I landed pretty much on Don. Our screams drowned out the soap opera broadcast and everyone came running to the barn to see how we had managed to kill ourselves this time. By the time they arrived at our drop zone/crash site, Don had almost managed to start breathing again. Those tough, military demeanors were made considerably less fierce by the tear tracks plowing through the mud on our faces.

The real fun began when they determined that we weren't seriously injured and Mama saw what we had used for our parachutes.

I think for the next five years every penny Don and I earned, sometimes at what seemed to us very hard labor at less than minimum wages, went into the satin pillow case fund. We learned a valuable lesson. If your mother has something that is really special to her, *leave it alone.* It's not worth putting yourself in the kind of peril which was more dangerous than war itself.

Back Then

I have no idea how the children of this era will feel about the times in which they grew up when they reach my age, but I feel lucky to have been born and reared when I was. Although there were trials, tribulations, war, cruelty, and hatred, my childhood memories are of a much gentler, safer, and more enjoyable lifestyle compared to today's world.

The early 1940s, in spite of looming—and then actual—world war, were years when kids knew how to play without adult supervision and could do so, for the most part, in safety—except for the spills, thrills, scrapes, bumps, and bruises we inflicted on each other and ourselves as we created things to do.

Summertime was our most special time because, with longer days, we could be out running, laughing, and inventing games with our own made-up rules until that hour when our folks called us in for the night. We didn't have to worry about staying out and missing our favorite television shows, because TV didn't exist in our idyllic West Texas world. I never even saw a television set until I was a sophomore in high school, when my mother purchased a Hoffman Easyvision black and white set with a sixteen-inch screen surrounded by a halo of soft, pale green light. There were radio programs, like Tom Mix, the Shadow, Amos & Andy, Fibber McGee and Molly, and lots of others, but these were entertainments to be enjoyed at times when we couldn't go out and play.

My grandparents' house, which now is a repository for files and records from Shannon Hospital, was on East Twohig in San Angelo, down the street from the Cactus Hotel and catty-cornered from what was then the main fire station. Across Magdelen street to the east was Robert Massey Funeral Home. The kids in the neighborhood—and there were lots of us back then—knew the firemen and the guys at the funeral home, who also drove the ambulance, and they unobtrusively looked out for us.

Tom Biggs was the fire chief back then. The summer I had surgery, he came to see me and told me when I got better to come to the station and he would see that I got a ride in a fire

Once a cowboy always a cowboy.
This is me long before the Biscuits years.

truck. I held him to his promise. Twice, as a matter of fact, because I had two surgeries that summer. Don and I showed up and we were taken for a spin in the county tank truck. I even got to go upstairs and see where the firemen slept while on duty. Then I slid down that shiny brass pole, coming to rest on the coiled fire hose at the bottom.

Can you imagine anything like that happening today? OSHA would have a hissy fit!

Another benefit of my hospitalization that summer was getting to ride home in the funeral home ambulance. Back then, any surgery was serious. Recovery was a lengthy process, including a couple of weeks in the hospital and a few more spent in bed at home. The guys from the funeral home who showed up to take me home were probably in their twenties or at most early thirties and I was about ten, so we had a great time. They tossed me on the gurney, strapped me in, and made the two and a half block trip from Shannon to home with the siren wailing and tires squealing. What excitement.

Another great thing about being close to the fire station was the volleyball games the firemen played in the evenings. The competitions were fierce but friendly. Kids came and watched, and sometimes they would let us join the game. There was no drinking or cussing, just lots of laughter and teasing. And the playground equipment was just a few steps away, so if we lost interest in the game, we could get on the swings, with heavy board seats and chains instead of ropes. I doubt that government safety regulations would allow such dangerous things to exist in today's world.

There was also the merry-go-round which sat on a pivoting steel post that allowed the riding part, of heavy two-by-twelve splintery lumber, to go up and down while spinning as fast as we could push. There was a well-worn rut beneath the seat, hard packed and rocky, which caused many a scraped knee, elbow, or nose, and the spinning seat had definitely loosened (or extracted) quite a few teeth.

If I close my eyes and concentrate, I can still hear the ear-splitting three-note whistle of my uncle T.B. signaling us that playtime had ended and baths and beds awaited our homecoming. Occasionally, we dared to pretend not to hear, although that whistle carried over much of downtown San Angelo. It wasn't very long after that when Aunt Louise's even more penetrating voice rang through the night air, "Donald Henry Odam, you get home this very minute," and we knew we had pushed our luck to the limit and called it a day, always with the expectation of an even better one to come in the morning.

We didn't have TV, video games, cell phones, pagers or other modern marvels, so we had to use our imaginations. We could sail the seas or drive through the jungle in nothing more that a good, sturdy cardboard box. We could play football, baseball, or basketball with no adult referees, making up and changing (to our advantage) the rules as the game progressed. We could range for several blocks around our neighborhood without our parents having to worry about people who did unspeakable things to their beloved children.

We could *go out and play!* What a wonderful difference.

Hot Lunches

I lived with my grandparents during my grade school years. We had a wonderful lady who worked for them—cooking, cleaning, and helping rear me. Her name was Mary Jones, but during the course of her employ, she became Mary Gray. Between her influence and the friendship I had with her sons, James and Lennie, I was blessed by a complete lack of racial bias. Mary was a wonderful cook, and I spent many happy times sitting on the kitchen counter watching her make biscuits, cornbread, and delicious meals, all the while quietly singing or humming "Ol' Time Religion" hymns.

Pop, my grandfather, insisted on hot bread with the noon meal, along with cloth napkins and something for dessert. I grew up with a wondrous variety of foods, including boiled tongue, sweetbreads, calf liver, and brains and eggs.

Whatever delicacy graced our table was meant to be eaten, or at least tried, by any younguns seated there.

The only trouble I ever had was when we had boiled squash. I resisted it with every fiber of my being, but to no avail. So I would place the mandatory bite from a quivering fork into a finely-grimaced mouth, chew once, then make a bee line for the bathroom. There I would gag, hawk, and carry on with the appropriate amount of drama as I discharged the squash into what I considered its proper receptacle, the toilet. A duo of these occurrences was sufficient to insure that I was no longer required to eat squash, which I have since learned to enjoy. But please don't offer me rhubarb or anything containing kidneys.

Having been raised so well fed, a crisis arose, at least in my grandmother's eyes, when I reached the ripe old age of six and headed to Lamar Elementary School for Miss Lyda Gibbs' first grade class. The school had no cafeteria. In fact, there was barely room for its six grades of one class each, along with an office for Miss Gibbs—who was also the principal— which she shared with our part-time school nurse.

Mom, my grandmother, was not about to allow me to be saddled with an abomination such as a sack lunch . When my mother and Aunt Louise were girls in school, Mom brought their lunches to them all during their grade school years at Lamar. For me, she came up with what I still remember fondly as a truly inspired solution. I was to walk across the alley to Steve Manitzas' restaurant, The Ranch House, for a hot meal.

Most folks my age and older from anywhere in the vicinity of San Angelo will remember the Ranch House and Steve, the world's most patriotic Greek/American. This was *the* place to eat in San Angelo, along with Sam's Chicken Shack and the original Little Mexico, unless you wanted to drive all the way to Lowake, which was not always an easy task during the war, what with gas and tires being strictly rationed.

Every morning Mom reached into the bottom drawer of her bureau, where she emptied her coin purse every evening, and handed me two quarters. At lunch time, I trundled across the alley into the Ranch House, walked to the bar at the end of the enclosed sun porch, plopped myself down on a stool, and waited for Steve.

I never ordered. He would greet me in such a way that I always felt like a most-valued customer, then say, "Don't worry. I fix you something good." Moments later my lunch would arrive. It was always a large, divided dinner plate with meat, two vegetables, a salad, bread, and then another plate containing dessert, along with my choice of tea or milk. The price was always fifty cents—no tip necessary.

I remember meat loaf, fried chicken, chicken-fried steak swimming in cream gravy, fried fish, and a wealth of other West Texas homemade delicacies, a hot roll or cornbread, along with delicious pies, cakes, or a dish of real hand-scooped ice cream.

Being the good, obedient child that I almost always was, I cleaned my plate, drank my tea, wiped my hands and mouth (on a cloth napkin, of course), left my two quarters beside my plate, and—filled with nutrition and warm feelings—headed back across the alley. I was ready to play on the boys' side of the school yard, which was separated from the girls' side by a high hedge and vigilantly patrolled by Miss Gibbs or one of the other teachers. In spite of being totally sated, I managed to stay awake for the afternoon portion of the day's lessons—due to a healthy respect for her and her paddle.

Having been a teacher in modern day public schools, I hold absolutely no envy of today's children and their up-to-date dining facilities. I know what a real school day meal ought to be—bellying up to the bar at Steve's Ranch House for a heaping fifty-cent plate of lovingly-served delights.

Spiderman O'Bryan

How many time have you heard the expression, "Boys will be boys"? I suppose that still holds true today, but it was definitely a fact in my younger days. Fear was for sissies. A dare was never ignored. We were invincible. At times, we wished we were *invisible*, as well. Sometimes there were consequences to that mode of thinking.

If there was any possible way, regardless of how perilous the prospect, to climb anything—tree, pole, truck, house, or whatever—it got climbed. The only time I can recall "chickening out" for even a moment was my first time on the high diving board at the Municipal Pool down by the river.

Don and I spent lots of time there when we were in Angelo. We incurred the piercing whistle of the lifeguard on more than one occasion for running, diving into the shallow end, or using our superior splashing technique on squealing girls.

The low board was no challenge. We did cannon balls, ugly duckling dives (they didn't qualify as swan dives), one and a quarter flips, for which we paid the price of loss of breath, and our own clown dive creations. But the high board had not yet lured us to its heights. One fateful day, ol' big mouth me got to wondering, out loud of course, what it might be like way up there. That's all it took for Don to go clambering up the concrete steps.

When he achieved the prestigious peak, he called for me to join him. I experienced a brief flash of common sense and shook my head. That was all it took for him to start chanting, "Scaredy cat, scaredy cat, stay down there and be a rat!"

The dare was made. I had no choice. I didn't know nine feet could be so high as I cautiously ascended, step by step, clinging to the metal rails.

I have to admit that it was quite a view. I could almost see Mom and Pop's house across the river on East Twohig. I could see Little Mexico café and the honky tonk where Ernest Tubb used to sing for change in the parking lot. I could see Fort Concho. But most of all, I could see the depths of the pool far, far below. It also occurred to me that the railings stopped shortly after the board began its projection into outer space.

Don fearlessly walked to the end of the board, turned around to heckle me and immediately fell off into the water. Being overwhelmingly concerned for his safety, I scooted back down the steps in case he needed to be rescued. But he came up laughing and hollering how fun that was. And now, he said, it was my turn.

It took about three trips to the end of the board (followed by two retreats and lots of fussing from others waiting in line) before I took the plunge into what I imagined would be my final act in this life.

I survived. Don was right. It was fun. After that, there was no stopping us, at least until my first two and a quarter flip. I was splotchy red for several days after that.

My greatest climbing feat was my ascent of the Cactus Hotel. I walked by it every morning on the way to school, but I was usually looking for other things, like dropped nickels and pennies on the sidewalk. One day, when I was in the fifth grade, I happened to notice the faux balconies on the second floor of the hotel. On closer examination, I discovered that the building was constructed in two-foot sections of concrete, each separated by a two-inch high and one-inch deep mortar line, perfect for hand and toe holds.

One quiet Saturday morning, when few people were out and about, I decided to make my climb. Being inured to heights through my diving expertise, climbing to the second floor held no hint of fear, nor an ounce of sense. The first step was the hardest, because the ridges didn't begin for about four feet above the sidewalk. After a few failed attempts, I managed to get a hand hold at the six-foot level and pulled myself up.

I recalled reading about the human fly and considered myself right up there on his level, even though in truth I was only about eight feet high. Just as I was reaching for the next level, either Jim or Roy happened by to open the barber shop and saw me.. Jim, I believe it was, told me in no uncertain terms to get a certain part of my anatomy down from there at once.

In retrospect, I'm grateful, because coming down was lots harder than going up .That sidewalk really began to appear harder and much farther down as I prepared to descend. I made it back to earth safe and as sound as I was when the adventure began. Jim proceeded to assure me that if he ever caught me pulling a dumb stunt like that again, he would make sure that the spanking he gave me wouldn't even close-ly compare to the one I would get at home.

I guess to some extent I proved myself educable, because that ended my Spiderman/Human Fly days. But every now and then, when I walk by the Cactus, I wonder if maybe, just maybe…

Skinny-Dippin' in the Concho

Have you ever been skinny-dipping? I tried it once and it completely cured me.

We always wore bathing suits, even when swimming in the stock tank at the ranch. This was mostly because there were girls or women around, but also because we were aware of some of the critters in the water with us—turtles, catfish, water snakes, etc.

My skinny-dipping experience just kind of happened by accident during Easter vacation. It was a gorgeous spring day with the sun shining, not much wind blowing (a West Texas rarity) and the temperature in the lower seventies. That really felt nice and warm since we'd gone through a really cold winter.

Don and I were out exploring. I was twelve and Don eleven. As our safari progressed east down the north side of the river, I have no doubt we were deep into philosophical discussions of the meaning of life, the potential benefits of nuclear science, and other ponderous subjects. Life was good. We were happy. School was out. What more could anyone ask?

All of a sudden, there it was. A small clearing appeared, ending at the river's edge with a huge flat boulder jutting out over the water. Then a truly unique event came to pass. Don became the idea man and I jumped (or fell) into the role of man of action. I should have realized what was happening and foreseen trouble, but everything had been going so well.

Don's brainstorm consisted of four words, "Let's go skinny-dippin'." What a great idea! Here we were, seemingly far from civilization. We had come upon the perfect spot. It was a splendiferous day. The sun was warm, so the water ought to be, too. Right?

I immediately began shucking clothes. Off came my shirt. Then my boots and socks. Finally, my britches. All the while, Don stood there, lost in contemplation from having such a brilliant idea. I was on the verge of dropping my drawers when the most terrifying of sounds invaded our edenic spot. GIRLS' VOICES!

We had somehow overlooked the well-worn path leading down to our would-be swimming hole. Out of the trees popped three young ladies about our age. There I stood in my relatively clean Jockey shorts, with a look of abject horror on my face. I was extremely shy as a youth, and the idea of being seen in my underwear by a bunch of girls was more than I could bear (or bare).

I immediately took the only path I could think of to rescue what remained of my dignity. I leapt into the waters of the Concho. The eight-foot drop was nowhere near as exhilarating as the sixty-degree dark brown river. The only thing I've ever experienced that was colder was the night I parachuted into an ice-coated stock tank in Germany. Every smidgen of breath left my lungs as I sank into the murky Concho.

I came up gasping for breath, choking on muddy water, and deeply shocked by the chill of the still winter-cold river. I returned to the surface three shades of blue darker than when I went in. Of course, fully-clad Don and his newfound companions were highly amused by my escapade. They peered over the edge of the giant rock and rained down laughter to add insult to my rapidly increasing numbness. I'm still amazed that I didn't break any teeth, because they were violently chattering.

Mr. Charming continued his conversation with the girls, at least until with my last remaining ounce of energy, I threatened his very life. He then politely asked if they would mind excusing us while he retrieved me from the ice floe. Reluctantly, the three little maids departed, leaving only echoes of glee. Don made his way down to the river's edge and, avoiding getting muddy or wet, helped me from the icy depths.

No sunlight has ever felt better. I was one giant goose bump, shivering so hard I shook off most of my wetness. Except, of course, my soggy underwear. Don held my shirt to shield me from any prospective peeking females while I shakily but rapidly shed my shorts and got into my britches. My socks and boots took a while to get on, but at last I was dressed.

Luckily for Don, I was too debilitated to toss him off the rock into the river, so we headed back to Mom's house. There wasn't much conversation on our return journey, because Don kept trying to disguise his giggling and I couldn't say anything nice and didn't want to give him the pleasure of hearing me complain.

To this very day, I retain extreme disdain for cold water. I promise you that I never again had any urge to go skinny-dippin'.

The Human Kite

Kids don't fly kites very often these days. The kites that do get flown tend to be store-bought creations fashioned of Mylar or rip-stop nylon with plastic or some other man-made material.

Our kites were most often of the homemade variety. Once in a rare while, someone might bring out a store-bought kite, which ranged in price from a nickel to the high-priced ones for a quarter (those were box kites, which I never could fly). We had a ready supply of newspaper, sticks, string, and flour paste. Our kites were usually constructed on the spot by us budding aeronautical engineers.

Our normal-size kites didn't provide too many thrills, aside from some truly daring tree climbing (mainly big mesquites with lots of potent thorns). Well, there was the power line incident which is still better left to your imagination, since the electric company may still have an open file on that case.

The real excitement came with our monster kites. Those were the ones we spent serious blood, sweat, and tears—and an occasional black eye or loosened tooth—creating and at least attempting to fly.

Once we built an eight-foot-high monster while vacationing on Lake Travis. I'm not sure where we came up with a thousand feet of heavy duty cotton twine, and I'm sure my mother carried to her final resting place the memory of the certain unmentionables we pirated for tail material. It was only by the grace of God that Don and I weren't yanked over that three hundred foot bluff, but the string broke at the last minute and we were spared.

Years later, I was relating that story to someone. That person recalled having been boating on the lake one day when a huge kite with a very unusual tail rocketed past them and crashed into the lake.

Our best kite adventure was our spectacular human kite. Mom had discarded a faded pseudo-silk, phony-feather-filled comforter. Don and I immediately recognized it for its potential—a priceless opportunity for creative, daring innovators such as ourselves. With Boy Scout knife and purloined sewing scissors, we carefully undid the hem around three sides and removed the stuffing.

What we had was an eight by sixteen foot tract of slightly faded pale purple kite material. PVC had not yet been invented, but there was a ready stock of very large cane, which, with much splicing, seemed sufficient unto the cause since Daddy had an abundance of bailing wire. The end product of our amazing feat of creativity was a sort of lop-sided, diamond-shaped kite of truly magnificent proportions—seven feet wide and fourteen feet tall, with hand-sewn leather straps for feet, arms, and waist to insure the pilot's complete safety.

That critter must have weighed twenty pounds. Don topped the scales at sixty-five pounds. Since I weighed in at seventy-two pounds, Don became the logical test pilot. I assumed the position of controller.

Daddy had this old hand-cranked windlass in the barn, and we reeled on about three hundred feet of fence wire and securely bolted that winch to the roof of the barn. A total lack of adult supervision blessed us with the freedom to attempt things like this.

It was a typical March day in West Texas, with a thirty-knot breeze, when we prepared to launch our attempt at tethered human flight. It took several attempts and considerable retracing of steps, having been blown across the barnyard several times, to get the kite and Don into position.

Probably the only thing that saved his life—and mine, too—was an extreme gust which arose while I was making my way up the ladder to the barn roof. It picked Don and the pleasingly purple airfoil up about eight feet off the ground and they did three or four 360 degree spins. Just then, a five-foot square of barn roof and the windlass departed the premises with a terrifying shriek, topped only by Don's vertigo-induced screams.

I recovered him after he hit the barbed wire fence about three hundred yards north of the barn. It took skill and perseverance to separate Don from his purple, cane-splintered, cactus thorn-pierced cocoon. Fortunately, he was much too dazed and disoriented to do me the life-threatening damage he had in mind. He came away with only a broken collarbone, a split lip and three days of decidedly unbalanced walking.

The folks, relieved by the lack of fatalities, decided they really didn't care to hear the whole story.

I learned quite a bit about barn roofing and decided to delay my plans to build a glider. Don has never quite overcome his fear of flying. So go fly a kite, but *be careful!*

Aunt Louise and the Dead Snake

The summer I turned twelve I had one of my greatest childhood adventures. Instead of Don coming to the ranch, I was invited to spend the summer with him, my Uncle T.B., and my Aunt Louise, my mother's sister, in the big city of Snyder, between San Angelo and Lubbock. At the time, my uncle ran a concrete delivery business, and their house was located very close to the town square, in sight of the old jail, on the banks of Deep Creek.

Deep Creek is a large draw that runs from sort-of northwest to kind-of southeast all the way across town. Like many West Texas waterways, it is usually dry. At the time, Snyder was dry not only from lack of rainfall, but also because the sale of alcohol was illegal.

One day, Don and I sat on the banks of the creek and watched the sheriff's children demolish several cases of confiscated bootleg beer by setting the cans on a tree stump and attacking them with hatchets. I figure they had to take at least five baths before they could get anywhere near the Baptist church because the foamy beer would spew all over them and everything else as each can was assaulted with the hatchet. It looked like they were having a wonderful time. We weren't completely certain they were keeping their mouths shut as the beer cascaded out.

One day, Don and I were exploring Deep Creek looking for whatever boys that age looked for, when we came to a place where, during those frog-drowning downpours, the water had eroded the soil along a curve in the draw. This left a cave-like formation with a ceiling about four feet high, receding into the bank of the draw several yards.

The Bermuda grass had grown down to the ground, hiding the recess. I may have mentioned that during those childhood days, I was the idea man and Don was the man of action. A lot of times my ideas came pouring out of my mouth before they had time to circulate in my brain. Of course, as soon as I spouted a suggestion, Don would be on it like a horny toad on a bed of ants.

"Wow, Don," I opined, "this would make a great hideout!"

I said that, having just peeked through the thick curtain

of grass, and it was no sooner spoken than in Don went. I followed right along behind him. We had indeed discovered a wonderful place. It was comparatively cool, a tiny bit damp with a soft dirt floor, and it looked a little eerie with the sunlight filtering in through the grass.

We were having a fine time crawling around exploring until I asked Don if he had noticed the water moccasin under his belly. It was amazing how a four-foot five-and-one-half-inch boy could stand instantly in a four-foot high space, turn like a crazed ballerina and be fifty yards down Deep Creek. Don stomped me down into the soft dirt and took out a good sized gash in the cave's ceiling as he made his escape.

Eventually, he realized that I wasn't behind him and he came back to see if the snake had captured me. That was when I asked if he had noticed that the moccasin was dead.

After the fight—and we became friends again—we reached a joint conclusion that a dead, four-foot water moccasin was just too good a treasure to pass up.

My Aunt Louise lived somewhere on the edge between fury and hysteria when Don and I were kids, and she had a definite dislike for anything remotely reptilian. So, naturally, we took that dead, four-foot, just-starting-to-smell- a-little snake back to the house to see what we could find to do with it.

Aunt Louise was nowhere to be found. We snuck (that's West Texan for "sneaked") back to the master bedroom and put the snake under her bed. I went to her spool cabinet, reeled off about eight feet of bright red thread, and tied it around the snake's neck. I laid the thread on her nice white bedspread. She was one of those people who, upon finding a loose thread, would wind it up around her fingers to throw away.

Don and I then headed for the back porch to await the outcome of our hilarious prank. Soon we were rewarded with a scream that sent half of downtown Snyder to their storm cellars and had us scurrying at top speed to our new-found hideout, laughing hysterically.

Eventually, reality set in. We knew we were going to have to go back and face *the wrath of Aunt Louise.* We put it off as long as we could, knowing that if we waited any longer we would be in even worse trouble, if that was possible. We spied Aunt Louise sitting on the back porch and knew she was waiting for our return.

Images of the horrors that awaited us were truly frightening. We put on our best hang-dog, golly-we're-sorry looks, and skulked up to face our fate. Surprisingly, she looked at us and grinned.

"You boys really scared me with that snake," she said, "but you're really lucky, because just before I discovered it, I had been holding a brand new box of straight pins, which I set down to get that thread."

This calm, quiet, smiling behavior was anything but typical of an Aunt Louise response. We knew if we got off with a belt or a board appropriately applied, we'd be doing real well. We were dumbfounded.

She looked us over. "You have certainly managed to get dirty," she said, which was true, since we'd been crawling around in our cave hideout. "I'm going to get your bath ready. As soon as y'all are cleaned up, I'll have supper ready."

Off she went to draw our bathwater. She soon returned and told us she had fixed us a nice bubble bath.

About halfway up the stairs, it dawned on us what had transpired. We had played the world's greatest practical joke, scared the living daylights out of Aunt Louise, and hadn't even got killed in the process. With gales of laughter, we raced to see who could get shucked of clothes and be first in the tub. It was a tie as be both jumped into a tubful of the prettiest purple bubble bath bubbles you've ever seen.

And it was another tie as we immediately exited the tub at top speed. Aunt Louise had laid the snake down the middle of the tub's bottom and we both landed on it.

We discovered something else. When we went into that tub, we were regular little boy pink and brown, but when we rose from the water, we were solid deep purple plumb up to our necks. Aunt Louise had put purple dye in that bath water.

That was a mighty long bus ride back home, and it was long sleeve shirts and Red Ryder gloves until that purple dye finally wore off. We never again played a trick on Aunt Louise.

My Very First Best Friend

My earliest memories include a most special friend – Johnson. A kinder, more caring person has never graced my life than my grandparent's yard man.

The first recollection I have of Johnson was a scratching on the screen wire of the sleeping porch early on Thursday mornings, when he showed up to do the mowing, watering, and everything else connected with keeping a good lawn.

I would jump out of bed, get someone to help me with buckling my sandals (I was only two years old) and, clad in shorts and a Buster Brown t-shirt, head out the back door. By then, Johnson had the completely unmotorized reel blade mower with the latch-on grass catcher whirring across the front yard on East Twohig Street.

Usually he would have a half-smoked five cent cigar in a soft-rubber holder clenched in his teeth. Johnson hummed unrecognizable melodies very quietly as he worked. At least he did until I began my barrage of never-ending questions.

Johnson had very little formal education, but he was a very wise man. He was about five feet six inches tall with a girth that expanded during my growing up years but declined as I approached middle age. He was almost bald with skin the color of a Hershey bar and had a very round face with a smile that could melt the hardest heart. He made me feel important, and I believe he took very seriously the part he played in helping to raise me.

Perhaps his most endearing trait in my estimation was his total lack of criticism. I knew he cared about me; he made me feel smart and important. Of the thousands of questions I posed to him, none were ever treated as foolish, even though many probably were. And they were always answered on the appropriate level, whether I was three or thirty-three. My great regret is that too many of his answers went in one ear and out the other. There are certainly times now when I could use some of his wise counsel.

Johnson began working for Mom and Pop the year I was born. He continued as a part of their household long after Pop died. No one ever actually knew how old Johnson was. My Uncle Ramon was county clerk at the time we figured

Johnson to be in the vicinity of sixty-five, so he was able to help him obtain a birth certificate so Johnson could draw Social Security.

He continued his proprietary overseeing of the yard work long after he was unable (or at least forbidden by Mom) to push that mower. He could still stand under the pecan trees with a water hose and be sure they were properly cared for. Johnson and Mom had some real fusses over his trying to do too much. She was one to talk, because she was still volunteering at Baptist Memorial Nursing Home well into her 80s.

After I finished high school, I always tried to get in a visit with Johnson when I would come to see Mom and Pop. It was a great moment when he would show up in his old, but always well-kept, Chevrolet, dressed in his either blue or gray pants and matching long-sleeved shirt, wearing his floppy straw hat, and still clenching that cigar in his badly deteriorating teeth. His smile was constant, and his soft, gentle voice would always convey his caring and pride in me, even when I wasn't necessarily feeling particularly proud of myself.

Johnson also worked for other people in San Angelo. He told me about an elderly lady who lived within a block of the Tom Green County Court House. Pop's business, Theo Montgomery Sand & Gravel, got the contract to dig the base-

Johnson and I got all gussied up for my grandparents'
50th wedding anniversary.

ment for the new Sears Building, which is now the Ed B. Keys Building, across from the courthouse. The well-packed caliche necessitated blasting to get down deep enough. My Uncle T.B. and my half-brother Hank's dad were supervising the blasting, and Johnson said that every time they set off a charge of dynamite, old Mizz so-and-so would call the police to tell them that it had blown out the pilot light of her water heater. Johnson would be called to come over and relight the pilot. He was probably one of the happiest people in town when they finally finished that project.

I had the sad but distinct privilege of representing our family at Johnson's funeral. He was ninety years old when he entered the nearer presence of God. What a flood of memories came to mind that day. The preacher asked me if I wanted to say something, but there was no way I could trust my emotions to attempt any words. But I certainly spoke to God that day, telling Him what a wonderful new friend would be sitting by the throne.

I don't know if they have lawns in heaven, but I know there are lots of youngsters who departed this life at an early age, and I have no doubt that they have quite naturally gravitated to the presence of this wise, gentle soul. I'd better quit because, for some reason, my vision has become a bit blurred.

An Occasional Stitch

Given the circumstances, our injuries were, for the most part, only minor. When you consider who we were and what we did, that's pretty amazing. I used to brag that the only bone I had ever broken was my little brother's arm. And that was definitely Don's fault.

We were practicing our wrestling moves in Mom's front yard. Mom and Pop's house was built on an elevated lot with a steep slope leading down to the sidewalk. Luckily for us, Pop and Johnson saw to it that the yard was totally free of grass burrs, so we could toss each other around, roll around, tackle each other in touch football, and remain confident that we would remain sticker free. Being a few years older, I could usually throw my brother Hank around, so I pitched him down the terrace.

He was sitting there recovering, leaning on his right arm. About that time, Don threw me down and I landed on Hank's arm. I heard an audible crack, then a considerable fit of squawking by Hank. From the commotion he created, one might think his arm was broken. Well, as a matter of fact, it was.

Hank was uncharacteristically unconsolable, and finally, more to placate him than from any fear of something being really amiss, Mother took him to the doctor. The X-ray justified his clamor. He had what they called a green twig fracture.

He returned looking mighty proud of the plaster cast on his forearm with his fingers and thumb sticking out. He got plenty of sympathy from all the grown-ups. Don and I thought he played it for all it was worth.

The next day, when my mother went to check on him at Lamar Elementary, we discovered the true seriousness of his injury. There was Hank, swinging on the monkey bars, hanging by his right hand.

Hank's little cracked bone was nothing compared to my first class, all-American, true blue broken nose. That happened one afternoon when Don and I were playing. We began arguing over something now long forgotten. Maybe words can never hurt you, but they sure can get you hurt. I got in Don's face and called him a liar. I caught a right hook squarely on my snout that put me flat on my back. When I arose, I was bleeding and howling.

Don went one way and I went the other. Mom ministered to me with a cold wash rag and cotton stuffed up my nose. Eventually, I recovered my composure and began to plan my revenge. In Mom's front bedroom was one of those chairs made of one-inch round bentwood with a round seat. That struck me as the perfect weapon.

I stuck my head out the door facing Don's house and began to shout, definitely not talking through my nose. "Oh, Don. You're a big fat liar! Where are you, liar Don? Don't you want to come play, Mister Liar? What's the matter, are you a coward *and* a liar?"

He must have figured out my scheme, because there was absolutely no response from the house next door. He had to have heard me, because the Grossclose kids heard me and they lived four houses down the block. Eventually, my voice gave out and my fury abated, probably from loss of blood. I gave up.

It couldn't have been more than thirty minutes later that all was forgotten and I was asking Aunt Louise if Don could come out and play. We were friends again. But I made sure I never again called Don a liar.

We had many other scrapes and bruises, but neither of us ever lost any permanent teeth or broke any more bones. There was that time Don slid off the front fender of his dad's old Ford pickup and sliced the back of his thigh clean to the bone on the license plate. I remember sitting outside the emergency room at the old Clinic Hospital on Beauregard while they sewed Don's leg back together.

My injury claim to fame came when I was in the fourth grade at Lamar. There was a steel chinning bar just outside the south door, in the playground next to the old Johnson's Funeral Home. I suppose I had unfulfilled aspirations to be a gymnast, although I'm not sure I actually knew what a gymnast was at the time. My brainstorm was to get out almost to the street and run at top speed. Then I would jump up, grab the bar, and make a 360 degree spin.

I made sure all my buddies were watching as I began my sprint. The initial concept worked well, at least up to about 120 degrees. It was pretty exhilarating until the g forces exceeded the strength of my grip on the bar. My next sensation was that of hearing one of those huge oriental gongs, kind of like the one they used in the J. Arthur Rank films.

I painfully awoke in the school nurse's office, with Miss Gibbs, the principal, hovering over me. She had already called my grandmother, who arrived soon after my return to consciousness. That was not a way I would recommend to get out of half a day of school.

I carry with me a tiny reminder of that escapade: a wee rock resides just under the scalp in the back of my head. I have no doubt Miss Gibbs, Mom, and perhaps quite a few others had thought for years that I had rocks in my head. Now they could prove it.

Bicycle Polo

X Boxes and Play Stations are pretty tame compared to the kinds of games we played. Kids nowadays might get a slight case of carpal tunnel syndrome or perhaps a sprained thumb, but those minor maladies don't hold a candle to the possibilities present in our creative play.

We made up all kinds of games involving roller skates, stilts, and pogo sticks, but one of my favorite—though short-lived—competitive sports was bicycle polo.

All the kids in the neighborhood around Mom's house had bikes. On the north side of the Masonic Lodge, where the now-vacant Texas Employment Commission building stands, there was, during our day, a vacant filling station/tire dealership. It had a huge concrete lot behind the building which was ideal for cycling.

Mom had bought Don and me a croquet set, perhaps hoping we would confine our play to something a little more refined. After several smashed feet from trying to hit our opponent's ball out of the neighborhood, we set out to discover other possibilities for mallets and wooden balls.

San Angelo had several polo players, and their games were written up in the *Standard Times*. I was inspired.

"Let's play polo," I said.

"We don't have any horses," replied one of the resident smart alecks.

"But we all have bikes," I smugly replied. That was all it took.

Imagine the havoc that ensued when three totally fearless young men lacking any protective gear set out to move a large wooden ball down the pavement with croquet mallets, while three more were equally determined to prevent that from happening. The crash potential was practically limitless.

The game proceeded vigorously until Don, who was on the opposing team, broke loose and looked like he was headed for a certain goal. That was when I discovered my secret weapon which halted his advance on scoring. It also brought us to the realization that perhaps bicycle polo was not the very best idea we'd ever thought up.

What I did was crank up my old Western Flyer to top speed, pull along side Don, and stick the handle of my mallet in his front spokes.

I never knew a bike could stop so fast, as I watched Don and his mount do a beautiful forward flip. In spite of a very unforgiving surface, Don bounced once and somehow regained his feet. At the speed he was traveling, I reckon he set a new forty-yard dash record before he finally got stopped.

By that time, I had zoomed on down the alley and was safely inside Mom's house. He eventually showed up carrying his wounded bike. Mom graciously offered to buy him a new front wheel, which somewhat allayed his anger. Bob Grossclose gathered up the croquet set, and that was the demise of bicycle polo.

The Great Bicycle Jump

When I was in the third grade, Pop, my grandfather, bought me a bicycle from Cullen Cole's bicycle shop. It was a full size Western Flyer with longhorn handlebars.

I was too small to reach the pedals, even with the seat at its lowest position. There was also one other small difficulty: I didn't know how to ride a bike.

"I'll teach you how," Don boasted. It mattered not a whit that his own bike was smaller, and therefore easier to ride.

At the time, we were living on Algerita Drive while the Twohig house was being remodeled by a truly great carpenter and handyman named Happy Adams. The house on Algerita sat on an incline overlooking Sulphur Draw. It had a very steep driveway. That was the venue Don chose for our initial lesson.

While Don tenuously attempted to steady the bike, I put my feet on the pedals—one up and one down. My arms were unable to reach the full extent of the handlebars, so with my wee little fingers I gripped the chrome next to the rubber grips with the streamers coming out the ends.

"Ready!" said Professor of Cycling Odam. Without waiting for my negative response, he used my shoulders to aid his vault to the seat. Away we went down the driveway. Luckily for us, there was no traffic on the street, because there was no possibility that I had any chance of even making an attempt to brake.

From that point, for me at least, it was a black (I had my eyes closed) and scream-filled few seconds that seemed to last an eternity. We plummeted down the driveway, across Algerita Drive, over the curb, with a tremendous jolt that sent Don airborne off the bike. I was still aboard, blind and yelling and praying that this wouldn't be my final moment of existence. The next thing I knew, I was upside down in Sulphur Draw with a giant two-wheeled demon forcing me under water.

Don recovered sufficiently to come to my aid—after he rescued the bicycle. Mom was not too pleased to see me looking like a near-drowned rat, but she was relieved that neither of us was seriously damaged.

Mom demanded that Pop return to the bike shop, where he rented a more suitable sized vehicle for me. I declined any further instruction from Don, choosing instead to teach myself. I definitely selected a considerably more level surface on which to learn, and happily succeeded fairly soon after.

I eventually grew into the Western Flyer. During my sophomore year in high school—that most tedious of times just prior to being able to drive a car—I painted that bike with numerous coats of shiny black enamel. I added even longer black streamers to the handlebar grips, and had an almost spit-shined black leather saddle seat installed. It looked fiercely awesome.

At the ranch, it was a couple of miles to the nearest pavement. My brother Hank and I would occasionally ride down the dirt road to the hard top. Hank had some little friends who lived there by the ranch to market road, and I would accompany him, not always enthusiastically, down there so he could play.

The Highway Department had dumped a big pile of dirt beside the road. It was about five feet high. When we arrived, I noticed that some motorcyclists, for whatever reason, had ridden their bikes over the mound, creating a packed-down path. Hank and his little buddies soon discovered the fun of riding their diminutive two-wheelers over the little hill.

Naturally, big brother (me) told them they were missing a real opportunity for fun. The paved road was built on a fairly long, not too steep incline.

"Let me show you how you can really put this to good use," said I, letting my mouth far outpace my brain.

I rode to the top of the slope, about an eighth of a mile from the dirt heap. Then I uttered those two words which more often than not lead West Texans into a heap of trouble: *"Watch this!"*

Although that Western Flyer, unlike its modern day clones, had no fancy gears to shift, by pedaling as hard as I could I probably exceeded forty miles an hour. In spite of the landscape flashing by in a blur, I managed to hit that track perfectly.

For a few glorious moments, life was grand indeed. I was flying! I was the inspiration for the boys-to-be in "E.T." I probably attained an altitude of close to twenty feet. It was amazing.

Unfortunately, the laws of gravity were still in force that day. That shiny black Western Flyer began to display a total lack of aeronautical ability, and so did I. The Good Lord must have been compassionately amused, for somehow my feet stayed on the pedals, and my seat and the bike's remained connected. Had that not been the case, my children probably wouldn't exist today.

The landing jolt sent shockwaves through my entire being. I managed to land on both wheels and remain erect, at least for a moment. Then, with a mind of its own, the front wheel of my bike attempted a ninety-degree turn to the left, but the rest of the vehicle and its passenger refused to follow. Instead, we completed the better part of a forward flip, then began a crashing down through the rocks and stickers in what we call in Texas a "bar ditch."

As I skidded to a stop, I firmly believe that the only thing that saved me from major harm or total destruction was the fact that this whole escapade struck me as being hilariously funny. Not just funny, but hilariously funny. There I lay, one major scrape in a pile of mangled Western Flyer, laughing like a lunatic. The four little ones were quite sure they were going to get nowhere near the hysterical maniac who lay bleeding beside the road.

Eventually, I recovered enough composure to stand up. What a sight that must have been. My clothes and my epidermis were shredded. I was covered in caliche dust, with various bits of roadside flora clinging to my wounds. There were tear trails down my dirt-streaked face from laughing so hard.

Hank's friends' mother called our house and Daddy came to get us in the pickup. He could only shake his head when he saw the condition of me and my bike. Mama said there weren't any scraps of my clothes big enough to go in the rag bag, nor was there enough Mercurochrome (what we called "monkey blood") in the bottle to treat all my scrapes.

The once-beautiful Western Flyer was beyond repair, and I really had no regrets because, for some reason, I really didn't care to ride it any more.

But the best part of the whole adventure remains that few moments when it felt like I was flying. That is a memory I will always cherish.

What a Ride

If you remember war bonds, ration books, victory gardens, and victory stamps, you've just dated yourself. That means you were alive and cognizant during World War II.

Tires, gasoline, and sugar were coveted items during that era. Chicken was a rare delicacy, since a lot of it went into C Rations for the troops. Mock chicken drumsticks were made from ground veal or pork, shaped like a chicken leg, skewered on a stick, and breaded. They were brought home and fried, but among the rarities of modern civilization, they didn't taste at all like chicken.

Pop had a large vegetable garden behind the house on East Twohig, and during the summer, we had tomatoes that tasted like tomatoes, Kentucky Wonder beans, really crunchy cucumbers, and, unfortunately, squash. There were also apricot, peach, and plum trees. A good number of apricots managed to get eaten prior to ripening, which gave rise to stomach aches. That meant a dose of Fletcher's Castoria. As a kid, those weren't difficult times at all.

There were opportunities for excitement and entertainment. I remember the traveling tent shows that would set up one block south of us on Concho Street. I can't recollect much about their performances, but they sold these boxes of pseudo-saltwater taffy that I just loved. Every box had a little trinket prize or sometimes a nickel or dime. Once I even got a quarter!

But the greatest moment of anticipation came when it was announced that everyone who bought a $25 War Bond would get to ride an elephant.

As an eight-year-old, there was no way I could possibly afford that huge amount of money. But that's what grandparents are for, right? My Papaw, Daddy's father, forked over the audacious sum of $75 so that my cousins Joe and Judy and I could acquire a seat on the pachyderm.

That night I was so excited I could barely sleep. I woke up every thirty minutes to look at the clock, just to be sure I wasn't late.

When morning finally came I ran down to the Texas Theater and met Papaw, Joe, and Judy. There she stood:

Queenie the Elephant. She was gigantic. Her leg was bigger than I was. On her back was a wooden contraption that formed a bench on either side of Queenie's massive back. The elephant handler had a five-foot stepladder to allow us to climb up to the step at the bottom of the elephant saddle.

Queenie had been giving rides since around 7:30 that morning, so she was warmed up and had walked out all her kinks. We eagerly awaited our turn. Queenie returned to her parking place in front of the movie house. She had a benignly benevolent expression on her face as she stood quietly. Giggling, laughing, joyful kids excitedly dismounted, clearing the way for us. It was here at last!

Joe, preceding me in age by a year and a couple of months had the honor of sitting closest to Queenie's head. I followed him so I could help Judy climb aboard. As I recall, there were four kids on each side. As the handler was moving the ladder to the other side, tragedy struck in a most unanticipated manner.

Joe was nattily clad in dark brown heavy corduroy pants, which, in the style of the day, had cuffs and wide legs. Queenie quietly and gently located the opening in one of Joe's pants legs, inserted her amazingly massive trunk, and sneezed.

My family is famous for totally unrestrained sneezes which can sometimes cause panic in a restaurant. But believe me, we in no way hold a candle to an elephant sneeze. Queenie could have blown out a brush fire two blocks away.

There's really no delicate way to put this. Joe's pant leg, from cuff to crotch, was completely filled with what can best be described as elephant snot. The only leakage was into his socks and shoes.

Joe emitted a full-blown howl that stopped traffic clear down on the corner of Twohig and Chadbourne. Judy and I had to join Joe in dismounting the elephant. Papaw made me accompany my cousins back to their house on South Austin Street. He first acquired a newspaper which he spread over the back seat of his Chrysler. That's where Joe sat. Judy and I sat up from with Papaw.

It was not a pleasant ride. Joe said unrepeatable things about Queenie and all her family. Papaw, who was a deacon at First Baptist Church, managed to ignore his comments. When we arrived at the house, Joe had a peculiar gait as he headed for the bathroom. I assisted my Aunt Lois in excavating Joe from his britches, which immediately went in the trash, along with his underwear, socks, and even his shoes. I never knew anyone could take that many baths in one sitting.

Alas, even though the war effort was generously aided, I never got that elephant ride. Cousin Joe denies any recollection of that event, but I notice he's particularly wary around elephants.

The Adventures Continue

Now that I have reached the ripe old age of three days older than dirt, one might expect at least a passel more circumspection surrounding me. Well, forget about it. Life continues to hold excitement and constant surprises for me as the cook for the I.O. Everbody Ranch.

Let's wrap this up with a couple of my present-day adventures. One happened a while back. We got word at the ranch that Red Stegall would be playing for a dance under the stars at Fort Concho, so the boys and I got all spruced up. We bathed, even though it was only Friday. We starched and pressed our newest Wranglers and even splashed on some foo foo. Then we headed to town.

We hadn't bothered to eat supper, 'cause we heard there would be food aplenty at the dance. When we arrived, it was a beautiful, not-real-hot spring evening. Red and the band were playing away. Folks were tripping the light fantastic across the shearing floor.

My tummy was growling, so I headed for the food booths to see what delicacies I could locate. Sure enough, there it was: Frito Pie with homemade chili. I bellied up to the booth and boldly requested one of those pies.

This little old gal with a chili-splattered apron picked up this dinky little bag of chips, which couldn't have held more than half a handful, ripped off one side, and dumped in a pitifully small dollop of chili. Then she sprinkled on a smidgen of grated cheese and handed me the sack, along with a white plastic spoon and a paper napkin. She didn't even offer to add any chopped onions or pepper slices.

To add insult to injury, she said, "That'll be two dollars." Not even a "please."

I had to reach back in my pocket for another dollar and a half and fork it over. As you probably figured out, I wasn't real happy.

There I stood, mini-sack in one hand, spoon and napkin in the other, with my blood pressure up quite a few points. I found an empty seat at a table and sat down to savor my two or three bites of high dollar supper.

The author as Biscuits O'Bryan   *The author as Rev. Monte Jones*

It was a puzzlement as to how to proceed. The bag would-
n't stand on its own, so I had to hold it. I was afraid to stir the
chili down too far into the chips, because it definitely held
the heat. So I just held on and dug in as best I could.

Have you ever used those little white plastic spoons?
Kids in the school cafeteria love them, 'cause you can shoot
a spit wad clean across the room. I scooped up a big corn
chip just brimming with hot chili and melting cheese, but
the tip of my spoon hung up on the corner of the sack,
unbeknownst to me. I had just headed it toward my mouth
when, sproing!

That larrupin' morsel flew right over my head. As fate
would have it, this young lady who could give Dolly Parton a

run for her money, just happened to be passing by. She was wearing a real low cut dress, and that enhanced Frito headed right into the crevasse. That gal raised such a commotion that Red and the band quit playing.

My mama tried to raise me to be a gentleman, so I whipped out my spankin'-clean bandana, licked it a bit to dampen it, and commenced to try and undo the damage.

That gal didn't seem to appreciate my ministrations. She screeched and called me some very inappropriate names. It seemed to rile her even worse when I commented that I didn't see why she was so upset, because there hadn't none of that chili got on her dress.

Fortunately, we got everything straightened out before the police arrived. To her credit, that gal even danced the Cotton-Eyed Joe with me before the evening ended. But I decided then and there that if I ever thought I might be somewhere where they're serving Frito Pie in a sack, I'm going to take along my own for-real spoon.

The other incident that I'm willing to relate took place last summer. Some of our deer hunters came out from San Antonio to check on feeders and blinds and clean out the camper they leave at the ranch. They brought me a big box of Fredericksburg peaches. They were those three-napkin peaches, the kind where the juice runs clean down to your elbow when you bite into them.

That was just the incentive I needed to get out my old White Mountain two-gallon, hand-cranked ice cream freezer, so I could whip up a batch of homemade peach ice cream. While the cedar tub was soaking, I peeled and chopped the peaches, covered them with sugar, and set them in the ice box. Then I beat my eggs, stirred in some cream and milk, and added a dab of almond extract, 'cause it really brings out the peach flavor.

I got all this mixed in the freezer innards with the dasher, put it in the tub, and poured in chipped ice and rock salt. Then I hauled it outside on the porch and told the boys if they wanted ice cream, they could crank the freezer. I sat down in the shade with a big glass of ice tea and supervised.

They were doing a fine job, going real slow at first. Then as the ice settled, we added more ice and salt. As the cream began to set up, the speed of the cranking was increased.

If you really want a good finish on home made ice cream, when it's really hard to crank you have to give it all you've got, going as fast as you can. They'd just got to that point when the boss came riding up and called them out for a chore. That left me with the hard, give-it-all-you-got cranking, but that's all right. I was ready.

The only problem was that I had no one to hold the freezer down for me. When the cream's almost done, that freezer walks around if no one's sitting on it. The only thing for me to do was to put my left arm on top and my chin on my arm.

If you know me, you know my moustache is fairly long. I was cranking at top speed when my moustache got caught in that thing whirling around. It jerked my head down and almost hare-lipped me. I saw stars and tweety birds.

When I came to my senses, I realized my lip was frozen to the top of that freezer and I couldn't get loose. I didn't know what I was going to do. About that time, one of the ranch dogs saw my face down on his level and he came over and gave me a big ol' wet doggie kiss. I wasn't too thrilled until I realized he had unstuck my lip from that freezer.

But my moustache was still wound up in that contraption. The only way I could get loose was to keep turning that crank backwards until I unwound my moustache. I'll be dad gummed if I didn't unwind that whole freezer of ice cream and have to start all over again!

So as you can see, the adventure continues. I hope you have as many fun times as I've had so far, but without the occasional pain. Just remember to keep your coffee strong, your chili hot, your bread fresh-baked, and always save room for a passing stranger at your table, 'cause you never know when you might be entertaining angels unawares.

Keep on cookin'.